Working with
Babies & Children

Education at SAGE

SAGE is a leading international publisher of journals, books, and electronic media for academic, educational, and professional markets.

Our education publishing includes:

- accessible and comprehensive texts for aspiring education professionals and practitioners looking to further their careers through continuing professional development
- inspirational advice and guidance for the classroom
- authoritative state of the art reference from the leading authors in the field

Find out more at: **www.sagepub.co.uk/education**

Second Edition

Working with Babies & Children

From Birth to Three

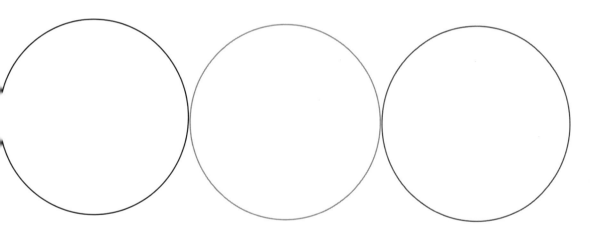

Jools Page, Ann Clare & Cathy Nutbrown

Los Angeles | London | New Delhi
Singapore | Washington DC

© SAGE Publications Ltd
1 Oliver's Yard
55 City Road
London EC1Y 1SP

SAGE Publications Inc.
2455 Teller Road
Thousand Oaks, California 91320

SAGE Publications India Pvt Ltd
B 1/I 1 Mohan Cooperative Industrial Area
Mathura Road
New Delhi 110 044

SAGE Publications Asia-Pacific Pte Ltd
3 Church Street
#10–04 Samsung Hub
Singapore 049483

© Jools Page, Ann Clare and Cathy Nutbrown, 2013
First published 2008
Reprinted in 2009 and 2010
This edition 2013

Editor: Marianne Lagrange
Editorial assistant: Kathryn Bromwich
Project manager: Jeanette Graham
Assistant production editor: Thea Watson
Copyeditor: Rosemary Campbell
Proofreader: Isabel Kirkwood
Indexers: Jools Page and Ann Clare
Marketing manager: Catherine Slinn
Cover design: Wendy Scott
Typeset by: Dorwyn, Somerset UK
Printed and bound by: CPI Group (UK) Ltd, Croydon, CR0 4YY

Library of Congress Control Number:
2012930902

British Library Cataloguing in Publication data
A catalogue record for this book is available from the British Library

ISBN 978-1-4462-0905-9
ISBN 978-1-4462-0906-6 (pbk)

*Jools and Ann would like to dedicate this book
to their children and grandchildren*

Contents

Acknowledgements

This book includes many examples of respectful and sensitive work with babies and toddlers, which reflect what happens in numerous settings every day. We would like to thank the many early childhood educators who have shared their work with us and allowed us to draw on their examples of practice for the material in this book, especially Julie Brierley and Heather Cobb. We are particularly grateful to Anita Johnston, Justin Mills and Kim Wailling (three MA graduates from the University of Sheffield) for allowing us to include extracts from their research. Our thanks go also to our colleagues at the University of Sheffield, School of Education, especially Jackie Marsh, Rachael Levy and Dylan Yamada Rice. We also thank Marianne Lagrange, Kathryn Bromwich and the team at SAGE. Last but not least we thank our loved ones.

Note on Terminology

We sometimes use the term 'parents' in its widest possible capacity. For example, foster parents, adoptive parents and those for whose role is in loco parentis – this may be the local authority in the case of looked after children (LAC) or grandparents where the birth parent is unable or unwilling to raise the child due to circumstance.

Throughout this book we often use the terms 'staff', 'adult', 'carer', 'educator' and 'practitioner' interchangeably to refer to all paid professionals who work with babies and young children. Where the professional role of the person concerned is pertinent we have stated this – e.g. teacher, nursery nurse, childminder.

Throughout the book we have used various terms synonymously to refer to the different stages of development in early childhood. We have used different terms to recognize the international language of early years. When referring to children aged from birth to 12 months we use the terms 'baby' and 'infant' and after the age of 12 months and up to the age of three, or when referring to a child who can walk, we use the terms 'toddler' and 'young children'. We use these terms to refer to *all* children, including children from all cultural, racial and religious backgrounds, children with physical and sensory impairment, and those with recognized health and social needs, as well as those living in poverty and difficulty.

List of Tables and Figures

About the Authors

Dr Jools Page is Director of the MA in Early Childhood Education programme at the University of Sheffield, where she teaches Early Childhood courses at Undergraduate, Masters and Doctoral level in the UK and overseas. Jools has worked in the field of early childhood education for over thirty years, and has significant experience in both caring for children and in policy-making roles. Before joining the Early Childhood Education team at Sheffield she played a key role, leading on policy and practice for provision for children aged birth to three, in the Kent local authority advisory service. Jools's research interests primarily focus on relationships between babies and their key adults and the rights of babies and young children, specifically those under three.

Dr Jools Page

Dr Ann Clare is an Early Years Foundation Stage consultant working for Trafford Children and Young People's Service. Ann originally qualified as a secondary school English teacher, before studying for her MA in Early Childhood Education whilst running a small nursery. Ann now supports students studying for their MA in Early Childhood Education at the University of Sheffield. Her main area of interest within the field of Early Years is babies and young children under the age of three.

Dr Ann Clare

Professor Cathy Nutbrown is Head of the School of Education at the University of Sheffield where she teaches on a range of early years courses from undergraduate to PhD level. She is author of over fifty publications on Early Childhood Education, including *Threads of Thinking: Schemas and Young Children* – now in its 4th edition. In June 2012 she reported on her independent Review of Early Education and Child Care Qualifications, 'Foundations For Quality', in which she made recommendations to Government to improve the quality of qualifications for those working with young children in early years settings.

Professor Cathy Nutbrown

Introduction

Your smiles are amazing – you first smiled when you were 26 days old and you've been smiling ever since! Now you smile and giggle with your whole body. What a joy you are.

(Extract written by a mother in her child's baby book)

Babies are amazing! In this book we seek to help early years practitioners to see the wonder of working with babies and young children. This book is for practitioners who want to rise to the challenge of working sensitively and respectfully with the youngest members of our society. This book is for people who want to create environments where babies and toddlers learn with their whole bodies. This book is for early childhood practitioners who want to know the utter joy of working with young and developing minds, bodies and souls.

Babies are amazing! Working with babies can be the most rewarding and the most challenging job. Adults who spend their days with infants and toddlers need recognition and support. This book recognizes their challenging and complex role, celebrates the potential of effective practice and offers suggestions of how to build on modern understandings of the importance of affection and attachment in relationships.

The growing workforce of early childhood practitioners has resulted in an unprecedented increase in the number of 'Under Threes

Professionals'. They work in a diverse variety of types of provision and hold a range of qualifications, from basic NVQ (Level 2) to Master's degrees and beyond. Some hold no qualifications at all. Within this diversity of provisions and practitioners, government policies have sought to address issues of equity in the quality of settings, particularly in the areas of curriculum, learning, teaching, planning and assessment. Changing government policies have led to new interest in how infants and young children learn, how best to provide for them in home and group settings, and how to evaluate the quality of the experiences they are offered.

Measuring the immeasurable

Is caring measurable? Is it not, at least in part, transcendent? Is using scientific instruments and methodologies to understand caring not in some way akin to 'searching for God with a telescope'? (Pence and McCallum, 1995: 27).

In this introductory chapter we set the scene by focusing first on the importance of vision, values and a sense of purpose for those who work with the youngest children. We consider what practitioners need – and need to do – in order to support the youngest children.

Who are we, what do we stand for?

Values

What is meant by 'values' in relation to early childhood education and care? What particular values underpin work with babies and young children? How can we distinguish 'values' from 'facts', 'knowledge' and 'beliefs'? Even if practitioners do not make explicit their personally held values it is certain that underpinning and driving their work is a set of core assumptions and values which is central to how they work with children.

Values in early education and care

It is not always easy to talk of values because they are subjective beliefs to which the concepts of objectivity and rationality do not always apply. It is difficult to measure values and difficult sometimes even to pinpoint the precise nature of how particular values are derived. What is clear is that nothing in relation to work with young children can be 'impartial', 'disinterested' or 'non-political'. In other words, nothing about work with babies and young children can be 'value-free'.

Can early education and care be value-free?

Values are central to the education and care of young children. How settings operate is informed by (and gives indicators of) the underpinning values of the setting. Physical care routines, creating menus and serving food, arrangements of resources, ways of talking with children, decor, daily routines, approaches to assessment, arrangements for key person approaches, relationships with parents ... all these things are important indicators of what is valued – what is important to the development of provision for young children. The ways in which practitioners choose to work with children, the learning theories which underpin their work, the degree of independence they afford to children, and their beliefs about and constructions of childhood itself incorporate a commitment (whether implicit or explicit) to specific values.

Professional educational practices and educational philosophies are interdependent – they cannot be held apart from each other. Values are an indispensable feature of early education and care – they cannot be denied because the 'value-free' early childhood setting does not exist. Settings are – to a great extent – evolved from the personally held values of practitioners who put political values (as laid down in policy documents) into action. Decisions about practice reflect much more than intellectual preference and learned knowledge – such decisions about working with young children are part and parcel of a commitment to particularly held values about education, learning, care, childhood, respect and rights.

What guides our practice? Why do we do what we do?

As Henry David Thoreau wrote in the 1800s, 'If a man does not keep pace with his companions, perhaps it is because he hears a different drummer. Let him step to the music he hears, however measured or far away' (Thoreau, 1995: 210). This highlights the individuality of each person, each child, each baby. And this is one of the values which underpins our work and much of the content of this book. Alongside this value is our belief that play is an essential part of every child's childhood. Different children need different opportunities – they need opportunities to 'bang on different drums', and they can do this when they play. And when they play they engage, have fun, collaborate, portray, improvise, act and … work. Some play is complex and difficult, and so it takes time – play cannot be hurried. No one ever heard of 'fast play', yet there are occasions when time to play is carved up into small chunks of time to fit in with other 'important' elements of the timetable – squeezed in between a television programme and lunchtime. As adults we need to remember that children need time to discover things – and when they do, it is for them as if that thing has never been discovered before. For example, the first time a child finds purple from a mix of blue and red paint is for her the first time purple paint has ever been made; the first time a little boy puts together words that rhyme it is as if he is the inventor of rhyme; the first time a child discovers how to make up jokes is for her the beginning of humour. And this process of discovery through repetition cannot be hurried – it needs time.

In the UK (as in the US) there is a sense of urgency about childhood – of hastening progress, of accelerating development. Is this born out of wanting the best for children or from some misguided belief that getting things fast is better? Somehow childhood is something to be got through so that we get to be adults as fast as possible. 'Fast food' does not nourish us – neither do 'fast childhoods', neither does 'fast play'.

And so, babies, toddlers and young children need time for recreation and re-creation. They need to play. The curriculum guidance for Oxfordshire in 1991 opened with these words:

> Gardeners don't plant runner beans in January to get an earlier
> harvest than their neighbours; if they tried, they would probably

get shrivelled and stunted beans. They fertilise the ground in the early months of the year, so that when the beans are planted – at the right time – they will flourish. (Oxfordshire LEA, 1991: 3)

One of the important ingredients of childhood is playtime – time to play – that unhurriedness that children are so good at. Free of the pressure of the clock or the calendar, children can learn. A key value for us, in developing early childhood provision, is that practitioners must allow children time. Never more so than in their first three years.

In order to be fully informed about their practice and to be able appropriately to interpret new policy initiatives in practice, those who work with babies and young children must remain aware of current issues in early childhood education and care. It is important that practitioners have opportunities for further professional development, to study for award-bearing courses, to read recent research, to attend conferences and to think about and discuss research and practice together. This is not something which should only be undertaken by managers or those responsible for leading services and settings, but is, we would argue, a responsibility of everyone working with and for young children. Being aware and professionally critical of policies and practices is an underpinning to respectful practices and respectful relationships.

Respectful relationships

Young children make multiple connections in their lives – and the opportunity to develop respectful connections with close adults is crucial. Respectful educators will include all children: not just children who are easy to work with, obliging, endearing, clean, pretty, articulate, capable, but every child – respecting them for who they are, respecting their language, their culture, their history, their family, their abilities, their needs, their name, their ways and their very essence (Nutbrown, 1996: 54).

Developing respectful relationships and practices means learning to live and work together in a setting, and this is not always easy. Difficult it may be, but efforts invested in building a community of practitioners, parents and children will pay dividends, for it is the most important element of early childhood education and care. Writing about issues of citizenship, Whitburn (2003: 175) describes the practices in Japanese pre-schools which she refers to as 'citizenship skills', which help young children to be independent, take responsibility, act as a member of a group and be self-reliant. She remarks on the importance of learning to live together and says: 'In a densely populated country, I am conscious that "learning to live together" is one of the most important and difficult tasks ahead' (Whitburn, 2003: 175).

In the intimacy of an early childhood setting, learning to live together is also the most important and difficult task and begs the question which the French social philosopher Alain Touraine asks: 'Can we live together?' We suggest that practitioners, parents and children need to develop the skills needed to 'live together' in early childhood settings, and that this can be brought about by seeing young children as 'citizens' in their settings, with rights to be consulted, to be treated with respect and dignity, and where adults take responsibility for meeting children's needs and creating positive learning environments. From a position when young children are seen as citizens, issues of respectful relationships can then flow; as Alderson et al. (2005) articulate, the difficulties arise in defining the relationship between 'citizenship' and 'childhood'. They note:

> Citizenship from birth entitles the child to a legal identity, and the right to expect certain services, protections and amenities from the state. Babies can easily be included in these concepts of rights. Secondly and alternatively, citizenship with its civil rights may be justified as a status that is gradually learned or earned or developed towards, and is granted by age, sex, or merit. Traditionally, English law has restricted children's rights and regarded children up to 21 and more recently 18 years as legal 'infants', literally 'not speaking'. Current English policy on citizenship education (QCA, 1998) slips uncertainly between education for future adult citizenship or the education of children who are citizens now. Traditional links between a set age of majority linked with citizens' participation or civil rights and the key right to a voice and to freedom of self-expression were replaced during the 1980s by competence or maturity. (Alderson et al., 2005: 31–2)

The notion that childhood is socially constructed through the beliefs, expectations and values of adults is widely reported (Alanen, 2001; James and Prout, 1997; Mayall, 2002). James's notion of the 'socially constructed child' is taken up by others and further demonstrated by Cunningham (2006) in a social history of 'childhood' in England since the Middle Ages. James and Prout suggest that:

> Childhood is understood as a social construction. As such it pro-vides an interpretive frame for contextualizing the early years of human life. Childhood, as distinct from biological immaturity, is neither a natural nor universal feature of human groups but appears as a specific structural and cultural component of many societies. (1997: 8)

However, as Morss (2002) demonstrates, such constructions of child-hood are complex and theories of social construction can themselves be deconstructed and reconstructed to satisfy the position of researchers and theorists.

Studies have shown children to be highly capable learners, not only cognitively but also socially and emotionally (Alderson, 2008; Dunn, 1987; Gardner, 1993; Hutchby and Moran Ellis, 1998; Nutbrown, 2011a). Mayall (2002) identifies children's abilities to challenge, nego-tiate and participate in social interactions with other children and with adults, and increasingly the traditional notions of a helpless child are being challenged, certainly in terms of learning competence and the study of education in the early years (Coles, 1997; Vakil et al., 2003). In this sense, then, we can argue that children can be seen as citizens, from the early years, because they are able to contribute to decision-making that affects them and express ideas and wants.

The ethics of early education and care

When we consider work with young children we must also consider the ethical and moral responses and practices in which we engage. Developing effective and respectful provision for babies and toddlers means much more than meeting a minimal baseline criteria for safety and qualification of staff. Effective and respectful provision for children means working to the highest ethical standards in developing relationships which result in positive experiences for all concerned. Noddings (2001) sees childcare as a role involving an ethical stance towards the role of the carer and his or her loving relationship with the children they care for. As we discuss in Chapter 8, to provide young children with secure attachments we need to consider the place of love in early childhood settings (Page, 2011a). Quality provision for babies and toddlers will be realized when we do not simply accept the baseline of minimal criteria – which in ethical terms would be 'first do no harm'. Quality provision for babies and toddlers will be realized when we move to a deeply moral and highly ethical position of ensuring that the respect, dignity and confidentiality of all concerned are upheld. The ethics of early education and care would take us to a position where little children are protected and respected in all aspects of their care. Ethical child care and education is something which is deeply human, highly individual and flexible to the needs of those it serves. An ethical response to early education and care also means respecting suffici- ently those who do the caring and the educating, and developing working conditions and remuneration which acknowledge the complexity and commitment of their roles. Ethically grounded early education and childcare also means sufficiently respecting young children to demand that those who work with them and care for them are trained thoroughly and are appropriately well qualified. We are not surprised to see some of the best practice being developed in baby rooms by practitioners who have themselves continued to study and possess specialist Master's degrees in early childhood education.

Learning from colleagues

Infants and young children need adults who know about children's needs, know about children's minds, understand different theories of learning, understand emotional literacy as well as literacy and numer- acy, and are highly developed in their skills and attitudes to support the healthy and holistic development of children's minds, bodies and souls.

Young children need well qualified practitioners who take advantage of opportunities to stretch their own minds – who engage in critical reflection on their own practice and participate in professional development programmes. The younger the children, the more crucial it is that their close adults are loving, caring, sensitive, 'attuned', informed, reflexive, reflective, alert and attentive. Children need to spend their days with people who 'think outside the box'. They need to spend their time with adults who ask 'why' – who know why they do what they do. Adults who can articulate their pedagogy make the best practitioners – for they can open themselves to self-scrutiny and reflect on the processes they have been involved in with the children. Children need adults who work with their eyes and minds wide open – ready themselves to learn, to think, to reflect.

Children re-create as they learn. A six-month-old baby amazes her parents with the tenacity with which she explores, how she uses every single second to find out, enjoy, request, repeat, seek. She is learning, as many six-month-olds learn – demanding opportunities, challenging some situations she finds herself in, seizing every moment, thinking about each experience, concentrating on simple things: a soft toy, a finger, a collar of a silky dressing gown, a spoon, a piece of banana, a reflection in a mirror, a sound and an expression (Nutbrown, 1996).

Every day young children are behaving like architects, astronauts, authors, builders, designers, drivers, initiators, inventors, originators, pilots, mathematicians, musicians, scientists … and so on. Young thinkers construct some wonderful and apparently bizarre reasons for why things happen, drawing on their present knowledge to create explanations which are logical to them at that time (Nutbrown, 2011a; Paley, 1981).

There is no more complex job than that of the early childhood practitioner, because working with babies and young children means working with the architects, astronauts, authors, builders, designers, drivers, initiators, inventors, originators, pilots, mathematicians, musicians, scientists … of the future. Today's practitioners are working with the youngest generation who will be entering the world of work and doing jobs that presently do not exist. They must teach these children to be flexible, imaginative and nurture their potential to be creative, confident and caring human beings. And in their busy discovering – of being other people and dreaming and creating – the job of practitioners is to help them understand the importance of all these things.

Practitioners need time to discuss their work together. They need time to share their observations of children and time to discuss their own interactions with the young children in their care. The range of professional development opportunities on offer now can provide for such discussions, and these, with time set aside within each setting for regular discussion and reflection, are essential ways of meeting the needs of professionals and in turn showing due respect to the children.

Is this the book for me?

This book is designed to meet the needs of a diverse young children's workforce by offering information about research and policy which informs respectful and effective practice. This book:

- discusses some of the theoretical underpinnings of early childhood practice with the youngest children
- provides an overview of some research studies into the learning and development of young children
- reflects on recent policies on services for children aged from birth to three
- considers learning and development of children from birth to three in an inclusive, international context
- presents case studies and living examples, to show how provision for young children in group settings and home care can be effective and appropriate
- poses questions for practitioners to reflect on how they support children aged from birth to three.

The emphasis throughout is on practical examples and ways in which high-quality provision can be offered to young children to support their learning and development. It is intended for the wide range of early years practitioners, whether studying for their first qualification or more experienced professionals undertaking continuing professional development.

In Chapter 1 we consider the place of research in work with babies and toddlers, and what those who work with young children need to know about research. We suggest that research is for all practitioners and identify some key themes in research on babies and toddlers. In Chapter 2 we also examine new views of the development of babies' thinking and the place of new attachment theory in modern practice. Then in Chapter 3 we give an overview of the development of policies in providing for the youngest children in the UK in recent times. In the context of the rapidly changing face of early childhood education and care we discuss the complex policy context in the UK; provide an overview of recent history of policy development; and consider the impact that the Every Child Matters agenda has had on training and qualifications for early years practitioners.

In Chapters 4 and 5 we focus on the importance of planning learning experiences for the youngest children. We explain why we believe that practitioners who have a sound understanding of child development are better equipped to support children's individual and holistic needs, and provide real-life practice examples from across a range of early years environments. We offer questions which we hope will inspire practitioners to think about how the scenarios could be professionally relevant in their settings.

Chapter 6 discusses the importance of understanding every child, and we explain the place of observation, record keeping and assessment to inform future planning and to document children's learning journeys. We also argue that working in partnership with parents is crucial to babies' and young children's learning and development.

In Chapter 7 we talk about transitions, discussing the inevitable realities of change and making clear the need for young children to be supported through the physical changes and the emotional transitions that are part of their lives. Chapter 8 ends the book, focusing on the subject of love, because love is an essential part of human existence and because love matters to our youngest children.

Much has changed since the first edition of this book was published in 2008, yet much has remained constant. Our values, philosophies and key messages from the first edition remain unchanged and permeate the book.

Chapter 1

What Do We Know about Children Under Three?

This chapter will discuss:
- The need for research and what it tells us about:
  o Literacy, language and communication
  o Learning, development, cognition and play
- Little voices – important messages

Why we need to know about research

In this first chapter we consider some of the things that research tells us about the needs and development of babies and toddlers. It is often the case that practitioners working with the youngest children know the children well, know the activities and environments which work best for babies and toddlers, and have learned alongside other colleagues how best to support young children's developmental and learning needs. There is much good practice to be shared and celebrated in the birth to three field of early years provision and such practices have often remained hidden. For it is only in the last decade or so that work with children under the age of three has been regarded as part of the field of 'education' – and even now some still struggle to acknowledge that children under three need 'education' as well as 'care'.

In the last two decades successive UK governments have recognized the importance of early education for children under five, and babies and toddlers are now firmly fixed in the education and care agenda of

12

government in the UK and other countries around the world, with issues relating to the quality of provision made for them becoming central to policy (COAG, 2009; Dalli et al., 2011; DfE, 2012a; French, 2007; Learning and Teaching Scotland, 2010; Tickell, 2011; Nutbrown, 2012; Welsh Government, 2011). With these shifts in policy, come new responsibilities for all those who work with and for young children. There is increased accountability (DfE, 2010, 2012a, 2012b; HMSO, 2006; Munro, 2011) – an inevitable consequence of increased recognition and funding (DfE, 2012b) – and there are added pressures to provide high-quality care and education which has the capacity to meet all children's learning and developmental needs (Penn, 2011; Sylva et al., 2004; Tickell, 2011). With this increased responsibility and accountability comes the need for all practitioners not simply to rehearse effective practices and to provide good experiences for babies and toddlers, but also to know *why* they do what they do. This is even more important in an ever changing world where economic policy levers and drivers can result in a shift in funding priorities, almost overnight. Practitioners must be ready to respond to change but, more importantly than ever before, practitioners must understand the research and theory which underpins their day-to-day work and decisions; for without such theoretical knowledge what they do can lack rigour and a rationale. It is like a building without foundations. Practice without theory, though it might *look* acceptable on the surface, is empty of a fully justified basis for what happens, and thus carries the danger of doing things 'because we do' rather than adopting (or rejecting) practices because there is a clearly understood basis for that decision.

Research is for all practitioners

Research is for everyone who work with young children. It is important to know what research can tell us about babies and toddlers and to know how others have observed and interpreted the things young children do. It is important to understand different viewpoints on work with children under three so that a variety of ideas can be considered and developed to inform modern practice. Research can provide a basis for challenging ideas or for adapting practice. Research-informed practice can make practitioners more secure in their practice, and more open to self-reflection in the light of new thinking and knowledge. Drawing on research as well as practice and experience can, in effect, help practitioners to draw a more detailed 'map' of the terrain in which they work. They can use the knowledge generated by others as well as their own knowing to guide their practice and develop their own unique pathway of interactions with young children.

What does research tell us about babies and toddlers?

In recent years studies of babies and toddlers have come more sharply into focus, particularly since UK government policies have begun to embrace the learning and development needs of babies and children under three within statutory provision. See for example: the English *Early Years Foundation Stage* (DfE, 2012a), and the Scottish *Pre-Birth to Three* (Learning and Teaching Scotland, 2010). The same is the case in Australia, where the first nationwide Australian *Early Years Learning Framework* (COAG, 2009) is now in place.

The landscape is changing. The boundaries of 'education' are no longer fixed at the school starting age. Therefore, we suggest that all research on and with our youngest children is important, regardless of its disciplinary origins. However, many studies are still concerned with literacy, language and communication and learning, development, cognition and play. There is still a need for more research on how babies and toddlers learn and develop, and for studies that help us learn more about the lives of our youngest children. Research that informs us about how babies and toddlers spend their time and who they spend their time with, helps us to understand how to plan for their individual and holistic needs. Early childhood education and care in the twenty-first century is informed, as Penn (2011) says, by a shifting global perspective of children and childhood. Nevertheless, the way in which young children learn and develop is central to our understanding of their needs, so in order that practitioners can plan for the specific needs of very young children they must have a thorough knowledge of child development.

Literacy, language and communication with babies and toddlers

In recent years studies in Australia, New Zealand and the US have focused on aspects of literacy (Dearing et al., 2009; Lee, 2010; Ravi, 2007; Riedl Cross et al., 2011). As Communication and Language is now recognized in the EYFS (DfE, 2012a) as one of the prime areas for learning alongside Physical and Personal, Social and Emotional Development, it is vital that the messages from research are utilized. In her research overview for the National Literacy Trust, Hamer (2012: 19) concludes that, 'The home learning environment, and in particular the communication environment, for babies and toddlers during the first 24 months influences their language acquisition and their performance at school entry'. Thus Hamer reinforces that it is what parents do in the early stages of development that really has an impact on the outcomes for children as they progress through life. In this overview Hamer recommends that practitioners be aware of this fact and work in partnership with parents to promote early literacy at home as well as in the setting, a strategy that has long been argued for and developed by Nutbrown et al. (2005).

This emphasis on the home learning environment is also seen in the UK where the attention paid to literacy and its importance in the early years has been evidenced by the Bookstart Programme which has grown over the years and has now become an established feature of early literacy promotion within the UK from birth (Bookstart, 2011).

In the US, Barlow (1997) reported on the effectiveness of the *Born to Read* programme which targeted children deemed to be 'at risk' of reading failure and developmental delay. In her review of the project, Barlow claims that the programme reached children 'during the years most crucial to brain development' (1997: 20). Most studies claim that early engagement with books is a 'good thing' for babies and toddlers. Many suggest ways in which parents might engage more fully in their young children's exploration of books, and emphasize the importance of spending time in talking with their youngest children. This is true of practitioners too. However, Macrory (2001) claims the emphasis needs to be on knowing and understanding how individual children make sense of language and how they use it, thus avoiding using books in a meaningless way with young children that they are unable to relate to.

Research into the development of language and communication includes studies of the beginnings of speech (Caulfield, 2002), the development of language in bilingual babies and toddlers (Pearson, 1998), the use and development of baby signing (Acredolo and Goodwyn, 1996; Goodwyn et al., 2000; Thompson et al., 2007; Vallotton, 2009, 2010, 2011a, 2011b) and communication with babies with hearing impairments (Yoshinaga and Stredler-Brown, 1992). In a recent study of babyrooms in England, (Goouch and Powell, 2012: abstract) found that: 'many of the practitioners were not routinely, incidentally or intuitively talking to the babies in their care, nor were they aware of the importance of doing so'. This highlights the continued need for those working with young children to understand the crucial importance of talking with babies and toddlers.

Learning, development, cognition and play

In a study of nearly 50 toddlers aged around 18 to 30 months in full day care, Kowalski et al. (2005) examined the toddlers' emerging pretend play. Using videotaped observations the research team assessed the play environment in terms of (a) the provision of play materials, (b) the quality of care and (c) staff attitudes towards play. The toddlers' weekly attendance pattern was taken into consideration when observations were analysed. They found that toddlers who attended childcare for at least four days a week had better play encounters with pre-school-aged peers than those who had less frequent attendance. Perhaps there is something to learn from this study about the benefits to young children of spending time in mixed age group settings rather than being confined to the 'toddler room' where they are separated from the older pre-school children. In a study of the experiences of children under three in day care, Clare (2012) found that children also benefited from the time they were able to spend with the older children in nursery settings. The benefits were recognized in the opportunities for children to become scaffolders of each other's learning as well as in the opportunities for children to engage in play and learning within a more family-like structure. Siblings were able to play alongside each other, younger children were able to be exposed to more challenging resources, and there was often less need for children to make high numbers of transitions as they moved through the nursery.

In a study of mathematical development of 50 one – three-year-olds, Miyakawa et al. (2005) conclude that it is important to present young children with developmentally appropriate tasks to better support their development in meaningful ways. They say, 'If an activity is at just the right level, children think deeply with intrinsic motivation' (2005: 300).

Little voices – important messages

Children's views are increasingly being seen as an important focus of educational research (Atherton and Nutbrown, 2013; Christensen and James, 2008; Grieg et al., 2007; Holmes, 1998; Lancaster, 2010; Lewis and Lindsay, 2000; Nutbrown and Clough, 2009; Nutbrown and Hannon, 2003).

Listening to young children's views and to their expressions of their needs and wants brings them 'into the centre' of discussions about policy, purposes and practices of early education and care. Ways of understanding children's learning have mainly relied on observation, of watching them (Drummond et al., 1992; Elfer, 2005; Nutbrown and Carter, 2010), but far less attention has been given to listening to children, and to the development of other ways of soliciting their views on matters of daily life and learning. It is the case that the 'voices' of vulnerable children have sometimes been attended to with the pioneering of specifically designed interview techniques, mainly in areas of difficulty, such as child protection and child witnesses in court (thus reflecting the interest in 'voice' in relation to oppressed and minority groups). But until recently there has been relatively little interest in understanding the perspectives of children on what we might call the 'ordinary, everyday aspects' of their own lives (Dyer, 2002; Filippini and Vecchi, 2000). Listening to babies and young children is an important role for practitioners.

For us, respectful relationships point to (and require) an inclusive approach to education and care where 'inclusion' means more than the shared location of children, families and practitioners. For us, inclusion means ensuring that all the children in the setting 'belong' in the fullest sense of the word. This means never ignoring or dismissing a small child's cries, and always investigating the protests of an ebullient toddler, as we see in the example below, and paying attention to the always quiet child, who never seeks attention – they belong too.

Billy was a lively two-year-old boy who enjoyed nothing better than being outside in the nursery garden playing with the big wheeled toys. He was fascinated with the 'big blue car', it was his favourite and he got very cross when it was time to come inside for a snack or to have his nappy changed. The nursery practitioners were finding it increasingly difficult to encourage Billy to come inside and he had started getting very angry – kicking, screaming and hitting out at anyone who came near to him, and the other children had begun to keep their distance. Billy's key person, Eliza, had gently broached the subject with Billy's mum who said she had been rather upset when she overheard another child refer to her son as 'angry Billy'. Eliza reassured Billy's mum that at two years old Billy was demonstrating his very powerful feelings and that it was perfectly 'normal' for children of Billy's age to find difficulty in regulating their emotions. Eliza talked with Sally, Billy's paired keyperson, who had noticed Billy was primarily becoming distressed when he had to leave the 'big blue car' behind to come inside. Eliza and Sally agreed they needed to try to reduce the reasons for Billy to come inside, thereby empowering Billy to feel that his 'voice' was being heard. They agreed that there were certain times of the day when Billy had to come inside, e.g. to have lunch or to have his nappy changed. However, they acknowledged that they did not always provide Billy with enough warning of a change to his routine. After further discussion Eliza and Sally decided to play a soothing classical piece of music to indicate it was time to start tidying away. Gradually, over time, Billy came to recognize that when the music came to an end (the track had been deliberately chosen because it was around six minutes long) he was expected to 'park' his car and come in from the garden. This solution worked well, not just for Billy but for all the toddlers.

A couple of weeks later Billy's mum told Eliza that she and Billy had attended a friend's wedding. As the bride began walking down the aisle Billy had said to his mum 'put car away'. She was puzzled at first then suddenly realized that the wedding music was in fact 'Pachelbel's Canon',[1] the same tune that Eliza and Sally used at nursery to indicate the end of outside play-time. The toddler team decided that now that Billy was familiar with the principle of the routine they needed to gather a range of music to use at tidy-up time. They wanted to ensure they gave the children an opportunity to appreciate music for pleasure as well as using it at key times in the day to help the toddlers to recognize when there was going to be a change to their routine.

Questions for reflection

1. How do you help infants and toddlers to have a choice about how they spend their time in your setting?
2. What strategies do you use in your setting to help young children to recognize a change is about to occur in their routine?
3. Supporting ebullient two-year-olds can sometimes be a challenge for parents and practitioners. What support is in place in your setting to help adults to recognize the norms of children's behaviour?

Nutbrown and Clough (2009) report a study of a professional development programme which involved 16 early years practitioners in small-scale action research projects to change aspects of the settings in which they worked, and, importantly, to involve the children in identifying the changes that were needed. The practitioners each developed an action research project in their setting and the following issues were addressed:

- involving parents in the setting
- making the outdoor play space a place where all children felt comfortable and secure
- reviewing the arrangements for transition from pre-school to the Foundation Stage unit
- changing the toilet area so that the children who were frightened were able to feel more at ease
- helping children to settle their disputes

[1] Canon in D composed by J. Pachelbel.

- finding ways to allow boys to have access to the home corner play space
- including children's views on their own progress and achievement in their assessment profiles
- making lunchtimes more peaceful and positive social times
- offering healthier mid-morning snacks
- developing new and workable practices on violent weapon play
- developing key person approaches with babies and toddlers so that their care is more attuned to their needs
- introducing baby signing to give them more autonomy and enable them to better communicate their needs and wants
- consulting children on new all-weather clothing to be purchased
- introducing Persona Dolls to help children learn more about other children's lives
- including more fathers on outings
- reviewing the pace and opportunities provided for children in day care from 8 a.m. to 6 p.m.

Reporting on the study, Nutbrown and Clough observe that:

> One of the things which is clear in all the examples in this study, is the implicit underpinning beliefs which practitioners hold about the children for whom they are responsible. And it is this crucial underpinning which, we suggest, enables practitioners to tackle the difficult, subtle and complex issues in order to create inclusive early years communities. The children's views on 'belonging' and practitioners' interpretations of how such views can be drawn upon to create more inclusive early years environments and communities are central. (2009: 21)

Following a review of the practitioners' projects Nutbrown and Clough (2009) conclude that:

- It is possible to learn children's views of inclusion and belonging, that young children have clear views which can be different from those held by adults.
- Children's own voices are central to any study of their perspectives,

and studies must find ways to 'listen' to those voices so that the views that young children offer can often be considered when making changes in practice.

- Children's personal sense of 'identity' and high 'self-esteem' appear to be the two most important issues to be addressed through curriculum and early years pedagogy. If young children are to successfully experience a sense of inclusivity and belonging in their early years settings, those settings must ensure that, at the heart of their work lie opportunities for young children to feel good about themselves and secure in their developing sense of who they are and how they 'belong' in their learning community. Having opportunities to express views about the things that affect them is crucial to their 'belonging' in their early years community. (Nutbrown and Clough, 2009: 30)

The concepts of 'belonging', 'being' and 'becoming' are at the heart of the Early Years Learning Framework for Australia (EYLF) (COAG, 2009). These concepts value children's sense of identity, thus being part of a family and community is to belong. When children belong this builds the notion that they are safe and free to explore in the 'here' and 'now', therefore valuing the distinct stages of childhood in their own right as opposed to as a preparation for adulthood. Finally, there is also the recognition of the rapid pace of change and the ever-evolving sense of identity which represents all that children are capable of and will eventually become. There are important messages contained within the EYLF, about listening to children and the development of a culture of participation (Lancaster, 2010; Sumsion et al., 2009). The Coram Family Listening to Young Children (Lancaster and Broadbent, 2003) project developed a framework for listening to and acting on the views and needs of children from birth to eight years. Lancaster argues that:

> For every child to really matter, early years professionals need to develop a listening culture; they need to build a set of RAMPS:
> Recognising children's many languages;
> Allocating communication spaces;
> Making time;
> Providing choice;
> Subscribing to a reflective practice.

These principles provide a sound framework to empower children in participatory processes. (Lancaster, 2006: 1)

In promoting this culture of listening to young children, Lancaster suggests that: 'The five principles constitute indicators that professionals can employ to steer how they involve children in making a positive contribution to their learning and well-being' (2006: 2).

Participatory learning is perhaps a term more generally associated with slightly older school-aged children (Cremin and Slatter, 2004; Fraser et al., 2004; Levy, 2008, 2009a, 2009b). Nevertheless, as Pascal and Bertram (2009) point out, since the ratification of the UN Convention of the Rights of the Child in 1991, practitioners have been keen to find ways to listen to the views of young children. Subsequently, there has been a growing interest in participatory approaches with three- and four-year-olds (Clark, 2005; Clark and Moss, 2011; DfE, 2010). The 'mosaic approach' (Clark and Moss, 2011) utilizes a range of methods such as observation, interview, activity-based games, and visual data as the basis for consulting with children. Clark (2005) suggests that listening to young children in a respectful manner can be a complex process and that young children respond best to familiar adults. Clark's point fits with an approach that Nutbrown (2010) adopted when she worked together with practitioners across England to find out about the likes and dislikes of 188 three- and four-year-old children in their early years settings. A key finding of the study highlighted the value children place on relationships with their familiar adults, as well as with their peers. Similarly, Stephenson (2009) combined the tools of conversation and observation over a five-month period to study a group of two- to four-year-olds in their childcare centre. Using a process of reflection, Stephenson found that she was able to 'stand back' from her initial interpretation, to allow for more meaningful themes to emerge from the data. She concluded that adult–child relationships played a significant role in the experiences of the young children at the centre.

There is a growing interest in research that considers the lived experiences of babies and toddlers (Berthelsen et al., 2009; Sumsion et al., 2011), and considers the development of the child within the context of their family and their own community. These studies are important if we are to make sense of what it is like for a child to grow up in an international society. We need to know more about babies and toddlers who spend time in home and group settings, for example. How we value very young children will undoubtedly shape their experiences. Therefore, as Bertheslsen et al. (2009: xiv) suggest, 'children's participation ultimately is the responsibility of adults and society ... To let someone take part in something also means that we (as educators) need to step back and give power to the participant (the child)'. As Nyland (2009: 32) points out, 'In early childhood group settings, many interactions are based around routines. Children have little freedom during the day but are constantly organized through daily schedules'.

Children's involvement in their play and their participation in the culture of learning and care in which they spend their days is essential if they are to maximize their potential. This culture of listening, really listening, can begin when babies are very young. Appell and David (1973) discuss the work of the Pikler Institute which advocates an approach to child-rearing and development based upon key principles whereby staff give their fullest attention to the children. The Pikler principles include:

- the value of independent activity
- the value of a special, favoured, affective relationship and the importance of giving it a form suitable to an institutional setting
- the necessity of fostering the child's awareness of themselves and their environment
- the importance of good physical health as fundamental to realizing other principles.

Appell and David (1973) note a fifth, and fundamental, principle of 'free movement' which is an essential underpinning to the other four. Pikler (1971: 57) argued that a young child had always to be free to move themselves, and their freely initiated movement led to babies' and toddlers' initiatives being in play 'every moment of the life of the young child, in every activity, including the moments of intimacy with the adult'. Pikler (1973: 61) also promoted a dialogue of mutual respect, created in the relationship between adult and child, if the child was 'able to pursue his or her desires with competence'.

Emmie Pikler's work in Hungary was built around her belief that babies and young children need to be offered an environment where they are respected and nurtured to become emotionally and socially mature individuals, able to adjust to the needs of others and of society. She believed that movement lay at the heart of cognition:

> While learning … to turn on the belly, to roll, creep, sit, stand and walk, [the baby] is not only learning those movements but also how to learn. He learns to do something on his own, to be interested, to try out, to experiment. He learns to overcome difficulties. He comes to know the joy and satisfaction which is derived from this success, the result of his patience and persistence. (Pikler, 1940: 73)

A team of early childhood researchers in Australia have been involved in a two-year project studying the lives of babies and toddlers who attend childcare. Through the use of an innovative technological approach, Sumsion and colleagues at Charles Sturt University have been attempting to see the world through the eyes of infants and toddlers. By using a webcam attached to a headband or hat and worn by the children in the project for brief periods of time, it has been possible to gain what has been described as a 'baby's eye view'. Early indications suggest some fascinating findings about how young babies socialize with one another in quite sophisticated ways. Yet, perhaps for professionals who spend their days in the company of infants, these early findings from Australia about children's interest in one another may not be so very surprising. Communication between babies in the first year of life is not a new subject of interest, for example a film of the same name was made by Goldschmied and Selleck in the 1990s, long before the technological explosion of more recent years. However, the everyday minutiae of young children's lives captured on film, over a two-year period, is original and distinct. The Australian project will undoubtedly contribute to our understanding of life from a baby's perspective.

In England, two researchers (Goouch and Powell, 2010) have been working with a group of baby room practitioners across two local authorities. The uniqueness in this particular project has been the introduction of a social network site, NING, set up as a private space where those in the project can discuss elements of their practice.

When we talk of babies, toddlers and young children, we must think of learning in a broad sense. When we talk of babies' learning, it is not necessarily talk about 'curriculum', in the traditional sense of the word, that we think of, but something else, something different. Infant-appropriate pedagogies are pedagogies of listening (Rinaldi, 1999; Scott, 1996), of looking (Elfer, 2005, 2011) and of loving (Lally and Mangione, 2006; Page, 2011a). It has also been long established that it is the warm, responsive and interactive relationships that key adults make with young children that enhances their disposition for language and learning (Bruner, 1983; Landry et al., 2006; Rogoff, 2003; Vygotsky, 1978). For little children, learning is about self and place and space and relationships. The traditional language of education does not always enable us to say what it is we need to say when we are trying to conceptualize, identify and articulate the intricate, moment-by-moment development of young babies. It is not always enough.

In the next chapter we reflect on how research affects our under-standing of the learning and development of infants and young children.

Further reading

Alderson, P. (2008) *Young Children's Rights: Exploring Beliefs, Principles and Practice.* 2nd edn. London: Jessica Kingsley.

Clark, A., Kjørholt, A.T. and Moss, P. (2005) *Beyond Listening: Children's Perspectives on Early Childhood Services.* Bristol: Polity Press.

Johansson, E. and White, E.J. (2011) (eds) *Educational Research with our Youngest Children: Voices of Infants and Toddlers.* International Perspectives on Early Childhood Education and Development 5. London: Springer.

Lansdown, G. (2005) *Can You Hear Me? The Right of Young Children to Participate in Decisions Affecting Them.* The Netherlands: The Bernard van Leer Foundation.

Chapter 2

Looking Beyond What We Already Know about our Youngest Children

This chapter will discuss:
- The need to broaden the research lens in light of:
  o New views of the development of babies' thinking
  o New interpretations of attachment and well-being
  o Addressing ethical issues
- Why research from different disciplines matters
- Why inclusion matters
- Why love matters.

Broadening the research lens

Research that can contribute to our understanding of the learning and development of infants and toddlers, and can tell us something of how systems and policies can work for them, is of vital importance. However, so-called 'educational' research alone does not provide a sufficiently broad information base to answer all our questions about the learning and development of the youngest children. Two areas of research have, in recent times, been shown to add an important dimension to our knowledge of young children and have become key to current and future understanding of young children. These two areas, which here we call *new views of development of babies' thinking and new interpretations of attachment and well-being* have provided supportive perspectives on babies' and young children's learning and development, and have contributed to a fuller understanding of the complexity of the task entrusted to those who work with them. These two aspects of research provide not so much new implications for practice, as a validation of many existing practices and ways of providing for and working with young children. Insights of research in other disciplines have prompted deeper thinking and necessitated clearer articulation of our rationale for the environments and routines created for children under three. We discuss these aspects of provision later in the book, but first it is important to consider what these two fields of research can offer practitioners.

New views of the development of babies' thinking

Not long ago it was thought that newborn babies did not feel pain and that young children could not see the world from anything but their own perspective (David, 1999: 87). Observation has always been an important tool for learning more about what young children can do, and modern observational methods – using film – are building on earlier learning theories developed by such theorists as Vygotsky (1978, 1986) and Piaget (1955). Modern visual and audio recording techniques have enabled researchers and practitioners to create a fuller knowledge base about young children. Recent studies of babies, conducted using film viewed over and over again, have enabled researchers to look more closely at the detail of babies' behaviours, making it possible to develop a clearer picture of their capabilities (Gopnik et al., 1999a; Sumsion et al., 2011). Gopnik et al. (1999a) suggest that it is at times difficult to grasp the amazing phenomenon of how young children think. Their summary of babies' development in thinking is split into three elements: 'Foundation', 'Learning' and 'Other People'. Their Foundation element is where babies are able to translate information and interpret their experiences in particular ways to predict new events. In the Learning element babies use their experiences to modify and reshape their initial representation, so ending up with more complex and abstract representations. This process is ever evolving and children play a dynamic role by exploring and experimenting. The third element applies to the Other People who care for the children actively and unconsciously, promoting, encouraging and influencing children's representations.

In their book *The Scientist in the Crib: Minds, Brains and How Children Learn*, Gopnik et al. (1999b) draw on theories of cognitive and developmental psychology to demonstrate the capacities of young babies and toddlers to learn, and illustrate the complexity of their learning abilities. Developmental psychology has provided some evidence to help us understand why some elements of practice have always been enjoyed by babies. For example, Gopnik and Schulz (2004) have shown how infants and young children have the prerequisites for making causal inferences particularly in their ability to learn from imitation. Meltzoff and Prinz (2002; see also Gopnik, 2009; Sumsion et al., 2011; Trevarthen, 2010) have shown how babies can understand and imitate some quite complex actions of others, and illustrate how this can be a powerful tool for learning social behaviour. This imitation is clearly seen in the work of Murray and Andrews (2000), where babies were videoed and observed to mimic the facial gestures of the adult minutes after their birth. Both are evidence, if we needed it, of what is going on when adults play peekaboo with young children, and indications that such interactive exchanges between adult and child are much more than simple fun.

Studies in neuroscience (Greenfield, 1997; Greenough et al., 1987), the scientific study of the nervous system, have shed new light on how the brain develops, and so have challenged some long-accepted beliefs about babies. Nobel prizewinner Eric Kandel, a psychiatrist and neuroscientist, argued that the purpose of neuroscience was to help us to understand what happens in the brain. He wrote:

> The task of neural science is to explain behaviour in terms of the activities of the brain. How does the brain marshal its millions of individual nerve cells to produce behaviour, and how are these cells influenced by the environment …? The last frontier of the biological sciences – their ultimate challenge – is to understand the biological basis of consciousness and the mental processes by which we perceive, act, learn, and remember. (Kandel et al., 2000: 7)

Graham Allen was commissioned by the UK government to carry out an independent review of early intervention (Allen, 2011). The review

highlights the importance of understanding how the brain functions so that intervention strategies can be put into place for vulnerable children, who are at risk of damage to their developing brains. The two images on the front cover of the report, one of a healthy brain next to one which has been seriously neglected, illustrate the consequences of neglect on the brain development of children in the first three years of life. Allen's review makes sobering reading but the intention in his report is to make clear the importance of early intervention to ensure the best possible chances in life for all children.

It is not necessary for early years practitioners to understand the physiology of the brain, nor do they need to be fully conversant with the development and functioning of the nervous system. Nor is it necessary for us to be aware of the detail of the complex field of neuroscience and neuropsychology. Above all, neuroscience gives us a confidence to trust what we see in babies, and to trust that the complex and rapid development which takes place in the first year of life is fuelled by nature and supported and extended by the environments and relationships in which children are nurtured. In their book *From Neurons to Neighborhoods: The Science of Early Childhood Development*, Shonkoff and Phillips (2000) draw upon a plethora of research to inform their thinking about how children think, learn and develop, which they summarize below:

- All children are born wired for feelings and ready to learn.
- Early environments matter and nurturing relationships are essential.
- Society is changing and the needs of young children are not being addressed.
- Interactions among early childhood science, policy, and practice are problematic and demand dramatic rethinking. (Shonkoff and Phillips, 2000: 4)

In an ever-changing world it is important for busy practitioners to take time to reflect upon their practice and to discuss with others what it is like to be a baby or toddler in an early years setting.

Questions for reflection

1. Thinking about the four bullet points above, what opportunities are there in your day-to-day work to think about and reflect upon the way in which young children learn?
2. Can such opportunities be built in to your working week?
3. What does the term 'vulnerable' mean to you, in the context of your daily work?
4. How do you provide a nurturing relationship to the young children that you are responsible for?

Neuroscience has now provided evidence of the capacities of babies which have been known to many parents for generations; for example, that young babies can distinguish one human face from another, and that even quite young babies can recognize a familiar face (Gopnik et al., 1999a). Such studies mean that we now *know* that babies can get bored and need interesting surroundings, company and stimulation. As Brierley (1994: 82) noted: 'The brain thrives on variety and stimulation. Monotony of surroundings, toys that only do one thing are soon disregarded by the brain'.

Video recordings of the eye movements of newborn babies suggest that babies can show preferences for certain objects and images (Gopnik et al., 1999a). That babies can differentiate between objects to seek out, for example, their chosen toy or comforter, is not news to many parents. However, such evidence from scientific research may well be a useful support to those working with the youngest children who no longer need to rely solely on instinct and personal observation but can draw on other research studies too. Studies suggest, as many parents of new babies have known, that babies quickly recognize familiar faces, and, although they may not call this process of human recognition 'habituation' (Gopnik et al., 1999a: 27), they know that their babies know them!

Other similar studies (Gammage, 2006; Meltzoff and Moore, 1999; Shin, 2010; Sumsion et al., 2011) have contributed to our knowledge of how babies and young children develop their understanding throughout the first three years of their lives. Such research suggests that babies are born with innate tendencies of curiosity and recognition and that adults can confidently harness these natural tendencies in order to support those early skills. By creating appropriate environments to stimulate their interests and support their learning and development, practitioners are building on babies' inbuilt desire to discover. 'Staff in infant/toddler rooms must make room in their very busy days to focus on each child, offering him or her the opportunity to experience the warmth and enjoyment of child-centred and responsive shared sessions' (Makin, 2006: 275).

In a study of visual stimuli to babies, Wailling (2005) identified three high-frequency triggers: noise, movement and being outdoors. Wailling writes:

> *Noise*, ranging from an adult calling the baby's name to an unex-pected clash of toys, immediately resulted in visual attention being given. … *Movement* – ranging from that of a pop-up toy to that of passing people – also attracted the babies' attention. … Movement triggered scanning and tracking responses in the babies as well as their sustained attention. … When *out of doors* the babies scanned and tracked their immediate horizons and once fixed on an object of interest, passing children, the black edge of the buggy rain cover, the movement of the garden shrub when they were being placed on the ground in the car seat before being strapped into the car, appeared almost hypnotised by the imagery. (2005: 52, original emphasis)

Trevarthen's work has become popular among some educationists, who believe it offers evidence to support growing assertions that babies *can* think and that their environments for learning should be tailored to support such thinking. Trevarthen (1977: 7), inspired by the work of Bruner, writes: 'I became convinced that an exceedingly com-plex innate mechanism foreshadowing the co-operative intelligence of adults and more general than the mechanism of language, was already functioning in early infancy'.

But we should not be seduced into believing that neuroscience is the key to understanding babies, and we should be careful not to tread uncritically into the realm of scientific research. Images of the brain and talk of young brains atrophying due to lack of stimulation can strike fear into parents and practitioners alike, and it is important to recognize the value of practitioner knowledge, practitioners' research and practitioners' experience. Neuroscience can offer us something, yes, but it does not offer everything and is not a substitute for understanding gained from other disciplines – it is not the Holy Grail. For while it can be useful for those in the field of education and care to learn from studies carried out in other disciplines, such as psychology, the sciences and, in particular, neuroscience, it does not necessarily take us so *very* far in changing practices. Hannon argues that while the results of the studies of neuroscience are interesting: 'They have limited implications for early childhood intervention and education in the sense of changing what is currently already done on the basis of non-neuroscience research or custom' (Hannon, 2003: 8). Furthermore, as Oates, Karmiloff-Smith and Johnson (2012) point out, although our knowledge of the importance of brain studies is increasing, we cannot and should not allow these studies on their own, to shape every aspect of policy and practice in early years, without further scrutiny of how such studies can be useful to us in the context of what we already know about young children and alongside other equally important research. Scientific evidence that babies can think, that stimulation is important, has led some parents and practitioners into dangerous territory, and to the so-called 'hot-housing' of babies and young children. In the US, psychologists Golinkoff and Hirsh-Pasek (2004: 3) write of the dangers of the ever-growing market in baby intelligence equipment and information: 'The baby-educating industry had found a receptive audience of parents eager to enrich their offspring. One survey shows that 65 per cent of parents believe that flash cards are "very effective" in helping 2-year-olds develop their intellectual capacity.'

Similarly Crain worries about going against the grain of nature and urges:

> Children enter the world with an inborn growth schedule that is the product of several million years of biological evolution. They are pre-eminently 'wise' about what they need and what they are ready and not ready to do … If baby is hungry, we should feed her; if she wants to play, we should go ahead and play with her;

if she is sleepy we should let her sleep and not rouse her to be fed. The baby follows nature's laws so we can safely follow the baby's cues. (Crain, 2003: 11–12)

New knowledge about the development of babies' thinking must be used in concert with findings from other research. Taken together with the findings of research, such as discussed earlier in this chapter, and with new thinking about how babies develop relationships and secure attachments with close adults, we obtain a fuller picture of babies' learning and development. Perhaps the most important point for practitioners to remember in their day-to-day work is, as David et al. assert:

> babies focus first and foremost on people, and then on the objects and materials around them (Gopnik et al., 1999[a]; Goswami 1998; Mandler, 1999; Murray and Andrews, 2000).
> It is these 'messages' that we can take to help us understand early development and learning – that right from birth, young children are active learners, deeply interested in people, who are trying to 'make sense' of the world around them. (2003: 46)

New interpretations of attachment and well-being

It is only natural that some parents may become jealous if they feel their child is forming a close bond with another unrelated adult, fearing perhaps that their child will no longer need the parent. However, although this is unlikely, as Goldschmied and Jackson point out, some parents need time to adjust to the new relationships their child is making outside of the family:

> Some parents may need help to understand that sharing love and affection with another caregiver is not like sharing an apple or a sandwich where the more people the less there is for each. Love is learned by loving … by the end of their first year, most children will have formed attachments to several different people. Their

love for their mothers is in no way diminished by this. (Goldschmied and Jackson, 2004: 44)

Fundamental to young children's healthy development, and crucial to the development of their thinking, are the parts adults play in their lives and in their all-round growth and development. Positive and close relationships with adults are crucial for all children – indeed for all human beings. We know that people need other people in their lives and seek out people with whom they can spend their days and their lives. Close, intimate and trusting relationships are essential to the well-being of every one of us. Human beings, deprived of the company of other human beings they like and love, will suffer. And the development of close and safe relationships is never more important than for young children who spend time in day care – away from their own homes and parents.

The early nurturance of very young children and the importance of consistent high-quality attachment between the caregiver and the child are in themselves recognized as the vital components in optimal brain development; a part of every child's birthright, and pivotal features in carefully crafted loving, educational and socio-emotional experience from birth. These are essential ingredients if the brain is to achieve something akin to its real potential, and if humans are to grow into fully functioning, creative and caring adults (Gammage, 2006: 235).

Attachment Theory points quite clearly to the need, in particular for young children, to be in the care of warm responsive practitioners. In 1953 Bowlby argued in his famous study, *Child Care and the Growth of Love*, that an infant forms a relationship with its mother which is special and different from the relationships he or she forms with other adults. What Bowlby described as 'monotropy', was never without controversy because it was said to have disregarded the close relationship a baby might also form with their father, siblings, grandparents, and so on. Bowlby suggested that the bond between mother and infant in the first six months is so intense that, if broken, it would cause *irreparable damage* to the baby.

Drawing on Bowlby's Attachment Theory, young mothers were told that leaving their children would have long-lasting, damaging effects on their babies However, in a further study, *Attachment and*

Loss (1969), Bowlby argued that his earlier work had been misinterpreted and that his theory had been misunderstood: 'It has sometimes been alleged that I have expressed the view that mothering should always be provided by a child's natural mother, and also that mothering "cannot be safely distributed among several figures" (Mead, 1962). No such views have been expressed by me' (Bowlby, 1969: 303).

Bowlby's Attachment Theory is a clear example of why questions should be asked of researchers, and why research should be scrutinized before its findings are used to inform and develop policy and practice. The children in Bowlby's study had been separated from their mothers – indeed from all members of their families – for long periods of time and were reared in residential institutions or had spent long periods in hospital. It is little wonder, then, that the children showed signs of suffering from a lack of close involvement with loving adults. There is a danger in using research for purposes different from those intended. Interpreting findings about a specific group of children, with specific needs and living in particular (and different) condition from many other children in society, and generalizing these to apply to all members of society, is dangerous. (Bowlby's study is part of the history of work with children in hospital, and he might well claim to have played some part in changing the shape of children's nursing and of attitudes to the involvement of parents in the recovery and well-being of sick children.)

More recently Vorria et al. (2003) examined the quality of attachment to caregivers of a group of Greek infants reared in a residential nursery prior to adoption at around the age of two years. They showed how the children's capacity for attachment was related to the children's cognitive and psychosocial development, their behaviour, temperament and the sensitivity of their caregivers. Vorria et al. (2003) found that the majority of infants reared in residential group care showed what they called 'disorganized' attachment to their caregivers, and that those babies who were 'securely' attached were observed to express more frequent positive affect and social behaviour, and to initiate more frequent interaction with their caregivers. Shin (2010) investigated adult–child interactions and infant–peer relationships in nursery settings. Her findings suggested that the characteristics of infant–peer relationships are different to adult–child relationships. However, because the subtle signs of intentional communication between infants and toddlers are often overlooked by early childhood practitioners, Shin suggests that her study provides further evidence that practitioners have a significant role to play in encouraging growing friendships between young children. We can conclude from these two studies that positive attachments support children's well-being and are vital for learning, but such studies of attachment which include children in routine home and day-care settings have been lacking until quite recently.

Others have contested Bowlby's theories (Cassidy, 2008; Melhuish and Moss, 1991; Rutter, 2002), arguing that the security of the mother–child relationship is also dependent on the skills and abilities of the mother, and that mothering skills are not *necessarily* innate. As Cassidy (2008: 15) points out, relationships are 'hierarchical rather than interchangeable', which supports the view that infants can cope with being separated from their mother and that she is not likely to be replaced in her child's affections provided the child receives sensitive caregiving from an adult who is closely attuned to their needs. We think that for practitioners working in professional roles with infants and young children there are two key messages to bear in mind here: (1) high quality caregiver relationships are central to emotional development (Carroll, 2001; Elfer et al., 2012; Schore, 1997) and learning (Sylva et al., 2012) in infants and toddlers; and (2) relationships take time to develop (Cassidy, 2008). Thus there is a compelling argument for young children who attend day care to be given not only opportunity but *time* to become closely attached to one or two special adults – key person(s) – rather than being indiscriminately cared for by a range of people (Bain and Barnett, 1986).

Lee (2006) studied the development of relationships between three babies (6–11 months of age) and their caregivers in a childcare setting in New York City. Using observations, video recordings and interviews, Lee found both common and unique patterns of relationship development. The study shows that the children took between six and 11 weeks to build firm relationships and that the infant–caregiver relationship is two-way and reciprocal. The daycare context, Lee suggests, can have a significant impact on the development of close and supportive relationships between carer and child. Lee concluded:

> Building a firm relationship between infant and caregiver was a mutually beneficial and meaningful experience for both the infant and the caregiver. Relationship development also made for easy and smooth communication, sharing of thoughts and emotions, and mutual understanding between infant and caregiver. In addition, the infants and the caregivers made an effort to fine tune their behaviours in response to each other's development and change continuously, which is crucial in maintaining a firm relationship. (Lee, 2006: 146)

Although Lee's study focused on only three babies, there is an important message here, as we have already mentioned, about allowing babies time to 'settle' and 'attach' – a process whereby one human being learns to connect with another cannot be hurried.

In many communities all over the world babies are cared for in extended families where grandparents, aunts and older siblings share in childcare – the babies in these families have the opportunity to 'attach' to key family members from the moment of birth. As David (2006: 30) reports: 'Grandparents in ethnic minority communities can often be seen as providing the strongest reason for families maintaining minority languages'.

Attachment Theory has had a troubled past, and (as is the danger that findings from neuroscience will *also* be misunderstood and misused) so Attachment Theory has, at times, been used and manipulated throughout its history for economic and political ends. The apparent misrepresentation of Bowlby's work about the mother–child attachment bond has long been debated – variously used as a 'stick' with which to beat working mothers, as a politically expedient tool, in relation to the economy and the workforce, and as a rationale for flexible working hours, and so on.

Sensational at the time (and perhaps – in part – responsible even now for the 'guilt' expressed by many mothers who return to work and 'leave' their baby in home or day care), some considered Bowlby's theory to have been used to promote politically expedient ends. At the time, servicemen were returning from the Second World War, and jobs (which had been largely carried out by women during the war years) were needed for the men. Perhaps 'Your baby needs you' was a better phrase to utter than 'We'd prefer the men to do these jobs now'! Bowlby's study became the object of political debate and was used by post-war pressure groups to argue that women should stay at home to rear their children. Working around the same time, Winnicott (1953, 1957), a paediatrician and psychoanalyst, developed the concept of 'containment' or 'mental holding', and the 'transitional object' (often referred to as the comfort blanket). The point here is that babies not only need to be held physically but also to be 'held in mind' (Miller, 1992). Winnicott's work has helped professionals to understand the needs of stressed and distressed children and to support children, particularly at times of transition in their lives, while his notion of the *good-enough mother* (1964), is also useful in seeing a mother whose physical and emotional attunement to her baby helps her baby to adapt without trauma to changes, including the eventual realization on the part of the baby that she or he is separate from his or her mother, and has also been influential in developing family and educational practices. For Winnicott the adult *is* the emotional environment. Thereby, as Fonagy et al. (2008) explain, it is *how* the adult responds to the baby's non-verbal clues and intonations that distinguishes whether the baby is being cared for by an adult who is warm, loving and in tune with the child.

Addressing ethical issues

This also causes us to raise issues about the ethics of research. All research, especially that involving children, must be conducted to the highest of ethical standards. For example, Wailling (2005) carried out a research project to determine what visually attracted two five-month old babies in their homes and in childcare settings. Wailling went to considerable lengths to consider the ethics and rights of the babies. The carefully planned minutiae of her approach to the research was striking (Table 2.1).

Table 2.1 *Wailling's ethical framework*

	Ethical issues which may arise	Action to be taken	Key reference
Research design	Minimizing the risk of significant harm during the research design and in conducting the field study	Identification of possible risks in the use of electrical equipment	Australian Association for Research in Education (AARE) (1999, p.3)
	Use of videotaping in baby's home/care setting	Letter sent to interested participants outlining project and its aims including a breakdown of equipment to be used and a section for questions	Society for Research in Child Development (SRCD) Ethical Standards (1991) x ref principles 2, 6, 7, 8, 11, 12, 13 & 14
		Discussion with adult participants re: research questions, expectations, level of involvement (proposed length of video recording, agreeing dates to review recordings and discuss findings) and how the findings are to be presented (x ref confidentiality and anonymity)	
	Informed consent of parents and carers	Use of consent slip – name, tel no and e-mail address given of academic supervisor, released to verify research status of researcher	University of Sheffield dissertation guidelines (2004, p.23)
	Acknowledgement that participants have the right to withdraw at any time	Availability of proposed ethical code of conduct that governs research and how it will be adhered to	Graue and Walsh (1998, p.57) Morrow and Richards (1996, p.103) University of Sheffield dissertation guidelines (2004, p.23)
Baby's rights	To use non-intrusive research methods	Video recording schedule to take into account baby's routine and preferences if known	x ref initial interviews with parents and carers
	Baby becoming distressed when recording	Stop recording, time length of stoppage, include this in the analysis of research method, resume recording when the parent/carer feels confident that the baby is comfortable and alert	Christensen and Alison (2000, p.10) Graue and Walsh (1998, p.60)

Continues

Table 2.1 Continued

	Ethical issues which may arise	Action to be taken	Key reference
	Jeopardy — if videoing brings to light circumstances which jeopardize the well-being of the baby — e.g. baby left with feeding bottle propped against a pillow	Stop recording and take interventionist action if baby is at risk of physical danger — i.e. choking	SRCD Ethical Standards (1991) x ref principle 9
		If baby has been at risk of physical danger, inform parent/carer of duty of care to report incident, leave setting, write down observations using a narrative style, sign and date within one hour of leaving setting, inform Child Protection helpline (number available in local Area Committee Child Protection booklet (acquired January 2005) follow advice and procedures, telephone setting informing them of my wish to discontinue research project	AARE (1999, p.4)
Professional conduct	Sharing findings and reporting results — avoiding giving advice, commenting on the care of the carer, abilities of parents	Conduct interview to discuss findings of recording and completed questionnaire. Consider strengths and weaknesses of interviewing	Cohen et al. (2003, p.27)
		Flexible interviewing methods and considering ethical issues when interviewing	Clough and Nutbrown (2002, p.107) Cohen et al. (2003, p.281)
		Careful transcribing	Cohen et al. (2003, p.281)
		Consider appropriate methods of recording interviews — tape recording, note taking	Cohen et al. (2003) p.292
	Building a sense of mutual trust — clear agreement as to the length of videotaping/who is to review recordings (x ref anonymity) how findings are to be presented in the dissertation, disposal of recordings (agreement that all recordings made will be passed on	Letter sent to participants, agreement outlining clearly what involvement involves, how results are to be reported	SRCD Ethical Standards (1991) x ref principle 2
		First meeting between researcher and participants to outline proposed length of video recordings, overview of questionnaire, indication of length of follow-up interview and how findings will be presented.	SRCD Ethical Standards (1991) x ref principle 7 & 3

Ethical issues which may arise	Action to be taken	Key reference
to the baby's parents, x ref incentive – the recordings to provide a unique record of the baby's history)	Agreement to be involved in research sought (signed permission slip signed by parents, carers and dated) Acknowledging that participants have the right to withdraw at any time	SRCD Ethical Standards (1991) x ref principle 4 BERA Ethical Guidelines (1992, p.2)
Personal misconduct – 'what if' scenario – what if money from the setting is missing following my visits?	If requested make available CRB disclosure and personal references of good conduct	SRCD Ethical Standards (1991) x ref principle 2, 7, 11, 13 & 14
Confidentiality – showing/discussing recordings with those who are actively involved in the research project	Conduct feedback sessions to discuss findings of recording and completed questionnaire Consider appropriate methods of recording feedback sessions Consider ethical issues in interviewing	Graue and Walsh (1998, p. 60) Cohen et al. (2003, p. 246)
Building a sense of mutual trust Building a sense of mutual respect Ensure that the questionnaire is clear and easy to complete and its completion falls within the agreed boundaries of research project and participant involvement	Outlining aims of dissertation Pilot proposed questionnaire and evaluate feedback and make amendments	
Entry into field Finding participants Approaching 'go between' agencies LEA childcare development officers, NCMA co-ordinator Approaching interested c/minders, key workers in day care settings and the parents of babies in their care	Outline aims of dissertation Discuss code of research conduct	University of Sheffield (2004, p.23)

Continues

Table 2.1 *Continued*

	Ethical issues which may arise	Action to be taken	Key reference
Gaining consent of participants	Ensuring that parents/carers give informed consent	Obtain written consent Obtain consent of any adult/child who is framed in the video recordings	x ref research design and use of consent forms
Data collection	Put in place procedures that ensure that all recordings/completed questionnaires and notes are stored securely and anonymity is addressed	Referring to participant babies using agreed names Use of locked cabinet to store field notes which contain contact details	SRCD Ethical Standards (1991) x ref principle 2, 7, 11 & 13
Leaving the field	Put in place procedures that ensure anonymity in all recordings/completed questionnaires, notes and findings	Strive to create relationship which is based on honesty and openness	BERA Ethical Guidelines (1992, p.2)
	Ensure that participants know how the outcomes/findings of the research are to be presented	Make available completed dissertation prior to submission for final marking in September 2005	x ref request for family to have a copy of dissertation/all recordings and notes
	Offer all original video recordings made in the baby's own home and in their care settings to individual baby's parent	Give verbal and written undertaking	x ref participation letter 3
Data analysis	Interview with parents/carers to share video recordings/researcher's interpretations and outcomes of the completed questionnaires		BERA Ethical Guidelines (1992, pp. 1–2) Cohen et al. (2003, p.292) SRCD Ethical Standards (1991) x ref principles 2, 7, 11, 13 & 14
	Avoid fabrication, falsification or misrepresentation of data		Graue and Walsh (1998, p.60)

	Ethical issues which may arise	Action to be taken	Key reference
	Present data analysis, outcomes and findings mindful to cultural, religious, gendered, and other significant differences		BERA Ethical Guidelines (1991, pp. 1–2)
Writing up	Write dissertation adhering to dissertation guidelines		University of Sheffield (2004, pp. 30–31)
Dissemination of findings	Distribution of dissertation – two copies to University of Sheffield	Two copies to the University of Sheffield	
	Distribution of findings to other agencies	One copy to parents of babies involved in research project (if requested)	
		In-house seminar session to colleagues (Ofsted Early Years)	
		Summary of findings to Dr A. Franklin, University of Sussex	
		Summary of findings to NCMA co-ordinator	
		Summary of findings to manager group day care setting	
		Summary of findings to participant childminder	

Source: Wailling (2005)

In the following extract Wailling (2005: 42–4) describes her ethical approach.

Consideration of ethical issues throughout this dissertation has been a constant theme. Primarily, my field studies have taken place in three domains: the family home, a childminder's home and in a day care setting. By video recording the babies in their own homes, I was aware that I was documenting private lives. Although the two childcare settings came within the remit of regulation and inspection under the national care standards (Sure Start/DfES 2003a; Sure Start/DfES 2003b), the boundary between private and public sphere was difficult to define. I was aware, for example, that gaining permission to video in the home of a childminder crossed both boundaries. My research involved her as a professional childcare practitioner, however the setting, the immediate environment, was part of her family life.

The way forward seemed to be in the use of an ethical framework, which could be developed and adapted to meet specific purposes relevant to my research. Marsh (2003), Parker (2002) and Chilvers (2002) successfully adopted an ethical framework as a working tool to document each step of their research projects, from research design to dissemination of findings. My use of such a framework evolved as the field study progressed to take into consideration aspects such as my role as a researcher and the 'what if?' scenario, for example what if I witnessed a situation which placed a child at risk of injury?

With the completion of the field study ... the advantage of using an ethical framework was that it could still be added to – especially with regard to the presence of children not directly involved in the research who 'wandered' into the viewfinder when recording was taking place. Recording non-participant children did not present itself until the last session of recording in the group day care setting but did need to be addressed. The key worker's own child came to her mum for a hug, an action which attracted the attention of the project baby. This resulted in a short recording of the baby's interaction with this older child. On discussion later with the manager of the setting it was decided that the permission given by all parents to photograph children in the nursery was probably sufficient to cover this scenario.

The completion of my ethical framework [Table 2.1] was a working document, often referred to and amended. Key references were taken from two sets of guidelines, the British Educational Authority for Research Ethical Guidelines (BERA, 1992) and the Australian Association for Research in Education Code of Ethics (AARE, 1998; Bibby, 1998). To supplement these guidelines other sources, referenced in the grid, were used to examine more closely issues such as children's rights and participation in research. It was important to consider if any adaptations were needed when working with babies. Such changes would influence not only the research design but also the presentation of the outcomes themselves. As Christensen and James (2002) highlight, research involving children does not require special techniques but research methods should take into consideration the 'concrete particularities' (p.ix) of the persons being studied.

The use of video recordings, as an appropriate research method, was balanced against babies' and caregivers' feelings. For example, the mother involved in the piloting of the video recordings felt that the tripod video recorder was intrusive, especially when she was comforting the baby, so I changed to a hand held camcorder. This issue becomes especially important, as Stone et al. (1974) argue, if infants are sensitive, as we must now believe, researchers must take serious account of the procedures that they use. Although the implications of research with children and involving children are well documented (Graue and Walsh 1998, Grieg and Taylor 1999, Cohen et al. 2003, Christensen and James 2000 and Mooney and Blackwell 2003), few studies discuss their approaches to research with babies under six months.

In the above extract, Wailling describes the method and process she adopted in her research project to ensure the ethical 'safety' and consent of those involved. It is now a mandatory requirement for researchers, including those involved in student programmes, to undergo a formal ethical review process (BERA, 2011). However, it is important to be clear about the difference between the ethical issues that Wailling so carefully addressed in her research and the institutional practice of complying with an Ethical Review in order to gain ethical approval to begin the research. Particularly striking in Wailling's research was her amendment of the use of the tripod when filming the mother and child, and this confirms the importance of establishing an environment of trust, confidentiality and indeed 'voice' for both participants. Ethical practices are an issue for practitioners as well as for researchers, and we return to this issue later in the book.

Some things never change, and the debate about the role of the mother is re-ignited from time to time by television programmes, other media reports and specific newsworthy events. The implications of Bowlby's controversial theory have been argued and debated for over half a century since it was first published in the 1950s. It has contributed to the ongoing controversy about day care for children, with critics of Attachment Theory claiming that secure attachment is not always necessary for healthy development and arguing that it may depend on cultural child-rearing practices (Göncü, 2010; Hennessy et al., 1992; Woodhead, 1996), and others such as Dahlberg et al. (2007) and Trevarthen (2004) arguing against attachment practice in nurseries, claiming it hinders young children's ability to make friends. However, as Elfer et al. (2012) make clear, the key person approach is not intended to diminish children's relationships with other adults and certainly not with their peers. More likely, as noted by Shin (2010: 298) the closely attached adult is more able to 'facilitate close peer relationships', as they will be more attuned to the child/ren. Much research suggests that babies, toddlers and young children fare best when they are securely attached to one or more familiar adults. The Effective Provision of Pre-School Education project (EPPE) (Sylva et al., 2004) and the National Institute of Child Health and Human Development (NICHD) (2002) emphasized the part played by the quality of interactions between staff and children in settings where children are cared for when away from their parents. 'The quality of the interactions between children and staff was particularly important; where staff showed warmth and were responsive to the individual needs of children, children made more progress' (Sylva et al., 2004: 3). This is not surprising – it makes sense that young children will want to be with adults who respond as if they like them and behave positively towards them. Babies and young children need to feel accepted, liked and loved if they are to feel comfortable about themselves and what they can do. High levels of self-esteem are an important part of young children's ability to develop resilience and independence (Roberts, 2002, 2010). The Well-being and Involvement scales developed by Laevers et al. (1997) give practitioners the opportunity to judge the levels of children's well-being at a particular moment in time, recognizing that when a child is in a state of high well-being the opportunities for sustained learning and development are heightened. 'Children with a high level of well-being feel great. They enjoy life to the full' (Laevers et al., 1997: 8). When there are high levels of both well-being and involvement Laevers describes this as being like a 'fish in water'.

Humans like to be liked and 'babies [in particular] like to be liked by their familiar adults' (Parker-Rees, 2007: 7). The role of familiar adults in affirming children's actions is crucial, because they can make or break children's feelings and increase or shatter their self-esteem. As McMullen and Dixon (2009: 112) point out: '…We build our most trusting and productive relationships between and among those individuals with whom we establish a reciprocal feeling that each relationship partner is valued as competent and worthwhile'.

Attached babies are often happier babies; babies who 'smile with their whole bodies' and who are secure and calm. 'When babies understand that what they feel is okay with the people around them, they have a better chance of learning to calm themselves' (Gonzalez-Mena, 2007: 20). Attachment is at the core of the 'key person approach' (Elfer et al., 2003, 2012) which provides clear evidence of the importance of close and specific relationships between practitioners, children and parents. Elfer et al. (2003) define the key person (KP) and the key person approach (KPA) as consisting of the close triangular attachments between the child, the key person and the child's parent/guardian or main carer (we return to this later in the book). It is a mandatory requirement within the EYFS (DfE, 2012a) to make provision for children to be assigned a key person. However, Page and Elfer (2013) demonstrate that practitioners do not always find it easy to cope with the emotional complexity of these close relationships. As Cortazar and Herreros indicate (2010), there is a need to find out what early childhood practitioners themselves already know about attachment theory and what strategies will assist them to understand more about how attachment relationships impact upon their day-to-day work with infants and toddlers.

Why research from different disciplines matters

The findings and the insights generated by Attachment Theory and subsequent studies on attachment and intimate relationships between young children and their carers, must – like any research study – be subject to informed, critical responses and used by sensitive and informed practitioners to create meaningful experiences for the children they work with. Brierley (1994) asserts that adults who work with young children have a responsibility to recognize each and every child's potential. This view is supported by Gopnik et al. (1999a, 1999b) who have shown that it is the confidence and reassurance of adults which gives the youngest children confidence to explore new things. In the 1930s Vygotsky called this 'scaffolding' the child's learning. So, studies by generations of researchers from a range of disciplines have come together to show how crucial and complex are the roles of early years practitioners in supporting the positive development of young children's relationships and learning.

As Gerhardt (2004) suggests, we have arrived at a time in which the emotional aspects of living and learning can be informed by different research disciplines. In other words, it is not only what babies and children *learn* that is important but *how* they learn – they need holistic approaches to learning. Educationalists, health specialists, psychologists, social workers, community workers and others can come together with families to support the whole development of children, and government policy is beginning to recognize the importance of young children's emotional development (COAG, 2009; DfE, 2012a; Learning and Teaching Scotland, 2010; Sure Start, 2006).

Why inclusion matters

The *Every Child Matters* agenda (DfES, 2004b) was a key to inclusive policy in practice with the aim of supporting parents from pregnancy onwards. Although the policy agenda has moved on, the 'joined-up' systems of health, family support, childcare and education services to provide *all* children with the best start possible chance in life (2004b: 2) are still relevant within early years pedagogy and indeed still exist within the remit of Sure Start Children's Centres (DfE, 2010), and this too is recognized by government (DfE, 2011). Though policy moves on and language changes, every child does *still* matter, so, keeping with the language of the ECM policy, we see that every child is important – all children are entitled to '*the best start possible in the vital early years*'. And so an inclusive position must lie at the heart of policies for children. A policy which is inclusive means meeting diverse needs in different ways – equality of opportunity and experience, not 'identikit childcare':

> All children are individuals, unique in their abilities, from a rich diversity of backgrounds, beliefs and cultures. All children have the right to be treated with respect, positive regard and dignity. Articles 29 and 30 of the *United Nations Convention on the Rights of the Child* (1989) state clearly that respect and recognition for the child's own cultural identity, values and language (and that of others), should be part of his/her education. (French, 2007: 10)

Inclusion is about partnership, it is about families, practitioners and government working together. It is about doing things differently and valuing everyone: 'Inclusion and responsive care are crucial if children's rights are to be promoted effectively. Through working closely with parents and other professionals, staff in early years settings recognise that all those involved with children and families have an important contribution to make' (Learning and Teaching Scotland, 2010: 20). And this recognition of diversity, difference, contribution and need must be in the consciousness of all who work with and for young children and their families. Nutbrown and Clough (2013: 2) see inclusion as 'a political and social struggle which foregrounds difference and identity and involves whole-setting and practitioner reform', having moved from being related solely to issues of learning difficulty to 'a central part of the governmental agenda for broader society'. Nutbrown and Clough represent the voices of children, parents and practitioners to highlight the importance of inclusion and the devastating consequences of excluding children and families because of who they are. They show how, for example, the exclusion of a travelling family, the racist harassment of a Pakistani family, violence and antagonism towards two gay parents, and the denial of a nursery place for a child with emotional and behavioural difficulties has a detrimental effect on those who exclude as well as those who are excluded.

A powerful recent study of the views of parents with disabled babies shows how parents can see their children as simply that, children. Goodley (2007) tells the stories of some parents who battle with the exclusionary practices of professionals – and sometimes of family and friends – to identify their children as the individuals they are:

> We're both from here, we've got a lot of family and friends here but further afield as well, we're very lucky. But even so we only had a couple of negative comments about 'oh I don't know whether to send a card' or 'I don't know whether to say congratulations or not'. And you kind of have to deal with that and just think 'well people are only perhaps a little bit ignorant and unsure as to how we have taken the news'. (Mother of baby boy with Down's syndrome)

The Parents of Disabled Babies Project (Goodley, 2007) also highlights the ways in which some parents see their babies, as babies first:

> But actually, why should you want to get rid of it [autism] anyway because I think some of the experiences that we've had with Ben are just amazing and very humanising really. I mean some of the things he's able to tell us, I really think that some adults would be struggling to find the words for that and the fact that we've worked very hard together to always find a way of understanding each other, it's sort of very enriching. (Mother of three-year-old son diagnosed with autism)

Inclusion matters because it is every child's right to have an education and be cared for in their community. Inclusion matters because it is every child's right to *belong*.

Why love matters

Gerhardt (2004) firmly believes that affection shapes a baby's brain. In her book, *Why Love Matters* (2004), she states that the *orbitofrontal cortex* is a vital part of the brain in relation to the development of emotions. She writes: 'What needs to be written in neon letters lit up against a night sky is that the orbitofrontal cortex, which is so much about being human, develops almost entirely post-natally. This part of the brain develops after birth and doesn't begin to mature until toddlerhood' (Gerhardt, 2004: 37).

Research tells us then that relationships, as well as being funda-mental for healthy emotional growth and development, are also crucial in terms of all aspects of children's learning and development. It is from this basis of secure relationships between children and prac-titioners that issues of practice in relation to children's cognition and learning development can be considered. Gerhardt has been arguing for the place of love in policy (Gerhardt et al., 2011), and Page's (2011a) research on mothers' views of love also has implications for practice, which we return to in Chapter 8.

Practitioners need to understand current research; they need to be able to take from research the essential pieces that support and inform their role and stimulate their thinking about their own practice; they need to be alert to research which is unhelpful and misinforming. Do they need to know about the precise location and function of the orbitofrontal cortex? Probably not, but – as we hope this book will demonstrate – they do need to know why attachment and love matter.

Further reading

Laevers, F., Declercq, B., Marin, C., Moons, J. and Stanton, F. (2011) *Observing Involvement in Children from Birth to Six Years*. Belgium: CEGO Publishers.

Nash, M., Lowe, J. and Leah, D. (2012) *Supporting Early Language Development Spirals for Babies and Toddlers*. London: Routledge.

Palalologo, I. (2012) *Ethical Practice in Early Childhood*. London: Sage.

Roberts, R. (2010) *Wellbeing from Birth*. London: Sage.

Chapter 3

Policies for the Youngest Children

This chapter will introduce:
- The policy context and its historical development in the UK in the twenty-first century
- Why Every Child *still* Matters
- Training and qualifications for practitioners

The policy context in the UK in the twenty-first century

Whatever one's role in working with young children, there can be no doubt that the policy changes in the past two decades have been huge. The face of early childhood education and care has changed beyond recognition from that of the late 1980s, and it is no longer the case that work with the youngest children sits in a policy vacuum.

Everyone who works with or for young children cannot help but be acutely aware of the extensive and rapid changes in care and educational policy in the UK in the twenty-first century. It is almost impossible to remain abreast of current initiatives, due largely to the overwhelming pace of change within the government plans for the sector. A key factor in the burgeoning weight of policy documents and guidance stems from the internet, which provides unlimited and unconstrained access to information. A further advantage of the internet is that information from around the world is accessible, regardless of time zones and distance. If you can click on it, you can get information about it! The drawback of this almost limitless resource is that the constant flow and change of information can be daunting, and indeed time-consuming. Busy practitioners often have to make their way through the plethora of information to find what they need. The labyrinthine qualities of non-linear text can open up new avenues of policy, thus making policy-related documentation and information ever more complex and detailed. As well as the information that practitioners can glean from the internet, they now have the potential to share their ideas and practice through social networking sites such as *Facebook* and *Twitter*, on a minute-by-minute basis. These sites are now entering the world of early years as childminders and group settings are using them to communicate and share with parents. So, remaining aware of policy developments and making sense of how policy affects day-to-day work with young children can be a challenge at the best of times, and an even more complex challenge when policy itself is shifting and changing. In this chapter we seek to unravel some of the tangles of policy and help practitioners to weave their own way through the historical context and content of UK policy as it relates to them and their work. Our aim in this chapter is to help practitioners to arrive at a point in the current context that enables them to recognize their roots, understand the key policy issues of their present work and thus be prepared to extend their own development by adding to their knowledge and understanding as policy continues to develop and evolve.

A recent history of policy development

In 1997 the Labour government under the leadership of Tony Blair took the UK by storm with their hitherto unprecedented policies to improve early education and childcare. The central aim of the National Childcare Strategy 1998 was to ensure: 'Good quality, affordable childcare for children aged 0 to 14 in every neighbourhood' (DfEE, 1998: 5). The childcare sector had just begun to implement the controversial 'childcare vouchers' system for funding state pre-school provision for four-year-olds (introduced by the previous Conservative government; SCAA, 1996). Discussion around types and quality of early years provision on offer at this time was heightened (Nutbrown,

1996) and there was scepticism about how changes in funding and the increased role of private and voluntary providers would enhance quality for children. The Nursery and Grant Maintained Schools Act (DfEE, 1996) gave the Office for Standards in Education (Ofsted) the power to inspect the quality of learning in early years settings, a move which, from the accounts of some providers, was later to prove controversial (Physick, 2005).

A list of the Acts of Parliament related to early years education and care since 1989 gives its own history of rapid and radical change and development, but also of massive investment in provision for young children as a means of addressing many social difficulties, including unemployment, crime, teenage pregnancy, ill-health and educational underachievement. We can only skim the surface here, but the following account indicates the extent and foci of change.

It was the 1989 Children Act (DoH, 1991) which marked the first step in bringing together the many different forms of services for young children (0–8 years) under one piece of legislation. Such an Act was much needed, because no such legislation had been passed since the 1948 Nurseries and Childminders Regulation Act (which it superseded). The Children Act 1989, when it came into effect in 1991, forced dramatic change in provision and affected all who worked with or for young children. Key effects of the Act were the identification of the positive contribution of day-care services (traditionally under the jurisdiction of social services departments), which had often been seen as 'Cinderella' services to the more prestigious nursery education which was the responsibility of education departments. The Children Act also pointed to practical solutions on strategies to 'join up' and coordinate services between education and social service departments. While local authorities were getting to grips with the demands of the Children Act 1989, other equally radical legislation focusing more specifically on the needs of children over the age of three years, entered the statute book. For example, the Education Reform Act (1988) introduced a 'National Curriculum' for children of five years and beyond, and brought with it apparent conflicts with aspects of, and indeed the ethos of, the Children Act. The Rumbold Report from the Committee of Enquiry into the Quality of Educational Experiences Offered to 3 and 4 Year Olds (DES, 1990) examined the educational experiences offered to children aged three and four, whatever type of setting they attended, and proposed that children of all ages should be offered comparable quality experiences to those of children in school. Perhaps prompted by the Rumbold Report (DES, 1990), issues of quality were hotly debated, for example Jackson (1992) suggested that because at this time the *expansion* of childcare places was seen as a priority within the private and voluntary sector, issues of quality of care aspired to in the Children Act would be virtually impossible to provide. For parents, affordable childcare was important, but independent providers needed sufficient financial return and so there was a danger that quality might be compromised. Hence Jackson suggested that the government may well lower standards instead of investing in the sector to raise standards, maintain quality and ensure the benefits for children. Two decades later the argument for quality *and* affordability is still underway, and June 2012 saw the launch of a commission to investigate the cost of childcare in England under the leadership of the Ministers for Children and Familes, and for Health.

So what did the National Childcare Strategy 1998 mean to practitioners working with babies and children under three years of age? There was much talk of improved services for all children, and in his Foreword to the National Childcare Strategy, Prime Minister Tony Blair stated that childcare in the UK had been 'neglected for too long', promising to address regulation of day care services, the quality of registered provision and develop a framework of qualifications for those working in the sector. However, there was little specific reference to the youngest children – those under three, and a need for clear guidelines to ensure that the care provided for them was appropriate to the ages and stages of the children was identified (DfEE, 1998: 4). In addition, while the 'free' educational places for three- and four-year-olds were welcomed, concern remained about the rise in costs of places for babies and toddlers.

Initiatives such as the *Early Excellence Centre Programme* (DfEE, 1997) set up in 1997 were intended to develop models of good practice through a range of services designed to meet the local needs of communities. In addition, in their 1998 spending review the government introduced *Sure Start* (DfEE, 1998), an early intervention programme for young children under the age of four years in areas of high deprivation in the UK. There were numerous projects and developments, however, and although there was much discussion about the National Childcare Strategy, its impact was not felt by many practitioners who were outside such initiatives and working in a 'hands on' capacity until sometime later.

In 2001 in direct response to a government Green Paper (DfEE, 2000b) Abbot et al. were commissioned to develop a framework for effective practice for children under three. *Birth to Three Matters*: *A Framework to Support Children in their Earliest Years* (DfES, 2002a) was launched after consultation with practitioners, children, parents, policy-makers and researchers. In the initial stages, there were concerns about 'curricula for babies' or the development of a 'watered down' version of the *Curriculum Guidance for the Foundation Stage* (DfEE, 2000a). Elfer (2002) advised that the framework, while developing practice, should also inspire policy-makers and should offer guidance to practitioners on their relationships with young children. It was felt that practitioners needed help in striking the delicate balance between offering physical care and attention, and in forming an emotional bond with the child – not one that replaced the affections of the parent and evoked feelings of envy towards the practitioner, but one which appropriately supported the child.

Changes and far-reaching policy developments did not end with the launch of *Birth to Three Matters,* in fact quite the opposite. In November 2002 a report was published in response to the Interdepartmental Childcare Review. This review, led by Catherine Ashton (DfES, 2002c), set out the government's intentions for the Spending Review for 2005/06 and reform was still on the agenda. While the review identified the many ways in which the government had implemented the initiatives set out in the 1998 National Childcare Strategy, it acknowledged there was still much to do to achieve the aim of providing good quality and affordable childcare. The Inter-departmental Childcare Review (Sure Start, 2002) recommended an increase in childcare provision and a total reform in the delivery of services.

The review of policy continued with the Early Years Foundation Stage (EYFS) (DCSF, 2008) which introduced the revolutionary concept that care could not be separated from learning and development, and so the EYFS was introduced, bringing together the Birth to Three

Matters Framework and The Curriculum Guidance for the Foundation Stage. The EYFS put a duty of care on practitioners to observe and plan for all children in their care irrespective of their age.

Again, in an ever-changing world, the EYFS was reviewed in 2011 by Dame Clare Tickell under the auspices of the newly formed coalition government. After a national consultation the renamed Department of Education launched the new framework in 2012 with an emphasis on supporting families to recognize the importance of their children's early development as indicators of their future learning. The Tickell Review (2011), along with the reports from Frank Field (2010) and Graham Allen (2011), brought parents into the picture as being key components of their child's learning and future aspirations. These reports, along with the Munro Review (2011), identified the need for early intervention and child safeguarding and protection. The Nutbrown Review (2012) recommended a raising of standards and quality of qualifications for those working with young children, and again highlighted the importance of quality experiences for the youngest children. This series of high-level independent reviews providing advice to government presents strong evidence for intervention and justifies the coalition government's continued support for the principles of the Children's Centres, as described later in this chapter, and the funding of places for the 40 per cent most vulnerable two-year-olds to access funded childcare places. Munro, in her summary, sets out:

> … proposals for reform which, taken together, are intended to create the conditions that enable professionals to make the best judgments about the help to give to children, young people and families. This involves moving from a system that has become over-bureaucratised and focused on compliance to one that values and develops professional expertise and is focused on the safety and welfare of children and young people. (Munro, 2011: 6)

The extent and nature of this reform has been on a scale hitherto unprecedented, with the main emphasis on funding and responsibility for service delivery devolved to local authorities, with the express purpose of meeting the needs of local communities. Sure Start Children's Centres were primarily established in the 20 per cent most disadvantaged electoral wards of the country but the long-term vision was always to provide a children's centre in every community, thus providing universal access to good quality childcare, early years education, health services, family support and parental outreach, as well as a base for childminders.

The impact of not only the 2002 Inter-departmental Childcare Review but also a number of successive reports commissioned by the government has seen a programme of change at both national and local level, with continued and increasing difficulty for those involved in keeping up with the pace of change. It has been an even more difficult task to demonstrate how the new initiatives and funding streams have become embedded in the practice and culture of early years service delivery and provision. Never in the history of childcare has there been such a rapid change to the sector than in the period since 1989.

Why Every Child *Still* Matters

However, despite the reforms suggested in the Inter-departmental Childcare Review 2002, there is no doubt that the biggest and most radical change was brought about by the Green Paper, *Every Child Matters* (DfES, 2003). The Lord Laming inquiry into the tragic death of Victoria Climbié (aged eight years and three months), who died at the hands of family members who should had been responsible for her health and well-being, heavily criticized the numerous missed opportunities by a number of organizations who could potentially have saved her life (DfES, 2003). The inquiry proposed what it called 'Radical improvement in opportunities and outcomes for children, driven by whole system reform of the delivery of children's services' (Every Child Matters, 2005b: 3). The *Every Child Matters* website detailed the strategy of change as follows:

> The *Every Child Matters* Green Paper was published for consultation in September 2003. In March 2004, the Government published *Every Child Matters: Next Steps*. The new Children Act 2004 provides the legal framework for the programme of reform.

Every Child Matters: Change for Children published in December 2004, brings together all the ways we are working towards improved outcomes for children, young people and families into a national framework for 150 local-authority-led change programmes. (Every Child Matters, 2005a)

This programme for change was drawn up following consultation with children and young people as well as practitioners, providers and local authority departments, and has been linked to five key outcomes of well-being both during childhood and in later life:

- being healthy
- staying safe
- enjoying and achieving
- making a positive contribution
- achieving economic well-being.

By basing the programme for change around these five outcomes it was suggested that the gap between disadvantaged children and their more advantaged peers could be reduced, thus bringing about better outcomes for all children. The programme for change was largely welcomed, there being no denial of the need to protect and safeguard all children while at the same time offering them the freedom to enjoy, achieve and make a positive contribution that could result in achieving economic well-being. But (there is usually a 'but') these reforms are so radical, so far-reaching and so rapid that it is possible to lose sight of 'the child' who is at the centre of this massive agenda. The only action for all concerned was for practitioners, service providers and others involved to respond positively in taking the agenda forward. The hard part was (and remains) getting to grips with, and remaining abreast of, and – at times – an unwieldy and challenging set of change initiatives. The *Common Assessment Framework* proposed a standardized approach to joining up 'integrated front line services' across all disciplines, thereby affecting the early identification of additional resources and services beyond the universal commitment to all children. An *Integrated Framework* comprises a database of information about children across the five Every Child Matters outcomes. *Every*

Child Matters: *Change for Children* (2005a) has required a total overhaul of the working practices of, and fundamental ethos behind, all the UK's 150 local authorities. Those who work in early childhood education and care, work in a culture which has changed, in some ways, beyond recognition to that which existed up until the mid-1990s.

In this context of rapid shifts in policy and culture of childcare and education, timescales have been fast moving. The impact of the programme for change was first experienced by early years and childcare providers in October 2005 when their work with young children was measured against the five outcomes in the inspection and registration process conducted by the Office for Standards in Education (Ofsted, 2005). This was the first time that an inspection had measured directly the impact of the *Birth to Three Matters*: *A Framework to Support Children in their Earliest Years* (DfES, 2002a), and the first time that inspectors were asked to make specific judgements about provision and outcomes for babies and toddlers.

As this brief outline of policy developments in England shows, it is the pace as well as the radical nature of change that has been felt by the sector. Indeed, the layer upon layer of policy and change meant that no sooner had practitioners started to implement the sound guidance within the *Birth to Three Matters Framework* (DfES, 2002a) than the consultation for the *Early Years Foundation Stage* (DfES, 2006a) began. It set out to combine *Birth to Three Matters* with the Foundation Stage to produce a new statutory curriculum framework for funded provision for children from birth to five years. The intention to consider a curriculum for learning and development that spanned the whole age range from birth to five was made very clear in the document *A Choice for Parents, the Best Start for Children: A Ten Year Strategy for Childcare* (DfES, 2004a), and the EYFS (DCSF, 2008; DfES, 2007) replaced the *National Care Standards for Under Eights Day Care and Childminding* (DfES, 2001), the *Curriculum Guidance for the Foundation Stage* (QCA, 2000) and the *Birth to Three Matters Framework* (DfES, 2002a). The EYFS (with its 69 early learning goals on which five-year-olds should be assessed) was received by many with caution (Ward, 2007). The early years and childcare sector still seemed to feel marginalized and left behind in this huge policy drive towards country-wide education and care provision for young children. Fears remained about the babies, and in particular there were worries that babies would be subjected to formal 'education' virtually from the minute they entered nursery at a few months old.

These concerns for the very youngest children continue with the publication of the revised EYFS (DfE, 2012a) and the introduction of the *Progress Check* for children at two years of age as practitioners seek ways of measuring this progress.

When a child is aged between two and three, practitioners must review their progress, and provide parents and/or carers with a short written summary of their child's development in the prime areas. This progress check must identify the child's strengths, and any areas where the child's progress is less than expected (DfE, 2012a: 10).

When children begin to access care and education in an out-of-home setting it is imperative that the policies and procedures are in place to ensure that children and their families are safe and secure. When choosing a setting for their child, parents need to have confidence that the setting will work cooperatively with them to ensure the best outcomes for their children.

Early intervention

One of the most fundamental ways in which practitioners can ensure these good outcomes is through observing children in their play. It is through these observations and through tracking a child's progress that practitioners can identify if there are any areas where a child is not making developmentally appropriate progress. If this is to be done effectively it is incumbent on the setting to work in partnership with parents and external agencies to support the child. The statutory requirements of the EYFS (DfE, 2012a) clearly state that parents must be involved with, and consulted about, any interventions that are put in place. Providers must also have the consent of parents and/or carers to share information directly with other relevant professionals, if they consider this would be helpful (DfE, 2012a: 11).

If interventions are to be effective this collaboration is vital. Any strategies put into place within the setting also need to be adapted within the home to ensure consistency.

Sometimes the interventions of a setting are not sufficient and so the setting needs to work collaboratively with the local authority or health services to ensure that the child is referred for the most appropriate specialist support. The work of the setting does not end here, as once the specialist support has been accessed the setting needs to implement this advice and continue with their role of observing and assessing.

Many early years settings in England now engage with their local Children's Centre to support children and families; some of whom only need to access these services at a particular moment in time, whereas others have more specific and complex needs. Children's Centres can fund places in privately funded settings for either a child's individual needs or to give respite to families who may be experiencing difficulties.

The Children's Centres were established to provide support to families within 'pram-pushing distance' of their homes through a multi-agency approach (DfE, 2010). The teamwork between agencies is intended to offer a model of support in a joined-up way, resulting in more effective outcomes for children. Children's Centres are now firmly established and the present coalition government has committed to their continued support, although this is and is likely to be an ever-changing picture, as political and economic demands affect the services which can be offered as universal.

Safeguarding

In spite of the recommendations of Lord Laming (DfES, 2003) following the death of Victoria Climbié and the resultant implementation of the Every Child Matters agenda, there have continued to be child abuse cases which have shocked the nation, two of which became high-profile cases. The first of these was the persistent abuse and subsequent death of Peter Connelly, generally referred to in the press as 'Baby "P"'. The toddler was just 17 months old when he died at the hands of his mother and step-father, despite being on the local authority child protection register and having been examined the day before his death by a paediatrician who failed to notice the little boy's injuries

(Powell and Uppal, 2012). The second case which caused not only media frenzy but public outcry was that of nursery worker, Vanessa George, who was convicted of a string of child abuse offences, including taking and distributing indecent images and the sexual abuse of babies at the nursery where she was employed (CPS, 2009, www.cps.gov.uk/news/press_releases/161_09). These cases make for haunting reading. Nevertheless, in the case of Vanessa George, it was only through multi-agencies working together that the full nature of these crimes was uncovered and the perpetrators brought to justice.

As a consequence, the revised EYFS (DfE, 2012a) has made some changes to the statutory early years framework in the ways in which settings follow procedures with regard to the safety and protection of children in England. Early years settings must now have clear safeguarding policy and procedures which cover the use of mobile phones and cameras (DfE, 2012a: 13, para. 3.4). As discussed earlier, the ever-changing world of the internet, social networking and the common use of mobile phones have opened up the debate about protecting the most vulnerable members of our society from the misuse of such technology.

One issue highlighted in the Safeguarding and Welfare requirements (DfE, 2012a) of the revised EYFS is the role of the adult in identifying and addressing any safeguarding concerns as follows:

> Providers must train all staff to understand their safeguarding policy and procedures, and ensure that all staff have up to date knowledge of safeguarding issues. Training made available by the provider must enable staff to identify signs of possible abuse and neglect at the earliest opportunity, and to respond in a timely and appropriate way. These may include:
>
> • significant changes in children's behaviour;
> • deterioration in children's general well-being;
> • unexplained bruising, marks or signs of possible abuse or neglect;
> • children's comments which give cause for concern;
> • any reasons to suspect neglect or abuse outside the setting, for example in the child's home; and/or

- inappropriate behaviour displayed by other members of staff, or any other person working with the children. For example, inappropriate sexual comments; excessive one-to-one attention beyond the requirements of their usual role and responsibilities; or inappropriate sharing of images. (DfE, 2012a: 14, para. 3:6)

One phrase within this which sometimes challenges practitioners is, 'excessive one-to-one attention beyond the requirements of their usual role and responsibilities', whereas elsewhere in the framework it talks about the key person having, 'a settled relationship for the child and build[ing] a relationship with their parents' (DfE, 2012a: 18, para. 326). This statement about closeness poses a particular dilemma and challenge for practitioners when considering their familiarity with young children, and in particular with babies. It is important that practitioners are helped to recognize that this does not mean that they cannot cuddle babies or hold them close, especially at times of settling in, distress and also during personal care routines. Their role is about establishing a close bond but not making it so over-intense that the baby has his/her independence taken from them. Yet, it is understandable that a level of concern may exist amongst even the most well-meaning and thoughtful practitioners, leading to a heightened level of concern about how to interpret this policy into daily practice. Munro (2008) draws our attention to the strengths and limitations of 'intuition and analytical reasoning'. Munro claims it is important to recognize that to rely solely on either human emotion on the one hand or factually based evidence on the other hand is to limit the understanding of child protection issues. Feeling uneasy about a situation or a person can be grounds for concern, but to be considered reliable requires further factually based evidence. However, for professionals working with babies and young children emotions form the bedrock of human relationships and are an important part of getting to know families. Munro claims that:

Traces of a negative attitude can, however, be seen in the managerial approaches that are common today wherein workers are expected to record facts and decisions but little attention is paid to recording or discussing emotions. A system that seeks to ignore emotions is in danger of leaving them to have an unknown, possibly harmful impact on the work, and is also neglecting a rich source of data to help us to understand what is going on. (Munro, 2008: 14)

It is perhaps unsurprising then that in her final report to the government, Professor Munro claimed that the very systems that had been set up to protect young children from harm were in the end culpable (2012). Thus, she recommended that the system should change. The government accepted Munro's recommendation to put the child at the centre and to aid professionals to readily access appropriate help, instead of being constrained within a plethora of complex bureaucratic policies and procedures. Importantly, for the early years workforce, Munro argued for professionals to receive support and 'practice-focused supervision', which Tickell (2011) had also advised in the EYFS review. As a result of these recommendations the revised English EYFS requires early years providers to: '… put appropriate arrangements in place for the supervision of staff who have contact with children and families … Supervision should foster a culture of mutual support, teamwork and continuous improvement which encourages confidential discussion of sensitive issues' (DfE, 2012a: 17, para. 3.19).

Training and qualifications for early years practitioners

Central to the quality of provision are the skills, knowledge, understanding, sensitivities and capabilities of the practitioners who work with the children. In the UK, the Office for Standards in Education is responsible for the registration and inspection of early years and childcare providers according to a set of minimum *National Standards* which were set as the minimum baseline for quality (DfES, 2001). Inspections were carried out under Part XA of the Children Act 1989 as introduced by the Care Standards Act 2000, and where nursery education was provided, under Schedule 26 of the School Standards and Framework Act 1998. The standards only required half of the staff to hold an NVQ level 2 or equivalent qualification appropriate for the care and education of children. However, there was a requirement for the supervisor of the setting to be qualified to or to be 'working toward' NVQ level 3. A large, full day care setting employing 30 staff could meet legal requirements with half the staff (15) unqualified and 15 with a level 2 NVQ and the supervisor and the deputy 'working toward' (not necessarily having achieved) a level 3 NVQ. The setting could still be judged as satisfactory and meeting the outcomes of the National Standards in terms of staff qualification. As Graham (1997) notes, it is unthinkable to imagine sending older children to study for their GCSEs with half of the teachers unqualified. Why, therefore, can it be even remotely acceptable to do just that to babies and young children, who, by virtue of their age, are among the most vulnerable people in our society? Why is it acceptable to leave them with practitioners who are not qualified to work with them? It is interesting to note that some of the work cited in this book is written by practitioners who hold Master's degrees, and who therefore have a strong sense of the importance of research, as well as sensitive, respectful, innovative practice. Pugh (2001) suggests that research reports over the past decade have pointed to a number of issues related to training and qualification which require attention. She cites the following concerns around the quality of experiences offered to children:

- a chronic shortage of trained staff in all sectors
- a lack of qualifications among those working with children under five years of age in the private and voluntary sector
- a huge range of different qualifications
- the inappropriateness of the content of teacher training for nursery and infant teachers, with a curriculum that neglects child development
- the high proportion of teachers in reception classes in schools who are not trained to work with such young children
- a lack of funding for training, whether through the NVQ route or through teacher training
- a lack of interface between the developing Early Years National Training Organization (responsible for accrediting NVQ-related qualifications taken by playgroup leaders, nursery

nurses, childminders, etc.) and the Teacher Training Agency's role in training teachers (adapted from Pugh, 2001).

Despite the minimal requirements for qualifications, government ministers in 1999 appeared to recognize that increasing the number of early years and childcare places was dependent on having: 'A highly skilled workforce' and that 'Working with children is a demanding, skilled profession' (DfEE, 1999a: 1). A high-level recruitment campaign was launched to raise the profile of a career in early years and play work.

However, despite the opportunity of access to free training, introduction of the minimum wage and the adoption of the European working time directive, the government still failed to recognize and properly address the very low pay and often poor working conditions of staff involved with children in early years and childcare settings. Penn (2000) suggested childcare would continue to be a gendered occupation, with a high turnover of staff, until social policy was challenged. As part of the government's strategy to build a suitably skilled workforce, the ultimate vision was the establishment of good quality provision for children through the establishment of a single qualifications framework (DfES, 2005) to support the careers pathway of those working in a range of roles with children, young people and families. It set out the required knowledge and skills in the following six areas of expertise as the most basic level in order for an individual to practise, hence the title, *Common Core of Skills and Knowledge for the Children's Workforce*:

1. Effective communication and engagement
2. Child and young person development
3. Safeguarding and promoting the welfare of the child
4. Supporting transitions
5. Multi-agency working
6. Sharing information (DfES, 2005: 4).

'The single biggest factor that determines the quality of childcare is the workforce' (DfES, 2004a: 43; see also DfES, 2005). The government commitment to a workforce reform strategy in a bid to improve quality came some 15 years after the Rumbold Report (DES, 1990) which highlighted the importance of the workforce. The need for highly trained professionals with respectful values and attitudes, and with the skills and knowledge to interpret the needs of young children and their families, is consistently acknowledged. However, the pay offered to some members of such a profession is, and will be, a major factor in recruitment and retention – until it is resolved. With the long-term goal to ensure all full day care settings are led by degree-qualified staff, this can only stand a realistic opportunity of being realized when pay and conditions are appropriate to degree-level recruits. Many day-care setting leaders and their staff (regardless of their qualification) currently work for low pay and in poor conditions. Professor Lesley Abbott led the team that launched the *Birth to Three Matters Framework* which became the practice guidance for all those working with children in England aged birth to three. This guidance was subsumed into the EYFS (DfES, 2008; DfE, 2012). However, the original document can be located on the Early Years Foundation website: http://www.foundationyears.org.uk/wpcontent/uploads/2012/04/Birth-to-Three-Matters-Booklet.pdf. To quote Abbott: 'I would fight to the death the view that anybody can look after young children and work with them; they have got to be the finest minds and the best trained people working with young children' (Page, 2005: 110).

Calder (1999) argued that the solution was to create a programme of study which supported the multidisciplinary approach and the profession of 'educarer'. This led to the development of early childhood studies degree programmes which supported the need to offer integrated multi-professional training. In 2006, in the wake of government proposals, the Children's Workforce Development Council (CWDC) was set up with the task of bringing about early years workforce reform. Its remit was to establish a workforce with the necessary skills of those required to lead the new single quality framework of care and education proposed by the government:

> The Children's Workforce Development Council (CWDC) aims to improve the lives of children and young people. It does this by ensuring that the people working with children have the best possible training, qualifications, support and advice. It helps children

and young people's organisations and services to work together, so that the child is at the centre of all our services. (CWDC, 2006b)

In 2011, following advice in the Tickell review (2011), the government commissioned Professor Cathy Nutbrown to lead an Independent Review for Government on the qualifications of those working with young children. The Nutbrown Review, *Foundations for Quality*, was published in June 2012, making 19 recommendations designed to strengthen the qualifications for those working with young children, and enhance the quality of experiences for children in home and group settings. The report begins with Nutbrown's new vision for the early years workforce as set out below:

A new vision for the early years workforce …
Babies and young children must have the very best early education and care. If those working with young children have the necessary skills, knowledge and understanding, they have the potential to offer the formative experience all young children deserve, supported by the significant Government investment in the early years. This means that the Government and the sector need to prioritise the training and development of all early years practitioners.
   My vision for early childhood education and care is one where:

• every child is able to experience high quality care and education whatever type of home or group setting they attend;
• early years staff have a strong professional identity, take pride in their work, and are recognised and valued by parents, other professionals and society as a whole;
• high quality early education and care is led by well qualified early years practitioners; and
• the importance of childhood is understood, respected and valued.

There are examples of excellent practice that meet these aims, but this is not the case in all settings, and the time is right to set our sights higher and demand excellent work with all young children across the sector. This requires:

- An increase in the number of qualified teachers with specialist early years knowledge who lead practice in settings, working directly with babies, young children, and their parents, using their pedagogical expertise to support young children's learning, play and development.
- Early years teachers who lead, and are supported by, an effective team of early years practitioners, qualified at a minimum of level 3, with all staff taking professional pride in their work, and continually seeking to extend and develop their knowledge and skills.
- Those who are working towards early education and childcare qualifications to be taught and supported by qualified and knowledgeable tutors, who are experienced in the early years. Tutors, as much as the practitioners in the setting, must take pride in their professional development, and regularly engage in practice in settings, ensuring their skills and pedagogy are current.
- Only those candidates who are confident and capable in their literacy and numeracy are able to enrol on these level 3 courses. Level 3 qualifications must be rigorous and challenging, requiring high quality experiences in placements, giving students time to reflect on and improve their own practice.
- A rigour of qualification such that employers can have confidence that those who hold a recognised qualification have the necessary depth and breadth of knowledge and experience to be ready for work in the setting.
- Employers who support new members of staff, and take the time to induct them to the setting and their role, and ensure they have good support and mentoring in place for at least their first six months. (Nutbrown, 2012: 11–12)

The Review argues that enhanced qualifications for all who work with young children are essential because children's experiences in the first few years can have a lasting impact on their later development, social interactions and life outcomes. Drawing on a wealth of evidence, the

Nutbrown Review pointed out that if these experiences are positive, if children experience high quality early education and care, this can have a lasting, positive impact on educational outcomes, and more. The report made clear that because children learn much in sustained interaction with other children, as well as with adults, so young children need to spend time with adults who are attuned to children's learning and development needs, and who can support their play and foster early interactions between young children. Furthermore, the Review called upon evidence which shows that high quality early years provision can narrow the gap in attainment between economically disadvantaged and non-disadvantaged children. Nutbrown argued for enhanced qualifications including a new birth to seven teacher qualification, because high quality provision makes a difference to children, and graduates with Qualified Teacher Status (QTS) have also been shown to enhance the learning and development of the very youngest children. Poor and mediocre provision, on the other hand, will not benefit children, and could even cause them more difficulties.

It remains to be seen how government will respond to these recommendations, which have been widely supported by the early years and child care sector (Mahadevan, 2012), but if they are enacted in their entirety this could herald the largest and potentially most successful early intervention programme that England has ever seen.

Early Years Foundation Stage (EYFS)

The *Early Years Foundation Stage* (EYFS) was launched in 2007 and became statutory in September 2008, with most local authorities offering multi-agency training on the EYFS aimed at all sector providers who would be putting the EYFS into practice from September 2008. Maintained sector providers were trained alongside non-maintained sector practitioners. Teachers in reception classes and nursery schools were trained alongside children's centre staff, childminders and practitioners from the private voluntary and independent sector. The plan was to bring together – through joint training – an overlapping multidisciplinary workforce who, as they became familiar with the EYFS, would identify the challenges it presented to them. The EYFS stated that where good quality already existed, providers could be assured that the messages from the previous policy documents were firmly embedded within the EYFS. This multi-agency training continues with the introduction of the revised EYFS (DfE, 2012a) and can be evidenced in the promotion of all agencies working together to support and identify the needs of children and their families (Allen, 2011; Field, 2010). However the now limited resources mean that training is patchy and there is still a lack of depth in understanding the learning and development needs of the youngest children. The EYFS alone will not bring about improvements in quality – for that it is important to have a highly skilled, knowledgeable and understanding workforce.

There remains a feeling of massive change in early childhood care and education programmes in the UK and elsewhere. Melhuish and Petrogiannis (2006) suggest that the significant rise in the proportions of working mothers (especially those with children under three) has resulted in the rapid increase and demand internationally for child-care (for example, in the US, and southern Europe). In New Zealand research has played an important role in the shaping of early educa-tion provision for children aged three and above, with government funding for programmes such as the Te Whāriki curriculum (Melhuish and Petrogiannis, 2006; Smith and May, 2006). In Australia the Early Years Learning Framework (COAG, 2009), intended to set the stan-dard for quality childcare and education in the country, was launched. The face of early childhood care and education is subject to change around the world, and this is the case too in many countries where the rearing of the youngest children has been seen traditionally as inter-generational, albeit with less haste. Kapoor (2006: 9) reflects: 'India is the ninth most industrialised country in the world undergoing rapid industrialisation and economic and social change, but early childhood care and education has been a low priority'. In China the *Shanghai 0–3 Year Old Children Plan of Care and Education* (2003) led to the develop-ment of programmes for babies and children under three years of age becoming part of the kindergarten system (Shenglan, 2006). The recog-nition of the needs of children under three in Shanghai was largely the result of research studies which suggested that early experiences affected their later life in school performance and beyond (Shenglan, 2006).

Around the world early education and care is developing as economic and social policies and events demonstrate the necessity to provide for the youngest children as part of family development. As Gammage (2006: 241) asserts: 'We do not need childcare, or kindergarten, because imaginary "feckless" women go to work outside the home; we need it from necessity, as secure and loving provision in settings which support and supplement the family, and which enable rich attachments and happy learning experiences for our children'.

Further reading

Dalli, C., White, E.J., Rockel, J., Duhn, I., with Buchanan, E., Davidson, S., Ganly, S., Kus, L. and Wang, B. (2011) *Quality Early Childhood Education for Under-Two-Year-Olds: What Should It Look Like? A Literature Review*. Wellington: Ministry of Education, New Zealand.

David, T., Goouch, K., Powell, S. and Abbott, L. (2003) *Birth to Three Matters: A Review of the Literature*. London: DfES.

The Economist Intelligence Unit Limited (2012) *Starting Well: Benchmarking Early Education Across the World. A Report from the Economist Intelligence Unit*. London: The Economist.

Trevarthen, C., Barr, I., Dunlop, A.W., Gjersoe, N., Marwick, H. and Stephen, C. (2006) *Review of Childcare and the Development of Children Aged 0–3: Research Evidence, and Implications for Out-of-Home Provision Supporting a Young Child's Needs for Care and Affection, Shared Meaning and a Social Place*. Edinburgh: Scottish Executive.

Chapter 4

Planning for Early Learning and Development

This chapter will discuss:
- Our understanding of how young children learn and develop
- The role of the adult
- Stages before ages or ages before stages?
- Secure relationships
- Patterns in children's learning and development
- The *real* treasure basket
- *Real* heuristic play
- Beyond the treasure basket

Understanding how young children learn and develop

In this chapter we focus on planning learning experiences for young children from a child development viewpoint. We consider child development from a variety of perspectives, drawing on examples of good practice from a range of settings and experiences taken from the diverse multi-professional under-threes workforce.

Our aim in this chapter is to make the sometimes complex models of child development and theories of learning accessible and meaningful to those who work with young children and to demonstrate the importance and usefulness of underpinning knowledge in developing respectful, developmentally appropriate practice work with young children.

In the US, the *National Association for the Education of the Young Child* discuss how in 'developmentally appropriate practice': 'Good teachers understand typical development from birth through age three. Knowing how the youngest children learn and develop helps professionals closely attune to individual children and their families – in all their variety' (NAEYC, 2005). For 'teachers' we should, in this instance, also read 'practitioners' because everyone who works with young children needs to have a secure knowledge base from which they help babies and young children to learn and also to make judgements about their learning and developmental needs on a daily basis. Teachers and other practitioners may have different roles, but all need a similar grounding in basic understanding of how young children develop and learn, whatever their roles and responsibilities. The term 'developmentally appropriate practice', in the US, is taken to refer to, in early childhood programmes, serving children from birth to eight years. The NAEYC documentation sets out 12 key principles of child development and learning that inform developmentally appropriate practice (NAEYC, 1996: 12).

Katz suggests that in developmentally appropriate approaches to the curriculum, decisions 'about what should be learned and how it would best be learned depend on what we know of the learner's developmental status and our understanding of the relationships between early experience and subsequent development' (1995: 109). This statement gives rise to a number of questions. How can educators know what should be learned? How do practitioners decide what next to 'teach'? How are children's 'stages' of development determined? How can educators understand the connections between early experience and later development?

What constitutes *development* and what is *appropriate* development are always contestable issues. Some may emphasize the definitions given in policy documentation, others may prefer the findings of research. Many will draw on research to illuminate and interpret policy to help them to make everyday experiences in settings meaningful for each individual child.

Many studies of children's learning and development have sought to inform the planning of provision for young children. Examples include Athey's (1990) work on schematic development, Nutbrown's (2011a) study of curriculum development based on schematic theory, Reggio Emilia pre-schools' development of communities of learning through multiple modes of expression (Abbott and Nutbrown, 2001; Edwards et al., 1993; Malaguzzi, 1993), as well as the curriculum diversity of Te Whāriki developed in New Zealand (Ministry of Education, New

Zealand, 1995) and the Early Years Learning Framework in Australia (COAG, 2009). Such studies, and the rapid policy developments in curriculum and pedagogy, are evidence of the continuing quest for ways of creating approaches to learning and development which satisfactorily meet the developmental needs of all young children – internationally.

A fundamental element of any curriculum for babies, toddlers and young children is play. Play is central to learning, and for most children it is natural and unthwartable. Jenkinson writes of the crucial role of play in children's development and how one teacher combined the requirement to give young children homework with the importance of finding time for children to play (Jenkinson, 2001). Watching babies play is a joy – the emergence of the 'peekaboo' game, when toddlers know that their adult is not 'gone' but 'hiding', and watching the discovery of babies exploring the treasure basket are clear examples of developmentally appropriate provision for babies and toddlers. Such opportunities are given to young children at the appropriate time by supportive, responsive, respectful close adults. Planning for babies' and toddlers' learning and development also means planning meaningful opportunities for them to play and planning for meaningful relationships (Atherton and Nutbrown, 2013; Elfer and Dearnley, 2007; Page, 2011a; Pikler, 1940).

The examples in this chapter will show how a range of child development and learning theories can be of real practical use in understanding and interpreting young children's actions and developing an understanding of their needs. In this way, planning can be truly centred on what babies and young children need rather than simply on a notion of what young children in general may like or need. Planning which is informed by theoretical knowledge and close observation of individual children is more likely to result in learning and development opportunities which meet young children's particular needs and interests.

The revised EYFS (DfE, 2012a) summarizes the way in which adults should interpret how infants learn and develop by the presentation of a holistic view of the child and his learning and development. The formula:

A Unique Child + Positive Relationships + Enabling Environments = Learning and Development

is designed to encourage practitioners to see that for a child to learn and develop they first need to observe how a child is learning, and then decide what they can do and decide what they need to provide to enable the child to consolidate this into their learning and development (Early Education, 2012: 2).

The role of the adult – learning as a social process

Lev Vygotsky, a Russian-born psychologist and educational theorist, is perhaps best known for his emphasis on learning as an act of social interaction and his theory of the *zone of proximal development*. Born into a middle-class family in 1896, he became a secondary teacher and was interested in the processes of learning and in the role of language in learning. He then pursued his interest in psychology, studying Freud, Piaget and Montessori in particular. Vygotsky put forward the idea of learning as a social exchange, that young children learn through interaction with other children and with adults. He was convinced of the importance of interaction and relationships to young children's learning and wrote that:

> Learning and development are interrelated from the child's very first day of life … development is subject to the influence of the same two main factors which take part in the organic development of the child, namely the biological and the social … human learning presupposes a specific social nature and a process by which children grow into the intellectual life of those around them. (Vygotsky, 1980: 88)

The *zone of proximal development* was a key contribution to present understanding of the role of the adult (or another child) in children's learning, and is a cornerstone of present-day pedagogy where children work together in pairs or small groups, and of practitioners' use of patient observation to plan their interactions and interventions in children's play and endeavours.

Vygotsky would perhaps say that for learning to take place the practitioner and the child must be 'in tune' with each other – working in the *zone of proximal development*, where through social interaction the adult can, as it were, take the child by the hand and help them take another step – one which they might not take alone. What is also important here is that the practitioner does not try to make the child go too far – only to the next step – not further than they can cope with. Vygotsky's ideas are fundamental to those who see learning as an interactive process and, had he lived (tuberculosis brought about his premature death in 1934, aged 38), it is likely that yet more understanding of this important developmental approach to learning would have been available.

For any child the role of the adult is important, but perhaps this role is even more vital for babies and toddlers who have not yet mastered intelligible language. Brain research (Gopnik et al., 1999a) informs us that from birth an infant is programmed to learn, and it is the adult who can supply the experiences that help to develop the synapses that lay the foundations for future learning. It is no longer acceptable to place the least experienced adult in the baby room (though it is often the case), rather the most skilled and knowledgeable practitoners should be working with them (Mathers et al., 2011; Nutbrown, 2012). Knowledgeable practitioners can plan experiences which scaffold children's learning, and it is this sensitive interaction which will provide the infant with emotional security as well as a model for language development.

Planning for the role of the adults

Fifteen-month-old Rosie was supported by a practitioner as she joined in with the body painting. While some of the older boys ran up and down the large sheet of paper, daubing paint on themselves, each other and the paper, and two of the older girls sat on the periphery slowly and cautiously painting their toes and their tummies, Rosie sat, wearing only her nappy, on the lap of her close adult.

She had a small daub of lime green paint on a plastic dish. She dipped her finger in and smeared it onto her tummy – a look of deep concentration on her face. She lifted her finger to the adult's face. The adult smiled and said softly, 'It's green Rosie, green paint, on your tummy and on your finger!' Rosie touched her chin, leaving a green daub of paint there.

Later, with her feet on the paper and having been given a pot of yellow paint and a brush, Rosie continued to explore the paint. The look on her face seemed to say 'What is this?' And she smiled with some delight when she transferred paint from her own hand to that of the adult!

Rosie worked with the paint – touching it tentatively at first then using a paintbrush with some confidence – for almost 30 minutes. (Nutbrown and Jones, 2006: 28–9)

Vygotsky's notion of the *zone of proximal development* (ZPD) and the broader idea of learning as a social process, make it possible to identify ways in which children's learning can be supported by adults and older children.

This encounter with paint gave Rosie the opportunity for sustained shared thinking (Siraj-Blatchford et al., 2002); and support from her close adult, through materials ready to hand and in quantities sufficient for her to handle, 'permission' from those around her to participate, uninterrupted time to explore at her own pace and role models of the older children. Her close adult took Rosie into her *zone of proximal development* and enabled her, through this one-to-one encounter, to explore the paint in ways which might not have been possible if Rosie had been alone with the paint or if the practitioner was not so attuned to Rosie's needs and interests. This encounter shows how Rosie's learning came about through an environment which created opportunities for, and encouraged children to participate in, socially interactive encounters. First, Rosie had her close practitioner and, second (but not unimportantly), Rosie was able to be alongside the older children (Clare, 2012; Kowalski et al., 2005).

Questions for reflection

1. What does this observation tell us about Rosie's journey of exploration?
2. What role do knowledgeable others (adults and peers) have on Rosie's journey?
3. What does the time that Rosie spent on this journey tell us about her learning?

How can stages of development support planning?

Piaget trained as a zoologist and turned to psychology because he was interested in the connection between the biological and the logical. He is famous for his work on cognitive stages of development in children and the importance of young learners being able to assimilate new information and accommodate new knowledge into their existing understanding of the world.

Piaget's suggested stages of development were based mainly on his observations of his own children, and the detail of his studies has been subject to some disagreement. He outlined four stages of development:

1. Sensori-motor stage (birth to two years)
2. Pre-operational stage (two to seven years)
3. Concrete operational stage (seven to 12 years)
4. Formal operational stage (12 to adult).

Piaget argued that: 'The teacher-organiser should know not only his own science but also be well versed in the details of the development of the child's or adolescent's mind' (Piaget, 1937/1954: 77). He promoted the importance of understanding child development and his writings document many observations of children. His analysis of (what he called) 'egocentric' behaviour in young children is well known. For Piaget, overcoming egocentricity was the goal of development. As a constructivist, Piaget saw learning as an evolving process taking place when children interacted with their environment. Through such inter-actions Piaget suggested that children moved through his four stages of cognitive development. Some have questioned the basis of some of Piaget's theories; Donaldson, for example, in her book *Children's Minds* (1978) considered that Piaget's experiments were too abstract for chil-dren to really perform appropriately well. Many believe, in the light of their own observations and interactions with children, that some of Piaget's theories about young children's cognitive abilities do not accu-rately reflect the intellectual accomplishments of which many very young children are capable. However, in order to understand children's stages of development, many of his experiments asked children ques-tions or to perform tasks which were just too difficult for them, and Piaget's work (sometimes focusing on what children could not do) had a profound influence on educational theory in the twentieth century. One of the things that Piaget gave to early education was a sense of the importance of 'stages' of development as opposed to or distinct from 'ages' as central to development. But he attached clear ages to his own four distinct stages.

Susan Isaacs, said to admire much of Piaget's work, was also to chal-lenge his ideas by making her own observations of child learning through play and drawing on many other disciplines to interpret what she saw (Isaacs, 1933). Isaacs promoted a view of what children could do. Perhaps it is fair to say that Isaacs's approach of using observation to understand learning and development led to a more constructive approach to child development and a more positive view of what children could do, whereas Piaget's view of fixed stages (governed largely by age) led some to take a deficit view of what children could do. What children can do can be helpful in planning – because it can help practitioners identify what the next step is (where the *zone of proximal development* might be).

Planning for stages and ages?

The following example shows how knowing a child's age alone is not enough, but knowing her specific point of development (learned as a result of observation) can help to appropriately plan for her needs.

> Zoe, aged 22 months, has been with her childminder Lynne for nearly three months and has settled well; she loves to spend time in the garden with the other minded children. In a daily hand-over conversation with Zoe's mother, Marina, Lynne reassured Marina that while Zoe was as yet unable to put on and take off her own shoes to go back and forth to the garden, she could correctly identify the two separate shoes that matched together to make up the pair. Lynne had also noticed during a close observation of Zoe that the particular style of shoe Zoe wore made it more difficult for her to put them on independently. Lynne suggested to Marina that Zoe bring a pair of wellington boots with her to put on when she went into the garden. These would be relatively easy to take on and off with minimal assistance, thereby avoiding unnecessary frustration for Zoe. Marina was happy with the suggestion and Zoe enjoyed pairing her red boots together before sitting on the doorstep to pull them on. She equally enjoyed kicking them off again when she felt like coming inside to do something else.

Knowing what children cannot do – for example, 'Zoe can't yet put on her own shoes' – tells us only that we do not know enough about Zoe to plan for her needs. It then becomes the job of the practitioner to find out more about what Zoe can do – more observation is necessary – in order effectively to plan to meet her needs in terms of next learning steps.

In this example Zoe wanted to go outside at regular intervals during the day. Lynne was aware that she needed to assist Zoe in her efforts, but she also wanted to ensure that Zoe had an opportunity to 'do it herself' and to build on the knowledge and skills Zoe had shown in pairing her shoes and, later, her boots. It was only through this kind of close observation that Lynne was able to 'plan' for Zoe's needs in this way and thereby identify her *zone of proximal development*. However, at 22 months Zoe may well want to go in and out many times a day. Therefore careful thought to ensure that she was empowered and that Lynne did not spend most of her day putting on and taking off Zoe's shoes and away from the rest of the children made things better for everyone, and Zoe was able to make frequent trips into the garden and enjoyed swapping from slippers to wellies and vice versa several times a day! It really did not matter how old Zoe was – some children may need help with their shoes when they are much older – but knowing what children can do makes for meaningful support.

Questions for reflection

1. Looking at Lynne's role in this observation can you identify the ways in which she supports both Zoe and Marina?
2. How could Marina continue with this support at home?

Secure relationships

As we saw in Chapter 2, research into children's needs to develop secure attachments and experience positive well-being are key in young children's healthy development, and their development of thinking. Attachment theories are now embedded in policy around the UK, and the need for warm, responsive carers is well established. Chapter 2 introduced the work of Bowlby who, in 1953, argued that mother–baby relationships were different from other adult–baby or adult–child relationships and the controversy surrounding this pronouncement has already been discussed. However, Bowlby's later statement, in 1969, that his earlier work had been misinterpreted and that his theory had been misunderstood, did little to appease the guilt which many mothers felt at leaving their baby with another woman (there were few men working in childcare at that time), and has been seen by many as one reason why state provision for children under three has been so slow to develop. With changes in the economy, and different attitudes to women in the workforce, a reinterpretation of Bowlby's work has taken place and a twenty-first-century 'take' on his theories has given rise to a new understanding of the importance of helping young children to develop safe, secure, reliable relationships with their carers, and of the value of multiple relationships. Recent studies of children in group care have highlighted the importance of good quality interactions between staff and children to children's cognitive development: 'The quality of the interactions between children and staff were particularly important; where staff showed warmth and were responsive to the individual needs of children, children made more progress' (Sylva et al., 2004: 3). The importance of positive relationships between children and adults is now firmly established in policy, defined by the term 'key person' and 'key person approach' (DfE, 2012a; Elfer et al., 2012) which provides clear evidence of the importance of close and specific relationships between practitioners, children and parents.

As we have seen in the early part of the book, relationships, as well as being fundamental for healthy emotional growth and development, are also crucial in terms of all aspects of children's learning and development. But what does this look like in practice? How can we plan for secure relationships?

Planning for secure relationships

In this example a child seems to be troubled with the imminent arrival of a new baby in the family.

> Joe had been at nursery for nearly nine months. He had always been a happy child and at 18 months had settled quickly. His mum and dad worked split shifts at a local supermarket, and it was important that Louisa and Jade (Joe's paired key persons) worked closely with the family to ensure consistency for Joe. Louisa and Jade worked opposite shifts and their manager regularly supported them both with one-to-one sessions to discuss their key person
>
> *Continues*

Continued

role. Louisa and Jade had noticed (independently of one another) Joe's change in behaviour and they had attributed this to the imminent arrival of a new baby in the family. Joe had been used to quite a focused routine, with his mum dropping him at nursery and his dad collecting him. However, with his mum now on maternity leave, she did all the dropping and collecting and at differing times during the day, thinking that her new flexibility due to maternity leave would mean she could spend extra time with Joe. It was this upset in routine which seemed to trouble Joe the most. Unfortunately this had coincided with Louisa's annual holiday which meant that he was totally reliant on Jade and frequently followed her around the nursery, sobbing. Jade spoke to her manager in her one-to-one session and requested a shift change to coincide with Joe's attendance pattern until Louisa returned from her holiday at the end of the next week. She had previously checked that this would not be to the detriment of her other key children, and fortunately (for this week) her own circumstances enabled her to be flexible about her working hours. Jade shared her concerns with Joe's parents and everyone agreed that it would be best to return to Joe's previous dropping and collecting arrangements – this would not be easy when the baby arrived and would put extra stress on his mum, but they all decided to give it a go.

In preparation for the imminent arrival of the new baby, Jade had already discussed with Joe's parents his particular enjoyment of the role-play area. Joe had taken a liking to a particular buggy and chose a variety of teddies and dolls to wheel around the nursery. Joe's parents agreed to extend Joe's experiences at home and took him to buy his own 'baby' whom he named Leah. Jade ensured that 'Leah' was welcomed into the setting each day with Joe and went to great lengths to plan for experiences to include Leah, such as a bath for her at water play, a chair at mealtimes, a sleep mat at rest times and so on, all part of supporting Joe's sense of belonging.

Upon Louisa's return from holiday, she noted Joe's own 'new addition' to the family and the two practitioners worked together to support Joe to understand about the arrival of the 'real' baby in a few weeks' time. Joe had practised negotiating the nursery corridors with Leah in his buggy and demonstrated his skills when he eventually – and excitedly – introduced his baby sister Hermione to his nursery friends.

This setting has adopted 'key person' strategies, and the skilful and sensitively attuned practitioner decides to focus on key themes which she knows are fundamental to the child's development when planning his experiences. She is acutely aware that she needs to foster his sense of belonging and emotional well-being prior to him being able to move forward. He needs to know he is important and that he has a place within the various complex relationships he shares. At this point in time his emotional responses to the disturbance to his routine are exacerbated by his uncertainty about the forthcoming new arrival, thereby disabling his social and cognitive development. It is of paramount importance that the practitioner is respectful and seeks a solution rather than dismissing his feelings or distracting him with activities that at this time are meaningless to him. Understanding about theories of attachment and children's emotional development can be useful here in helping the practitioners appropriately to meet his needs. Knowledge of theory can sometimes support (or challenge) a 'gut instinct' or a 'hunch' and gives practitioners some basis upon which to make daily decisions.

Questions for reflection

1. How do you get to know the specific circumstances of your key children in the context of their homes, families and their communities, so that you are best placed to plan for the children for whom you have special responsibility?
2. How do the organizational demands within your setting allow for flexibility to address the individual needs of children such as Joe?

Learning through play

It has long been recognized, as Froebel (1912) suggested, that, 'play is the work of children' but the use of the word 'play' conjures up images of children occupying themselves but being engaged in doing nothing of any real value. It is important that the notion that play is of no consequence is eradicated and that professionals, parents, policy-makers and those working outside early years recognize and understand that play is the child's unique way of learning (Nutbrown, 2012; Wood and Attfield, 2005).

There has, however, since the introduction of the EYFS (DCSF, 2008) been a move by practitioners to see free 'unplanned' play as the only opportunity for young children to learn. Tickell (2011), in her report on the revision of the EYFS, recognized that it was important to get the balance between structured and unstructured play right. 'However, there is confusion about what learning through play actually means, and what the implications of this are for the role of adults' (2011: 28). Tickell urges that practitioners realize the importance of their role in children's learning and plan for it accordingly. Of course, there is a strong body of argument that to intrude on children's play and manipulate it for adult motives is wrong and thus causes what children do under these circumstances not to be play in the 'true' sense of the word (Broadhead et al., 2010). It is also important that the natural propensity to play and explore is not distorted so that the world of childhood play becomes, not play, but imposed activity in the guise of play.

For babies and young children the part that the adult plays in role modelling and planning for experiences is crucial, as demonstrated in the following practice example:

A group of babies and toddlers are sitting on the floor alongside their familiar adults. The adults have planned for the young children's creative learning and are challenging their thinking skills by supplying them with open-ended resources. These are CDs and straws strewn all around the space, but these resources have not been selected randomly. These resources have been presented to the children in an open-ended manner; no role modelling by the adults is necessary. They are observing to see what the babies and toddlers will do. It isn't long before the children begin to explore and experiment with what is in front of them.

One nine-month-old non-mobile baby reaches out to hold a CD; she looks at it, putting her finger over the hole before reaching for one of the straws. She then pushes the straw along the surface of the CD; she notices the hole and attempts to push the straw through the hole, though missing it on several occasions. This is when she looks to the adult, who has been watching with interest. She smiles reassuringly as if to say, 'Go on try again'.

The baby does so and this time is successful. As the straw pops through the hole, she bends her head to see it peeping through the hole on the other side; she grabs it and then begins to twizzle the CD on the straw. This learning (physical hand to eye coordination and creative and critical thinking) from a baby so young is remarkable and the adults begin to discuss how they can take this learning on to a different level.

With these same resources two toddlers are using the CDs in a completely different manner. One child is also fascinated by the hole in the middle, not to thread through but to look through. This fascination develops as the child and adult begin to 'spy' on each other in an act of reciprocity which gradually develops into a game of 'peek-a-boo'. This learning isn't physical but more social as the baby and adult turn take (a prerequisite for turn taking in conversation). The toddler looks on as the key person and baby interact. The baby looks down at her CD, she sees something so she holds it closer to her face and recognises the image reflected back at her. She excitedly shows her key person who affirms, 'Yes, it's Sophie. Can you see your face?' ... and so the learning goes on.

This learning stemmed from an adult planned activity to encourage exploration from some basic unsophisticated resources and which led to so many different learning outcomes for three infants. The role of the key person in this case study is to plan for the infants, to observe and assess but most importantly to 'be there' for support, affirmation and challenge. This is about the adult being there, being involved and having a shared experience. The role is one of interacting, being interested but not interfering and intervening with adult agendas which are of no interest and value to the baby.

Questions for reflection

1. Reflecting on the play of the first baby in this vignette consider the ways in which this learning can be developed and extended.
2. Looking at your own setting and practice consider the everyday resources in your environment which could be offered to babies at differing stages of development and which could challenge their thinking and creativity, as well as giving them opportunities to become involved and engaged.

3. Reflecting upon your own practice, with your key children, what are the current challenges that might be a barrier to providing experiences such as the one above into your practice?
4. What action could you take to begin to address these current challenges?

Schemas and children's learning and development

As generally understood in current early childhood pedagogy, schemas are 'patterns of repeatable actions that lead to early categories and then to logical classifications' (Athey, 2007: 49). Athey (1990, 2007) has made popular the incorporation of schema into early childhood pedagogy in the learning of three- to five-year-olds. More recent work has extended understanding of schematic learning to work with babies and toddlers (Atherton and Nutbrown, 2013).

There is no single or definitive definition of the term 'schema' and, although the current use of the term in early childhood education and care is that given above, earlier work (Piaget, 1977) identifies schemas as part of the study of cognitive structures of young children's developing minds. Athey (2006) gives a thorough explanation of the various roots and definitions of the term as derived from the work of Piaget (1969), Bartlett (1932) and Neisser (1976).

We now know more about the learning patterns (or schemas) of babies and how they might think and learn. Goldschmied (1987) demonstrates how babies, given safe, simulating and supportive opportunities, will use their senses and their developing physical skills to learn about the objects they encounter. Babies, as they suck, handle and smell, are in a world of discovery – they puzzle, enjoy social interactions with others and make attempts to communicate their feelings and their needs. Those who watch young babies see some of the early patterns of gazing and following with their eyes and some of those basic patterns of behaviour (or schemas) are quite obvious to the observer. As babies suck and grasp, they work on, develop and refine the early schematic behaviours which foster their early foundations of learning. Early patterns of behaviour seen in babies become more complex and more numerous, eventually being connected so that babies and young children co-ordinate their actions.

Toddlers work hard, collecting a pile of objects in the lap of their carer, walking to and fro, backwards and forwards, bringing one object at a time (Nutbrown, 2011a). They are working on a pattern of behaviour which has a consistent thread running through it. Their patterns of action and thought at this point are related to the consistent back-and-forth movement. The early schemas of babies form the basis of the patterns of behaviour which children show between the ages of two and five years, and these in turn become established foundations of learning.

Athey (2006) maintains that children will notice elements in their environment, depending upon their interests at the time, and that they have their own intrinsic motivation which must be facilitated by materials and support from adults. Athey focused on how two- to five-year-old children also work on particular patterns of behaviour. A number of such patterns of behaviour were identified by Athey as part of the *Froebel Early Education Project* (which collected and analysed over 5000 observations of 20 two- to five-year-olds over two years). These were named according to their characteristics. For example, a 'vertical schema' was so called because it related to up-and-down movements. Athey discussed children's 'action schemas', which led to aspects of learning and development, among which the following schemas were most prominent:

- dynamic vertical
- dynamic back and forth or side to side
- circular direction and rotation
- going over, under or on top of
- going round a boundary
- enveloping and containing space
- going through a boundary
- thought ('internalized data' and 'telling a story').

The actions and marks related to these descriptions of movement can be identified in young children's drawing and mark-making, but Athey illustrates how such patterns can be represented in children's play, their thinking and their language. Athey argues that patterns pervade children's actions and speech as well as their mark-making. Detailed descriptions and discussion on ways in which different patterns of learning can be represented through action, speech and mark-making are given by Athey (2006), who further illustrates in theoretical and practical terms how forms of thought (schemas) once identified can be nourished with worthwhile content. But by means of examples we could say that, for instance, if a child is focusing on a particular schema related to 'roundness', she or he is working on a circular or rotation schema. The form is 'roundness' and the content can be anything which extends this form: wheels, rotating machinery, rolling a ball, playground roundabouts, the spinning of planets! Similarly a child interested in 'up and downness' could be working on a vertical schema. The form is 'up and down'; related content can include using ladders, using the climbing frame, watching parascending or skydiving, riding in a lift or on an escalator. In the same way, if a child is interested in enveloping and containing schemas, the form is 'insideness' and related content may include wrapping presents, hatching chickens' eggs, en croute cookery, dressing up, mining and burrowing.

More recently Atherton has studied the learning and development of children from eight months to three years, and identified similar schemas of action, representation and speech which support and enhance young children's learning at home and in their Children's Centre (Atherton and Nutbrown, 2013).

Planning for children's patterns of learning

The following example shows how young children's patterns of learning, as identified through Schema Theory, might be planned for.

William, aged 17 months, was sitting cross-legged in the home corner. He seemed quite unaware of other things going on around him. Watching him closely, Michelle noticed that William was repeatedly putting a lid on and taking it off the empty bottle he was holding. Michelle (a less experienced practitioner) thought that he might like to put something in his bottle and shake it to make a noise, but William ignored her efforts. Instead he discarded the bottle and toddled (furiously it seemed!) to the other side of the room and began rummaging in a basket of 'treasure'. The basket was filled to the brim with sensory fabrics and was an Aladdin's cave of interesting and exciting items, but William rejected everything, discarding them on the floor until he got to the very bottom of the basket. Finally, he let out a pleasing sigh as he found what he had been searching for – another circular lid. He shoved it roughly in his pocket and made his way to the sand tray leaving the basket of 'treasures' in disarray. He stood at the sand tray for a few minutes watching the other children until he spotted Oliver with the big dumper truck. He seemed mesmerized by it and laid his head on the side of the sand tray watching the wheels go round.

Wendy, the room leader (and William's key person) returned from lunch and immediately picked up on William's interests. She explained to Michelle that William was interested in rotation – and this seemed to be his current pattern of learning; this, she thought, explained his determined efforts to find the bottle lid and the intensity of his observation of the dumper truck in the sand. Michelle did not know about patterns of learning and was unaware of schemas and told Wendy that she had mistakenly thought William had been behaving badly and that she had been about to chastise him for the mess he had made over at the basket of treasures! In fact Michelle even wondered if William had a behavioural problem or was ill when he did not join in with the sand play and just stared and stared. Wendy suggested that Michelle shadow her for the next week and that they carry out joint observations and use them to discuss how to extend children's schemas as a way of supporting Michelle's continued professional development.

In this example we can see how sometimes less experienced practitioners who do not have a deep understanding of child development and learning theories can miss important signals that suggest children's interests and levels of involvement. William was demonstrating a high level of skill, not only in his ability to concentrate and persevere in his efforts in the initial task of putting the lid on the bottle, but also in making the connection to where he would find other similar items. Sometimes practitioners like Michelle, though well meaning, can mistakenly intervene or dissuade children from following their pattern of interest, which succeeds only in upsetting and frustrating them as they are interrupted in their play. William was not interested in the basket of treasures, despite their appealing nature, nor was he interested in playing in the sand, but he knew exactly where to locate his items of interest and was very pleased with his achievements. The skill of the practitioner lies in observing William's interests and planning to extend his learning by offering him further opportunities to persevere with rotational schema. This might be on a large scale with circular items in the garden or when painting, or by adding to the collection of lids with differing sizes and colours for William's further exploration. Laevers (1997) would describe William as having high levels of involvement and well-being, his behaviour demonstrating that he was, as Laevers (2005b) describes, like a 'fish in water'. Less experienced practitioners may feel nervous about carrying out observations, and Lindon (2012) suggests the starting point is for practitioners to record what they notice children doing. Put simply, it becomes less daunting and thereby the barrier is lifted to enable the practitioner who knows the child very well to record their interests.

Questions for reflection

1. Michelle mistook William's schematic play for misbehaviour. How do you work with parents so that they too can become aware of this aspect of their child's learning as a positive learning experience?
2. Using this observation as a starting point, reflect on the schemas that the infants, toddlers and young children for whom you are responsible are beginning to display.

The *real* treasure basket

In this section we discuss the importance of following children's interests. Goldschmied pioneered the idea of using a basket full of items of interest for babies to explore and discover. It was in fact in the early 1990s that the treasure basket was first promoted in the UK. In the film *Infants at Work* (Goldschmied, 1987) she introduces her notion of the treasure basket designed specifically for babies who can 'sit up but not yet crawl'. She is quite specific about the design and contents of the basket and, importantly, about the role of the adult. This section, 'The real treasure basket', draws very specifically on the learning that can take place given the set-up as Goldschmied intended it (Goldschmied and Hughes, 1992). In working with the treasure basket it is important that everyone understands the purposes of it and their role in the session. However, as Goldschmied and Jackson (2004: 101) point out; 'perhaps one of the things that an adult may find it difficult to do at first is not to intervene, but to stay quiet and attentive'. The idea behind this concept is to provide young children with affirmation and an 'emotional anchorage' by their very presence. When practitioners reach a shared understanding, the learning experience for the baby is even more powerful (Page, 2007).

Jamie had been attending nursery full-time since he was three months old. He had a very warm and responsive relationship with Philip, his key person, with whom he had bonded from an early age. Philip was sometimes shy with adults and at 19 years of age still got embarrassed when his friends laughed at his choice of career. But Philip was determined and had begun to form effective relationships with his colleagues and the children in the setting. Philip liked working with the older children and had got to know Jamie's mum quite well and had chatted at length with her about her elder son Simon and his keen interest in football and cricket. At seven Simon was not in the least bit interested in the prospect of another new baby on the scene – his younger sister was quite enough! Philip had talked to Simon about his siblings and Simon seemed at ease in Philip's company. When Jamie was born Simon was invited to tea to see the baby and he offered to babysit Simon, Jessica and baby Jamie while their mum took a rest.

Philip was very natural with all the children, he did not profess to be expert at everything and could not sing lullabies quite as well as some of his colleagues, but he did seem to have a natural affinity with the children. When Jamie took up his nursery place, Simon was already well settled at school and Jessica with her key person. It seemed natural for Jamie's mum to ask for Philip to be her baby's key person. Although Philip had not worked in a group capacity with babies before, most of his key children had moved on to school and in discussion with his manager it seemed to make sense. In terms of Philip's continued professional development (CPD) and in

Continues

Continued

response to the request from Jamie's mother this seemed to suit everyone. Jamie was described by everyone as an 'easy baby' and his parents could hardly believe his apparently straightforward transition into the nursery.

At about seven months Jamie had shown interest in sitting up and Philip had been propping him up with cushions behind him which he really enjoyed as he explored his immediate environment. Shahin, the baby room team leader, suggested that Philip offer Jamie the treasure basket. Philip had not seen it in use before and was unsure about what to do. Unable to overcome his shyness to seek advice he merely put the basket next to Jamie but out of his reach. Philip selected some items and offered them to Jamie. He did not seem interested but instead his eyes fixed on a large heavy glass paperweight. His interest at first went unnoticed until Shahin sat beside Philip and discussed with him how best to offer the treasure basket to Jamie to sustain his interest and exploration. Philip was concerned about the health and safety aspect of the treasure basket and had chosen what he considered to be 'safe' items for Jamie to play with. Philip was worried that Jamie's mum would disapprove as she was very safety conscious. Shahin understood Philip's concern and decided that a broader view was required. Knowing that she had a staff meeting coming up, Shahin approached the manager of the setting to ask if the nursery practitioners could view the 'Infants at Work' film again – this would serve as a training session for practitioners like Philip who were relatively new to the setting. It would also be a refresher for the more established practitioners on how to introduce the concept of treasure baskets to parents.

Shahin suggested to Philip that he might like to work on a display in the baby room to explain to parents about the value of the treasure basket, and their approach to assessing the risk to the babies, and to set up a loan library of articles including the 'Infants at Work' film to support parents and colleagues in their understanding of the value of the treasure basket. Further to the display, Philip added a suggestion box for parents to raise privately any questions or queries they might have about the treasure basket. Parents could choose whether to remain anonymous and to have the question and the response posted on the display wall, or to direct the question to a particular practitioner and for the response to come back to them directly.

In this example it would have been easy for Philip, given his know-ledge of the family and his close relationship with them, to have made assumptions about how to offer the treasure basket resource to Jamie. Although Philip was shy, which did at times inhibit his relationships with his colleagues, he always put the interests of the children first. He was able to explain that he thought Jamie's mother might worry that some of the objects in the treasure basket were unsafe and this can be a real fear for parents and practitioners. 'Misunderstandings and wor-ries about safety need to be addressed through a participative approach to working in partnership with parents and ensuring that family and cultural concerns and wishes are respected' (Nutbrown, 2011b: 162). Fortunately Shahin in her role as room leader of the baby room was clear about her role as Philip's immediate line manager and role model.

Questions for reflection

1. How do you introduce the concept of the treasure basket in your setting to (a) parents and (b) colleagues to ensure there is a shared understanding about how the treasure basket is offered to babies?
2. Who takes responsibility in your setting for (a) risk assessment (b) replacing and replenishing items in the treasure basket to ensure both safety and cultural sensitivity?
3. Are there sufficient opportunities in place in your setting to engage babies in language and communication experiences outside treas-ure basket play?
4. How do treasure basket observations help you to plan for their patterns of play (schema)?

Real heuristic play[1]

The term 'heuristic' is derived from the Greek word *eurisko* – which means to 'discover or gain an understanding of' (Goldschmied and Hughes, 1992). Goldschmied's work promoted *heuristic play with*

1 An earlier version of this section appeared in J. Page 'Heuristic play', *Nursery World*, (2007) 107(4074): 15–18.

objects as it is most widely understood. *Heuristic Play with Objects* (Goldschmied and Hughes, 1992) and *People under Three: Young Children in Day Care* (Goldschmied and Jackson, 1994, 2004) have related the ethos and spirit of Goldschmied's view of heuristic play that is most familiar to practitioners.

Put simply, heuristic play consists of offering a group of young children a large number of different kinds of objects and receptacles with which they play freely without adult intervention. These are offered for a defined period of time in a controlled environment (Goldschmied and Jackson, 2004: 128). Goldschmied promotes such play sessions for toddlers – children who are in their second year of life – and key to the heuristic play experience is the abundance of materials to support children's innate desire to investigate and explore.

> Studies of day nurseries and childminders suggest that children between one and two get the least planned attention and are considered to be the most difficult age group by caregivers … they are often seen as disruptive, having lost interest in baby toys but still too young to be involved in the … activities provided for older children … This second year is one of extraordinarily rapid growth and development, but unless careful thought is given to how their particular needs can be provided for, the experience for children, especially in group care, can easily be negative and limiting. (Goldschmied and Jackson, 2004: 111)

As with the treasure basket, the ethos of the heuristic play session is to offer mostly natural materials, or objects made from natural materials, as opposed to those that are commercially produced. To ensure children are offered a quality experience it is important to provide plenty of sensory materials, enough for all the children who will use them during the session. Thought is needed when collecting, storing and arranging the objects for play. Practitioners need to carefully consider the type, size and sensory properties of the objects they provide, so that children can gain maximum benefit from their exploration of them. Heuristic play as discussed here is intended for children aged around 12–20 months when they are at the stage of exploring materials but not yet capable of using them in a way which could cause harm to themselves or others. Older children are likely to be more sophisticated in their explorations and may choose to use the objects as part of socio-dramatic play, potentially resulting in danger due to overzealous misuse.

During an heuristic play session for toddlers there is no 'right' or 'wrong' way to play. Heuristic play can be inclusive and often therapeutic. Unlike many commercially produced toys, whose play value may be limited, 'heuristic play' objects are natural items from everyday life that hold the potential for children to test out their own theories and to solve problems. It is not unusual for a child to be more interested in the wrapping paper, ribbon and box than the gift they once contained. This is because an empty box or a length of ribbon can provide endless possibilities to sustain children's natural curiosity. Laevers (1997) uses 'well-being' and 'involvement' indicators to determine the quality of learning episodes. He suggests that when children can be observed in activities that promote high levels of well-being, this supports their involvement; the two together being indicators of 'deep level learning'.

Provision of an array of materials such as different sized boxes, varying widths of ribbon, lengths of chain, corks and bottles, wooden clothes pegs, curtain rings, and so on, can help stimulate children to sort, select, balance, fill, empty and test out the properties of the things they find. They can discover for themselves if one type of material acts the same as another. A child pushing pegs into a bottle soon discovers she is unable to retrieve them – they are stuck in the bottle. Yet, when she drops a chain into the bottle and turns the bottle upside down, the chain falls out. Children in heuristic play sessions often persevere with the same task over and over again until they have had enough. This experience of exploration and discovery can support children's cognitive development and, as Gopnik et al. (1999a: 157) confirm, 'They [children] never start from scratch; instead, they modify and change what they already know to gain new knowledge'.

To make effective use of heuristic play sessions, settings must ensure that all practitioners thoroughly understand their role during heuristic time, especially when introducing these ideas to parents and visitors. Heuristic play does not have to be offered to a whole group of children at a time. It can be offered to one or two children, and in some mixed-age settings it can be particularly beneficial.

It is not a time for adult-to-adult conversation, or for lots of talking to the children, which is precisely why it requires careful consideration and inclusion in the overall planning, ensuring it is balanced with the provision of plentiful opportunities to support and encourage children's language and emerging speech patterns. The adult's role should not be underestimated. Quality planned experiences for children can best be provided by skilled and knowledgeable adults who know and understand the children's interests, and with whom the children have secure, trusting relationships. The key person is ideally placed to carry out this role as she or he will be attuned to the individual behaviour of the children and can be a facilitator for their patterns of play. Sometimes, detailed observations can be made of a child or small number of children.

Heidi had set out the room for a heuristic play session. The children arrived and started their explorations. Eighteen-month-old twin boys, Barney and Wilf, like to be close to one another. They share the same key person but have quite distinct and different personalities. Barney is shy and likes to take his time to check things out before attempting to explore. Wilf has a tendency to have a go at anything and noisily explores his environment. Wilf picks up one of the large tins and puts his face into it and shouts. He can hear his voice and he repeats the action. Barney stays close to Heidi who is sitting in a low chair. Heidi gestures to Barney as he picks up a large pebble and drops it into another tin. It crashes to the bottom. Wilf stops what he is doing and looks up as he hears the loud sound of the pebble crashing into the tin. Wilf toddles over to the tin and drops in another pebble but Barney winces at the sound. Instead, he sits close to Heidi and explores the bottle tops and chains that lie piled up on one another. Barney picks up the largest chain and gently lets it slip through his fingers. It drops to the floor, the fluidity and weight of the chain results in it coiling itself into another pile. Barney continues with his exploration, this time using a piece of rope. He holds the rope in one hand and the chain in the other and raises his hands up and down in turn, first the rope and then the chain. He lets them drop to the floor and then picks them up again. He repeats this action over and over. Heidi counts him doing this 15 times.

Meanwhile Wilf has found a selection of stones and is busy dropping them into any turned up receptacle he can find, laughing gleefully as each stone drops to the bottom. He waits to hear the sound the stone makes at the bottom of each container. He drops a stone into a tube with no bottom in it and, hearing no sound, investigates further. He puts his arm into the tube and as he reaches the bottom realizes he can touch the carpet. With the tube still attached Wilf lifts his arm and starts to giggle. Heidi smiles at him and gently removes the tube as she sees that Wilf is about to become a little distressed because he is unable to shake it off. Barney looks up at Heidi as she smiles warmly, affirming his attempt to investigate the chains and rope.

Sometime later when the children were clearly coming to the end of their play, Heidi begins to involve the children in clearing up the room. The children know what they have to do and immediately start to help to fill the drawstring bags with the things on the floor. The tidying complete, Wilf rushes to the door ready to go out, Barney hangs back and holds his arms up to Heidi. She offers her hands to the boys as they rejoin the rest of the nursery.

In this example the boys are the focus of Heidi's observation, although other children are present in the room. They are used to such heuristic play sessions and were familiar with the way in which Heidi had set out the room. Having plenty of materials, suggest Goldschmied and Jackson (2004), is one of the prerequisites of a good heuristic play session; it means there is sufficient for all children to do what they want to do. In this example the two children take two very different approaches to exploring the materials on offer. Because there is no 'right' or 'wrong' way to use the materials, the children followed their own individual interests, sustained their own level of involvement and made their own explorations. The practitioner in this case played her subtle and quiet (but nevertheless 'active') role with affirming smiles for Barney and intervention to help Wilf out of his tangle!

Much of the children's interest could be considered playful but there is also a sense of intense 'work' and 'thinking'. Adults keep overt interaction with the children to a minimum and their engagement is not one of intervention or of leading children's play. Rather, the adult role is to support children's own curiosity and give them quiet 'permission' to explore. Heuristic play sessions are different from other play experiences. Many opportunities exist when practitioners can talk with children or prompt a particular form of inquiry. But the point in heuristic play is to have added another dimension which facilitates children's natural exploration and creativity. Skilful practitioners will build upon their observations of the children and utilize their interpretations to inform planning for children's continued learning in other aspects of their day.

Treasure basket play and heuristic play are approaches which are non-gendered, non-stereotypical and inclusive. They can provide useful media for all young children's exploration as they are based on the use of one or more of their senses.

In practice terms you may consider involving parents, families and members of the wider community in collecting suitable items for heuristic play; for example, local restaurants may provide large catering tins. It can take several weeks or even months to gather sufficient items to offer in a session to a group of children. It is important that heuristic play sessions are offered alongside continuous play provision, but not necessarily every day (Goldschmied and Jackson, 2004). This is to ensure children derive maximum benefit from this carefully planned and unique session and not to routinize such explorations. Items such as chains, bottles and cones can, of course, be provided at any point in the continuous provision of the setting, and could be included in the 'enhancements' section of the Continuous Provision Planning documentation, as we discuss in more detail in Chapter 5, with the item name and the child's initials to make the link between an earlier heuristic play observation and the designated area (thus extending children's learning and development).

Questions for reflection

1. Thinking about your own practice, how might you plan for toddlers' exploration of natural objects?
2. Who is responsible for carrying out a risk assessment and checking the suitability of the items before, during and after use?
3. How do you introduce parents to the practice of heuristic play with objects?

4. Is there a shared understanding in your setting about the value of heuristic play with objects?
5. How does heuristic play with objects support young children's problem-solving skills?
6. How are heuristic play observations informing you about the children's patterns of play (schemas)?

Exploring beyond the treasure basket ...

Variety and quality, discovery and concentration, decision-making and problem-solving are themes that Goldschmied and Jackson (2004) identify when young children derive pleasure and enjoyment from the treasure basket. Children's enjoyment of play with a range of materials can be extended beyond the realms of the treasure basket. The principles of the heuristic play approach can be incorporated into other types of exploratory play. However, practitioners may wish to consider the types of play that children prefer to engage in. Play has long been argued as being a highly complex and skilful activity – 'children's work'. But the descriptions of play as 'ludic' and 'epistemic' (Hutt et al., 1989; see also Table 4.1) can be helpful in supporting our understanding of children's play and adults' responses to that play.

Of course, children themselves do not distinguish between different types of play as defined by adults, and these two 'types' are intertwined. Children need first to be provided with opportunities to investigate, explore and test out their theories (in epistemic play) before they can move on to the more imaginative or symbolic (ludic) play. Sometimes children are too quickly hurried on to symbolic play because of the adults' need to understand it or to see an end product. But the enjoyment and deep-level learning that takes place during the exploratory (epistemic) stage is crucial. Metaphorically we can imagine children first asking (of an object) 'What is this?'. Having found their answers to this question, they later move on to ask (of the object) 'What can I do with this?', and then come the imaginative and symbolic elements of play. We can think of extending heuristic play to include opportunities for exploration of other materials such as water, sand and glue. Holland (1997) describes setting up a gluing session

Table 4.1 *Characteristics of epistemic and ludic play*

Epistemic play behaviour	Ludic play behaviour

• is concerned with the acquisition of knowledge and skill problem-solving
• gathers information
• is exploratory
• is productive
• discovers
• is invention, task or work orientated
• is relatively independent of mood state
• has constraints which stem from the nature of the focus of attention
• needs adults to:
  – support
  – encourage
  – answer questions
  – supply information
  – be involved
	• is 'playful'
	• is fun
	• is lacking in specific focus
	• is highly mood dependent
	• has constraints which (when they exist) are imposed by the child
	• does not need to involve adults
	• requires that adults are sensitive to children's needs
	• can be changed by insensitive intervention
	• has the key features of enjoyment and fantasy
	• is unconstrained
	• is idiosyncratic
	• is repetitive
	• is innovative
	• is symbolic

Source: Holland, 1997: 120

with one- and two-year-olds, adopting Goldschmied's ethos and principles for heuristic play with objects. Holland provides a space set out with tables and chairs, enough room for each child at the table and each provided with a pot of glue and spatula, paper and cut-up tissue paper (Abbott et al., 2000). One-year-olds involved in exploring the properties of the glue show little interest in sticking the tissue paper, which, unlike the glue, does not interest them. Young children need time to watch, explore, create and just 'be'.

Lesley, a newly qualified practitioner, was very excited at taking up her new post at 'Meadowbank'. She could not wait to put into practice the skills and knowledge that she had learned during her last two years of initial training. She had enjoyed her placements and felt confident about working with one- and two-year-olds. At her interview, Lesley had talked about her fascination with children of this age, who, in her view, were no longer tiny babies, but with their emerging personalities and attempts at language were becoming more noticeable to adults outside the family.

As part of her induction Lesley observed a session which the setting referred to as 'exploratory play'. She followed the six children whose ages ranged from 13 to 16 months into the room set up for the exploratory play with paint session. The room leader had covered a large table with paper and individual pots of paint. The children were invited to sit up at the table, which was evenly spaced with chairs to enable the children to move freely. Within their reach were individual pots of paint in various colours, large pieces of coloured paper and a variety of brushes, rollers and mark-making tools. The children chose a place to sit, and the practitioners, including Lesley, sat at the side, close at hand observing their key children.

Lesley was fascinated by the quietness of the room, in fact it was quite a shock to her at first as she was used to the hustle and bustle of the toddler group room. However, she was struck by the children's exploration. She noted how attentive the practitioners were as they took time to write their detailed notes, while continuing to smile and nod at the children, affirming their 'voice'. One of the children seemed to dislike having paint on his fingers and began to cry. The practitioner gently offered him her hand and gestured to the hand basin where he went with her to wash his hands. She waited for him to decide what he wanted to do next. He climbed onto her lap and 'snuggled' in. Five minutes later he returned to his seat and started again to explore the blue paint. This time, as he started to put his finger inside the pot, he stopped, looked at his finger and said 'Oww – No!' and then picked up the stumpy brush and pushed it into the paint pot. As he drew it out again, covered in thick blue paint, he looked at it with a satisfied grin and watched it drip onto the table, it continued to drip as he moved his brush across the table and he watched it drip, drip, drip onto the floor …. On the opposite side of the table another child was completely immersed in paint from hand to elbow. He squidged and squelched the paint through his fingers, squealing with delight each time it made splurting noises and spat out into the newspaper. His key person noted his delight and pointed to his feet which were now bare as he had kicked his feet with such glee his shoes had fallen onto the floor beneath the table. She removed his socks, put some more paper and a pot of paint on the floor and watched as the child continued his exploration, dripping the paint off the paintbrush onto the paper and standing on it …

This example demonstrates Lesley's first experience of this type of exploratory play session. She was already familiar with the ethos of the treasure basket and heuristic play from her previous training but had not observed an extension with paint. She was at first quite shocked at the quietness and formal structure of the room layout and overall set up of the session. This seemed to be at odds with the way in which very young children would usually be offered what she had always termed 'messy play'. She also noted the almost total absence of language from the adults. At the end of the session, which lasted about 40 minutes, she was amazed that the children's explorations had been so intensive and uninterrupted. She was interested to know how the children's parents had reacted when introduced to the concept of the session. The room leader showed Lesley the photographs of the parents' morning when all the parents had been invited to find out about the treasure basket, heuristic play and how the setting planned to extend the sessions further into exploratory play with sand, paint, glue and water. The setting was located in what was considered to be an area of social and economic deprivation, and engaging with parents in a meaningful way was a key aim of the setting. Especially important was the establishment of a sense of trust within the community and for the setting to be able to share the philosophy and ethos of these types of sessions. It was important to allow parents to raise questions or concerns in order that they could reach a shared understanding about what their children did.

The room leader explained to Lesley about other ways in which parents got involved. She recalled a session for a group of teenage fathers who had been invited to observe the children in their play. The 17-year-old father of one of the toddlers was quite captivated when he saw his daughter's exploration of glue. He had recently taken up a place as an apprentice painter and decorator and could see ways in which he could extend the sessions with his daughter at home. A few weeks later he brought in some lovely photographs of the toddler sitting on lengths of wallpaper with a pot of glue in one hand and a pasting brush in the other. After that he regularly brought offcuts of wallpaper into the nursery and accepted the practitioners' invitation to help the three- and four-year-olds set up a painting and decorating role-play area.

Ideas for practice

■ Informing parents about exploratory play sessions that go 'beyond the treasure basket' is essential if parents are really to feel their contribution and opinions are valued. It is crucial that parents have opportunities to share their pleasure and concerns. It is important too, not to obscure key messages with professional terminology (such as ludic and epistemic play). Clear explanations will make it possible for all to share similar insights into what the setting is aiming for in offering such play provision. But it is important to know about research and to be confident and conversant with the terminology used.

■ Exploratory play can be inclusive. We have already established that there is no right or wrong way in exploratory play, and no intended visible result or outcome. Practitioners, in discussion with parents, can make adaptations and alterations to such sessions so as to facilitate opportunities for all children – including those with particular and specific needs – to be included and involved.

■ The role of the adult remains the same in exploratory play sessions as in the original treasure basket and heuristic play sessions. Goldschmied and Jackson's analogy helps us to appreciate the emotional confidence the adult offers just by being close by, attentive and interested.

> An adult may find it difficult … not to intervene, but to stay quiet and attentive. If we think for a moment how we feel when concentrating on some enjoyable but demanding activity, we do not want or need someone constantly to suggest, advise and praise our effort, we just want to get on with it, though we may be glad to have their friendly company. (Goldschmied and Jackson, 2004: 101)

Questions for reflection

1. Consider how the babies and children in the group relate to one another. How do their explorations change according to which children are sharing the session? Do children interact and experiment

with their voices when their friends are present?
2. How does an exploratory play session with two-year-olds differ from a similar session for one-year-olds?

In this chapter we have used some examples from practice to discuss some theories of learning and apply them to everyday practice with babies and young children. It is important to understand the meaning of particular terminology rather than to leave it shrouded in some sort of professional secrecy. Policy initiatives will come and go, and with them new and different terminology. When the Department for Education and Skills (DfES) launched the *Birth to Three Matters Framework* in 2002 (DfES, 2002a; the result of pioneering work led by Lesley Abbott), it was widely welcomed throughout the early years and childcare sector (Sure Start, 2003c). Even so, it took practitioners some time to make connections with the language used and to sort out the 'Aspects' and 'Components' in relation to young children. But the policy wheel turns quickly and these 'Aspects' and 'Components' have now been replaced in the *Early Years Foundation Stage* (DfE, 2012a) with 'Prime Areas of Learning and Development' and 'Characteristics of Effective Learning'. Even more difficult to grasp were some of the categories in the four broad areas of development. For example, the term 'Heads up, Lookers and Communicators', used to describe babies from 0 to 8 months, did not exactly roll off the tongue! But practitioners, parents, researchers and policy-makers know what is meant by terms like 'young babies', 'babies', 'infants', 'toddlers' and 'young children'. What is important is the achievement of a shared or common understanding, locally, nationally and internationally. Those concerned with babies and young children need also to recall work that has gone before. All practitioners in the twenty-first century must have a secure understanding of child development and how children learn as a bedrock to working with and for babies and young children. There are great responsibilities on the shoulders of practitioners, who are expected to analyse and interpret new policy initiatives so that they make a positive difference to the experiences of the children.

Further reading

Arnold, C. and the Pen Green Team (2010) *Understanding Schemas and Emotion in Early Childhood.* London: Sage.

Henry, L., Michael, B., Crowther, C., Evans, J., Mortimer, H. and Phillips-Green, J. (2007) *Senses – Play Foundations.* Dublin: Folens Publishers.

Hughes, A. (2010) *Developing Play for the Under 3s: The Treasure Basket and Heuristic Play* (2nd edn). Abingdon: Routledge.

Lindon, J. (2012) *Understanding Child Development: 0–8 Years: Linking Theory and Practice* (3rd edn). Abingdon: Hodder Education.

Chapter 5

Environments for Learning

This chapter will look at:
- Creating and organizing learning environments
- Planning for 'continuous provision'
- Environments for learning:
  o in a home setting
  o in a 'pack away' pre-school
  o in purpose-built provision
  o in a mixed age range setting

Creating learning environments for young children

Providing an active learning environment for infants and toddlers encourages their need to look, listen, wiggle, roll, crawl, climb, rock, bounce, rest, eat, make noise, grasp or mouth or drop things, and be messy from time to time. (Post and Hohmann, 2000: 14)

In this chapter we identify and discuss ways of creating interesting and effective learning environments for babies and toddlers. We are mindful that issues of quality in learning environments can be context specific; what works in one place does not necessarily work (nor is it always desirable) in another. Settings in city centres may well be organized and operate differently from rurally located provision. Quality in a relatively poor northern city in England may be differently defined from quality in a pre-school provision in New Delhi. Woodhead (1996) reminds us that quality is a relative concept, but not arbitrary. He writes:

Treating quality criteria as being relative rather than fixed, negotiated rather than prescribed, might be interpreted as undermining for programme managers, whose role is already difficult. If there are multiple perspectives on quality, are all attempts to identify and objectify criteria illusory? Is seeking agreement about quality as illusory as seeking a crock of gold at the end of the rainbow? … whilst we reject the idea of the crock of gold, we should not lose sight of the rainbow itself. Like rainbows, quality is not fixed and can be elusive … (Woodhead, 1996: 45–6)

Penn (2011) talks of the challenge to universal understandings of quality both at macro as well as micro level. She says, 'Quality is nothing if not relative, and there are no magic formulae, only many adjustments to suit each set of circumstances' (2011: 6). In relation to the quality of young children's learning experiences Brooker and Woodhead make the following point:

The concepts of development and learning are intertwined: development is a holistic concept, encompassing growth and changes in all aspects of the individual's physical, mental and social functioning; learning refers to the specific processes for developing knowledge, skills and identity … Development and learning are universal processes, but they take place in specific social and cultural contexts, including childcare and early education settings … Variations in children's development and learning are shaped by cultural values … supporting the child's development entails both respecting and supporting the family and community which carry the major day-to-day responsibility for the child. (2010: 1)

In a UK context, there are quality baselines in place designed to safeguard children and to offer them positive experiences, as well as to reassure parents that their young children are in 'safe hands'.

It is widely accepted (Elfer, 2011; Nutbrown and Carter, 2010) that in order to plan the best opportunities for children to learn we need to spend time observing them and noting their preferences, and this is an on-going process. However, before we really know children, when they first come into the setting and while we are getting to know them we need to ensure the environment is such that it positively facilitates children's interactions, interests and involvement. In the following examples we illustrate ways in which practitioners have used all aspects of the environments in which they work to enable babies and young children to learn.

Organizing the environment for children's needs

An experienced practitioner with a sound understanding of child development can plan to create an environment that reflects the likely needs of the babies and children in his or her care. For example, very young children will enjoy using all their senses to explore, and 'mouthing' in particular is a natural instinct. The *treasure basket* (Goldschmied and Jackson, 2004) offers a wonderful opportunity for babies usually between the ages of six and nine months (those who can sit up but not yet crawl) to use all their senses. In the same way a *heuristic play* session where toddlers can explore a large range of objects (Goldschmied and Hughes, 1992) can be offered to older babies and toddlers who are more mobile.

Even in a specially designed and purpose-built nursery, rules and regulations can place restrictions and constraints on what can be done – long before children even enter the building. There are some fine pieces of equipment which are commercially available and the available budget makes a difference to what can be purchased, however, equipping the environment does not necessarily have to be costly in order to offer high-quality opportunities for children. It is important that practitioners question the long-term play value of some commercially produced materials that can sometimes initially offer and promise much but turn out to be limiting (or even useless!). A nine-month-old baby who enjoys posting items through the fence will not necessarily derive the same enjoyment from a shape posting box that requires dexterity and fine motor skills that he has yet to develop. On the other hand as Thomas (2002) suggests, a large cardboard box with large holes cut out on each of the sides, large enough for him to post everything in sight, will foster his enjoyment and achievement.

We know that babies and young children respond well to familiarity and are likely to feel more secure when surrounded by familiar things. Thomas (2002: viii) suggests that babies often prefer '80 per cent familiar to 20 per cent new', certainly until children have grasped some meaningful language. She then proposes that the balance may change to '70 per cent familiar to 30 per cent new'. It is hardly

surprising, then, that when babies and young children are first introduced to a new environment the transition needs to be handled
sensitively. There should be plenty of opportunities for the child to
visit close adults and become accustomed to new surroundings and,
importantly, to begin to form relationships with the adults and children. (Thomas's study may prompt practitioners to consider what
they themselves feel comfortable with in terms of familiar/unfamiliar
experiences! How good are adults at coping with new experiences and
unfamiliar surroundings? All transitions in life can engender some
feelings of anxiety, even when adults have strategies to draw on to
help them cope with new things.) Each child is unique and their needs
differ. There is no blueprint for how long it will take a child to feel
safe, comfortable and familiar with his or her surroundings.

We know that bringing special items from home is often very important to babies and young children. These items, often referred to as
comforters or soothers (Post and Hohmann, 2000), can range from blankets, teddy bears, pieces of ribbon, dummies and even old nightshirts.
They can come in all shapes and sizes, and have interesting names too!
Something that perhaps started life as a quite ordinary muslin square and
was renamed dribble cloth by the family (a description of the purpose it
served) became affectionately known, when the child acquired language,
as 'Ribble' (the shortened version of a muslin 'dribble cloth' that the child
could say). *Uh-u, Gerr,* and *Muh-muh* are three other comforters we have
known! Sometimes inexperienced practitioners remove these special
items (which can look like dirty old rags) from children when they arrive
at their setting, mistakenly believing that the child is better off without it
– or that hygiene rules! There is nothing more traumatic than to witness
a small child crying desperately for 'tubby' – a small grubby blue teddy
with one ear that smells of home – only to be told by the practitioner that
he can have it at home time and to stop being 'silly'. Enabling environments offer babies and children 'cubbies' whereby they can leave their
comforters should they choose to, knowing that they will still be there
when they return. Children are much more likely to give them up and
become engrossed in their play if they are secure in the knowledge that
they can go and get their comforters *when they need them!*

Just as young children need their comforters from home for emotional security, our very youngest children should be cared for in
environments which reflect the home, suggests Clare (2012), and of

course childminders are in the perfect position to do this. However, whether it is appropriate for group care settings to replicate home environments is a constant source of debate (Dahlberg et al., 2007; Degotardi and Pearson, 2009; Trevarthen, 2004), particularly with regard to whether adult–child relationships inhibit interaction between infant peers. Nevertheless, in nurseries the numbers of children and adults in the space impacts on the environment; even more reason why sensitive caregiving by closely attuned adults is needed to help young children feel loved and cherished (DfE, 2012a; Elfer et al., 2003; Page, 2011b). However, when planning an appropriate infant/toddler environment the adult's role is to give careful thought to creating a space which is interesting, stimulating and secure for toddlers as well as babies who are not yet walking. It is important, therefore, to ensure that small children do not feel intimidated by the number of cots, buggies and high chairs which can unnecessarily dominate their spaces. Multiple pieces of rarely used equipment can take up valuable space which could be better used to provide babies who need to lie or sit with a quiet, calm, soft and cosy corner. It is important that environments for babies offer sufficient challenge for early toddling infants, but this should not replicate the rooms and environments created for older children. When looking at the environment and the resources, the adult also has to bear in mind the ever-changing needs of the very youngest children in their care; one week a baby can be crawling and the next s/he can be walking, and as a result the resources and the way in which they are offered needs to be adapted in order to maintain interest and involvement as well as challenge.

'Continuous provision' planning[1]

> Infants and toddlers in group care have no choice about being in childcare. Each part of the day, however, presents opportunities for choices and decisions they can make … what to hold, look at, or whether, how and how long to participate in an activity … making these choices and decisions on a daily basis and being able to change their mind from one day to the next tends to give children a sense of control over their day. (Post and Hohmann, 2000: 26)

[1] An earlier version of this section was published in J. Page (2006) 'Planning for under-threes', *Nursery World*, (2006) 106(4031): 13–20.

Having already established that to plan rich experiences for babies and small children requires skilful practitioners in the role of the key person (Elfer et al., 2012), the practitioner needs to define how to plan the environment space to support the child's interests from the outset. Practitioners might choose to use tools such as the Continuous Provision Planning (CPP) sheet illustrated in Table 5.1. It can be adapted to meet almost any area of the setting and used to plan enhancements to meet the individual and differentiated needs of children. Practitioners may find it useful to add a further column to indicate the broad area of development they are planning to foster in the child, or children, to support their further understanding of the purpose of a particular environment space. The CPP sheet can be enlarged or reduced to suit the setting and, if a blank copy is produced and laminated, planning can be on a wipe-on-wipe-off form. The 'enhancements' column will change most often, depending on the needs of the children in the area at the time, and so this form of planning becomes a practical tool for busy practitioners. It can be particularly useful when practitioners need to plan in mixed age group settings such as community pre-schools and childminder homes because (as the example shows) it can span the whole age range.

Points to consider

When planning the environment based on observations of the children, or when children are new to the setting, from the information shared from parents, practitioners might consider the following points:

- What activities are being provided and why?
- Are the resources inclusive?
- Can the younger children access the materials and equipment – can they make appropriate choices?
- Can children clear up after the activity has finished? What might the practitioner need to do to enable the child to become more competent in this task?
- How might adults be involved? What is the role of the key person? Are they supporter, negotiator, supervisor, observer?

Table 5.1 *Continuous Provision Planning sheet*

This would be used in designated areas of the room, e.g. book area, home corner, construction area and so on. The boxes would be extended accordingly to complete the appropriate information in line with observations and individual documentation to meet the needs of the children in the setting.

Resources	Organization	Areas of learning and development	Adult involvement	Possible enhancements
What is always available for children as part of basic provision with or without adult support?	Where are basic resources kept? How are they made available to children?	Why are these basic resources provided? What is the planned learning experience?	This will vary according to the ages of the children and the type of resource	This column could be changed regularly to support children's individual interests

Source: adapted from Salford EYDCP (2004)

The Continuous Provision Planning sheet can be used for other areas of the setting such as:

- exploratory play
- sensory area
- role-play area
- mark-making area
- physical area
- outdoors.

The whole emphasis of the document is the word 'continuous', in other words it is the stable environment – what children can expect to encounter for most of the day, every day. Therefore for items such as the treasure basket, heuristic play or 'islands of intimacy' (Goldschmied and Jackson, 2004) the practitioner would need to use a different planning tool (still based on the same underpinning principles) to plan for these opportunities.

Environments for learning in a home setting

In this first case study we consider how a childminder, faced with a tragic and possibly extreme request, organizes a home setting to make living and learning possible for grieving children.

Giles had been caring for his terminally ill wife, Barbara, and his three children – eight-year-old Felicity, three-year-old Robin and six-month-old Jenny – while still working as a mechanic. The family was still trying to come to terms with Barbara's diagnosis which came only three months after the birth of Jenny.

Felicity spent hours sitting on the bed talking to her mum, drawing pictures for her and practising her reading from the array of books that Felicity borrowed on her frequent trips to the library with her grandma. Robin was cross because he wanted his mum to play making tents with him and run around the garden like she used to do. Jenny, who was too young to *really* understand (though Giles sensed she knew that something about her mum was different), enjoyed her bedtime snuggles in her mum's arms, gazing into

Continues

Continued

her eyes before settling down to sleep in her cot next to their bed.

With the children all settled in bed and the evening meal cleared away, Barbara and Giles discussed the long-term childcare arrangements for their children. Barbara knew that she did not have long to live and especially wanted to ensure that she had a say in every aspect of her children's future. All the children had been attending a local childminder, Ruth. Giles usually dropped the children at 8.00 a.m. and collected them at 6.00 p.m. Ruth took Felicity to school with her own son, Martin, who was in Felicity's class, and collected them again at the end of the day. All the children had an excellent relationship with Ruth, although Robin had been very tearful during the last week after Barbara's recent spell in hospital.

Giles and Barbara decided to invite Ruth to their house to discuss every element of their children's needs both now and in the future. They had obtained some additional funding to support their changing childcare needs and Barbara listed all the things they wanted to discuss and the possibility of flexible childcare arrangements.

Twelve months later Robin (now nearly four years) waved to Felicity and Martin as they skipped hand in hand down the path to school. Robin turned to Ruth and said, 'Can we play that game now? You know the one I used to play with mum when she made the big tent in the garden'. Fighting the tears, Ruth smiled at Robin and said 'Yes let's do that' and ruffled his hair.

Ruth would always remember the day Barbara died and the family's sadness in the weeks and months that followed. Everything had changed for them, but as the family slowly began to rebuild their lives Ruth knew that she was supporting the family, especially Barbara, in her choices of childcare even after her death. It was important for Ruth to continue the professional relationship that she had always enjoyed with the family. And in order to do so, Ruth had received significant emotional support from the childminder network that she belonged to, and Giles had set up a direct debit payment so that Ruth was always paid on time – this added to the professionalism of the relationship. Following a specific request from Barbara, Ruth regularly looked at family photographs with the children, something which Barbara knew that Giles would find it hard to do as he was coming to terms with her death. But Barbara had known that for her children to cope, with Ruth's help, she needed to plan some times when they could talk about her and laugh and cry.

In this example we consider the learning environment in its broadest sense. The family all knew and trusted Ruth. She was a consistent, familiar adult in their lives. Barbara chose to spend as much time as possible with her children but to call upon the professionalism of Ruth as a childminder to support her wishes both prior to and after her death. Barbara and Giles were secure in the knowledge that, in the safety of Ruth's home, their children could explore their emotions and have a much needed space to laugh, cry and play (all of which make up the essential ingredients of learning in young children's lives) in the 'normality' of a familiar environment. Although the complexity of the situation could have been daunting for Ruth, she ensured she had her own support systems in place. She also considered it to be a huge privilege to have been able to work so closely and compassionately with the whole family. Giles needed to keep working to ensure a steady income for the family but was secure in the knowledge that his children had a safe, secure and loving learning environment in which to grow. With practical support from Ruth he was able to share in his children's achievements as well as come to terms with his own grief.

Ideas for practice

- A childminder needs to consider which parts of her or his home will be accessible to the minded children. Providing a space for privacy for children is essential, particularly when children require some quiet time for themselves. Getting the balance right can be a dilemma as health and safety is of paramount importance. But a cosy corner behind the back of the settee may be a perfect hidey hole for a toddler to crawl into to look at books, photographs or special items.
- The key person approach as defined by Elfer et al. (2012) makes it clear that support from the manager/owner/head of centre in group care is an essential ingredient to understanding and working within the close triangular relationship with the child, the parent and the carer. There is also a requirement in the revised EYFS for practitioners to receive supervision to cope with sensitive issues. If the childminder works alone then it is important to ensure that there are support systems in place to offer help and advice so that s/he can continue to offer a learning environment to the children in his or her care.

Questions for reflection

1. Although this is, perhaps, an unusual case there will be times when the adults in your setting need you to be this supportive. Consider how you, either as a childminder or a key person working in an out-of-home setting, would have responded to such a situation.
2. What emotional support do you think you would need to equip you to respond with sensitivity and understanding to the needs of this family?

Environments for learning in a 'pack away' pre-school

Many settings operate in conditions which are not purpose built for young children and/or in bookable space where all equipment (including furniture and large play constructions) must be stored when not in use. This can make the physical challenge of working in such settings significant and can also make planning and continuity problematic. This case study shows how one group used planning to support their aim to provide good quality experiences for the youngest children who attended.

Staff of the community playgroup had recently attended a workshop on the role of the key person and strategies for planning the environment more effectively. Before attending the training, the practitioners of the pre-school had struggled to organize their environment to show differentiation for the children aged between two and two and a half in their group. The older children seemed to be catered for quite well.

Following the training, and with further support from their birth to three consultant, the setting worked towards implementing the key person approach. They adopted and adapted the 'Continuous Provision Planning' sheet, paying careful attention to ensure that they recorded children's initials and their individual interests in a simple manner. They needed a document that could be updated regularly to differentiate learning intentions according to the needs and abilities of each child in order to plan for their next experiences. This simple but effective tool ensured that the offered curriculum was available to all the children and meaningful connections to observations of individual children were made. The dated documents provided records of children's individuality and progression, which meant that the setting was able to dispense with their previous, often meaningless, tick list.

Two months later the setting had an unannounced Ofsted inspection and practitioners were delighted to receive an overall judgement grade of 'Outstanding'. The inspector made particular note of the way practitioners had used their observations and assessment of the youngest children to support their sensitive and appropriate planning. The practitioners reflected upon the changes they had made and the positive effect on the quality of the children's experience. They recorded their findings in their Ofsted Self-Evaluation Form as evidence to support their development and continuous improvement.

When the setting received its final report, staff were very pleased to see that the inspector had acknowledged their recent training, noting its particular impact on their understanding and ultimate outcomes for children.

In this example the practitioners had not previously understood the importance of differentiated learning and had merely provided what might be called a 'watered down' version of a curriculum more suited to three- to five-year-old children. Training to support their initial understanding about working with children under three helped practitioners to rethink and revise their practices. It helped them to recognize that the youngest children's inability to become engaged in their planned activities was because what was provided for them lacked meaning and interest. They overcame this by providing a continuum of learning experiences based on their observations of the children's enjoyment and patterns of play. The marked improvements were noted by the Ofsted inspector, but, more importantly, by the practitioners themselves as part of their evaluation and reflection. Practitioners who work with children in mixed age group settings can face the greatest challenge in relation to setting out their environment, particularly when they are required to tidy away everything at the end of every session. Working in settings where every item of equipment and furniture has to be taken out and put away at the beginning and end of every session adds to the work of practitioners in those settings. This form of provision can still provide a rich and balanced set of opportunities for children, which is made possible through careful planning and by using the creative skills of practitioners and parents to organize time and labour-saving ways to set up the environment.

Ideas for practice

- A row of chairs can quickly be turned into a reading corner by draping material with ready-made see-through pockets suitable to hold books. It can be easily assembled and tidied away at the end of a session.
- Continuous Provision Plans for each designated area of the room enlarged to A3 size and laminated can be easily put up and taken down each day and help to remind practitioners of the items of equipment they need to have on offer – and where these need to be located. The inclusion of a removable 'enhancements' column (see Tables 5.1 and 5.2), which displays children's initials, can help to meet the needs of individual children (according to observations of them).

Questions for reflection

1. Think how in any setting, training that has been received by one practitioner is disseminated to other staff members and how this training impacts on practice.
2. How can group settings ensure all practitioners have an opportunity to attend training first hand?
3. In what other ways can practitioners access continued professional development (CPD) opportunities?

Environments for learning in purpose-built provision

Purpose-built nurseries can be seen by some as the crème de la crème of nursery provision and practitioners who work in a 'pack away' nursery may speak with envy about a neighbouring 100-place day nursery with wide open spaces, streams of light coming from the large floor-to-ceiling windows and the additional rooms for small-group activities such as a sensory room or parents' room. But to parents and children some large spaces can seem daunting, depersonalized and unfamiliar places – and, after all, it is the relationships which are most important. It is vital for parents and children to feel safe and secure in their environment, and to be familiar with the spaces in which babies and young children spend their day.

Table 5.2 *'Enhancements' column*
In this example the 'Possible Enhancements column' of the 'Continuous Provision' document is linked to the Book Corner as a designated area. It demonstrates how flexible this column can be and how it can be amended to meet the individual needs of children. Practitioners can align to relevant Frameworks or documentation as necessary to observe and assess children's progression and learning.

Possible Enhancements
In this column examples of resources may be listed to indicate how a basic book corner resource area can be extended (with adult support, preferably the key person). Other areas can be similarly planned.

- Include Thomas the Tank Engine series of books especially on Friday – links to J's interest in 'Thomas' and encouraging speech patterns since recent visit to the railway museum.

- Ensure the book depicting photographs of familiar faces of children and practitioners in setting is always available to support continuity for Emily's key children while she is away on holiday, especially 'F' and 'J' who are still settling in and are less familiar with Kate (Emily's buddy key person).

- Encourage 'R's parents to bring in books from home to reflect familiar things from home and from her family in Pakistan.

- Remove the hand puppets on Thursday afternoon as 'F' doesn't like them. Keep them in the 'special box' for the rest of the group who enjoy them. Karen (key person) to re-introduce slowly at 'F's pace over the next few weeks in line with his interests.

- Sue to check audio system is working effectively in the morning and after lunch so that the children can listen to music and stories, especially 'L' who is still adjusting to her new glasses and responds to close individual support after her afternoon nap.

Amelia was born with a congenital heart condition. Following heart surgery, she no longer suffered the bouts of sleep apnoea that had caused her parents such distress. She continued with regular check-ups at the hospital but otherwise had no difficulties. When choosing her childcare, Amelia's parents had particular ideas about the type of provision they wanted for her and the newly built nursery en route to the railway station suited their needs perfectly.

However, they still remained nervous and hesitant about leaving Amelia at nursery, and thought perhaps removing her daytime nap before she began and asking staff not to put her to bed during the day was the best way to overcome their worries about the sleep times. George, her key person, spent an afternoon with the family listening carefully to the parents' concerns and taking notes. He realized that it was imperative for him to build a close and honest relationship with Amelia's parents if they were to trust him. George asked for their permission to film Amelia in the nursery, 'warts and all' as he called it. They agreed, and for the next week George made a video recording of Amelia. The following week George invited Amelia's parents back to the nursery to watch the film footage with him. They soon realized that Amelia enjoyed nursery, that she thoroughly enjoyed painting, sand, water and mark-making. She also got cross, upset and frustrated at times – all very normal for a two-year-old. They saw that George sensitively attended to Amelia; he listened to her demands and supported her when she could not always find a solution. At nap time, the moment that Amelia's parents dreaded most, George ensured that after he had settled Amelia to sleep, he stayed close to Amelia. If for any reason he was called away other practitioners knew why it was necessary to monitor Amelia slightly more closely than the other children. The staff were used to this practice and often adopted a similar approach if a child had a cold or seemed slightly 'under the weather' during the course of the day.

After four weeks, Amelia was happily settled into nursery and really enjoyed all the mark-making activities. His careful observation and conversations with her parents meant that George could note Amelia's preferences and provide an enabling environment for Amelia to practise her new skills and make independent choices. In turn, her parents felt much more relaxed and were pleased with Amelia's new-found skills and independence.

In this example the 'learning environment' extends beyond the physical play space in the setting. It encompasses the whole of the nursery and particularly the bedroom, where Amelia's parents required a lot of reassurance regarding sleeping arrangements for Amelia.

The suggestion of an unedited film of Amelia gave the ownership and involvement back to Amelia's parents without the need to disrupt Amelia's routine. An experienced practitioner, George understood that Amelia's learning environment extended far beyond the nursery group room that Amelia was in and he recognized the importance of gaining the trust of her parents if he was ever going to be able to ensure that Amelia could make the most of the rich environment. To have gone along with Amelia's parents' original suggestion of denying Amelia her daytime nap would only have caused Amelia anxiety due to overtiredness. Amelia's parents would have been upset and frustrated to be greeted with a tired, crying little girl at the end of each day, and other children and practitioners would have found the whole situation stressful.

Ideas for practice

- When prospective families are viewing the setting prior to placing their child, it is important to try to ensure that they are given a clear opportunity to see all the spaces their child will spend time in. It can sometimes be very disconcerting for anxious parents to realize that their child is, for example, in the sensory room when they come to collect them at the end of the day when they are unaware of its existence.
- Sleep times can create anxiety for parents and children. Current policy suggests that children should be allowed, moreover encouraged, to follow their own routines and schedules (DfE, 2012a). Thus the environment should be created such that children, where possible, have choices about where and when they sleep and can go to their sleeping spaces themselves. There are several commercially produced low-level cots and sleep spaces but often a cosy corner made up with soft, suitable clean bedding and set out with each child's own items, such as teddy bears, blankets and comforters, can be perfectly

acceptable and appealing. This may or may not be in a separately assigned bedroom. Of course, safety is of paramount importance and all sleep areas (as is the case with all aspects of the nursery environment) must be established within recommended safety guidelines.

When practitioners are very familiar with the environment it can be easy to overlook or dismiss the feelings of children and their parents, who are reluctant to go beyond their usual space. We only have to think back to an experience when we entered unfamiliar territory, such as starting a new job or entering secondary school for the first time, to remember and understand the fears and insecurities of young children and their families – a point for periodic discussion at team meetings.

Questions for reflection

Fully inclusive practice that takes account of highly complex and cultural needs of children, and their families, take time to establish. Nevertheless, nurseries are committed to providing care provision for some children with highly complex needs, and always to thinking about inclusion in its broadest sense, not only for children with SEN.

1. In your setting are there systems in place to enable you to respond to such needs and how does the setting's Special Educational Needs Co-ordinator (SENCO) ensure that she or he is able to give support to all practitioners by knowing where to seek specialist advice and support?
2. Consider the different ways in which you would need to plan in order to meet the requirements of children with additional needs. Reflect on your IEPs (Individual Education Plans) to consider how they best meet the differing needs of these children.
3. How do you foster a sense of inclusion to help all children to feel that they belong?

Environments for learning in a mixed age range setting

Practitioners working with children in mixed age range settings face particular challenges. Traditionally pre-schools (once called playgroups) catered for children aged three–five years (Stevens, 2003) and were open for morning or afternoon sessions. As policy in the UK developed, so too has the expansion of childcare places (DfE, 2012c). Some settings have moved to offering full-day care and have also lowered the age group to admit children from two years old to help the sustainability of the setting, given that many children in England will start school the term after their fourth birthday (contrary to the statutory school age of the term after their fifth birthday). In addition, some settings will be offering funded places to two-year-olds as part of the Government's 15-hour entitlement to children in areas of disadvantage. In England, from May 2012 two-year-olds who live in households which meet the eligibility criteria for free school meals, along with children who are looked after by the state, became entitled to a 15 hours per week free early education place. This entitlement will be extended to a further 20 per cent of the least advantaged two-year-olds in the autumn of 2013, with this number rising again in 2014 when approximately 260,000 two-year-olds will be entitled to free funded early education (DfE, 2012b). The age at which children attend nursery and school has been part of a long-standing debate. For example, the inappropriateness of four-year-olds in schools has been an issue of concern for some time (Mills and Mills, 1998). However, some providers of early years and childcare services (particularly those in the private, voluntary and independent sectors) have offered places to two-year-olds for some time, often in order to remain financially viable. In some cases little thought has been given to how or why differentiation of the organization, curriculum and learning environment is necessary. Some settings have only accepted two-year-olds who were out of nappies – perhaps due to lack of changing facilities and practical arrangements – thus often placing undue pressure upon parents and children to get children toilet trained before they were ready. Some children, it must be recognized, will never stop needing nappies, some will never get to a point where they can use the toilet independently, and it is (quite simply) wrong that learning opportunities are denied to them because of these facts of their lives. However, while many may have come to recognize that the personal care needs of young children require more thought, this is not always the case with regard to the learning environment. In the next example the practitioner has already been worrying about the needs of the younger children and as she becomes more fully informed she takes the lead with her colleagues to find solutions to provide a more meaningful learning environment that offers some differentiation to the younger children.

Practitioners in a pre-school setting were concerned that the two-year-olds were finding the routines of the setting difficult. For example, circle time, which included a 'good morning' session, sharing of news and a story, was difficult for them. At a recent meeting the setting staff realized that their expectations of the two-year-olds were quite unrealistic and meaningless. During a lengthy debate several of the team felt quite challenged about how to proceed.

Having recently attended a workshop to extend her knowledge and understanding of children under three, Mary had been thinking deeply about the needs of her four key children in the group aged between two and three. She suggested that she spend some time with her children outside of circle time, following their interests. The rest of the team thought it made much more sense and decided that this practice could be adopted for all the two- to three-year-old children in their key groups. The correct staff-to-child ratio would be maintained but all the children would have an opportunity to have a voice and a choice! Effectively, 'small circles' were to be created, in different spaces of the room, providing a thoughtful and enjoyable introduction to the day and differentiated according to the needs of the children.

At their next staff meeting several weeks later, the team evaluated their new schedule. Mary had discovered that her children really seemed to enjoy the time to explore the garden area without the older children present. Kitted out with coats, hats and woolly scarves they learned a great deal about the weather, including the difficulty of reading a book on the big tree stump when the wind is blowing and the need to find a sheltered space! The older children, in their circle time, had been able to extend some of their thinking and had been working on a solution about turn-taking in the home corner, raised by Millie, a four-year-old, who complained that some of the children 'took over' the space. A lengthy and complex discussion ensued but over several days the children, with the help of staff, used practical strategies to test out their suggestions. Of course, there remained the problem of whether boys were to be allowed into the home corner – something that the girls would need more than a few days to resolve!

This example illustrates how the setting staff planned a session mainly for the needs of the older children. Although there are only four children under three in her group, Mary had long since recognized that parts of the session were meaningless and at times pointless for the younger children. Her recent attendance at the 'birth to three' training course had consolidated her views, and she decided to take action. She knew that story times are particularly problematic, but she was also aware how much the younger children enjoyed books, and she often spent time with them in the book corner on a one-to-one basis.

Mary raised the issue about how the practice in the setting did not meet the needs of the key children she worked with. She was pleased that her colleagues took the opportunity to reflect on the needs of their key children as well. Mary had noted the interests of the younger children when they were in the outside environment, and so followed their interests, which included sharing books and stories outside in their 'small circle'. The children learned more about the weather than they had done previously, as on a windy wintry day they could feel the wind on their faces and understood that they needed coats, hats and scarves to keep them warm – so much more meaningful than changing the colour of the clouds from white to grey on the felt weather chart in a centrally heated room!

Ideas for practice

- The outside environment provides endless opportunities for children to explore and learn, and should be considered whenever possible as continuous with the inside, forming an integral part of provision. It is important to consider how babies and very young children might use the outside environment, particularly if there is no easy access to a direct outside space or when the inside environment for the youngest children is in an upstairs room.
- Practical outdoor clothing suitable for children (and practitioners!) will help to ensure that everyone enjoys the environment regardless of the weather. There is no fun in being cold and uncomfortable outdoors, and settings may need to consider buying outdoor clothing for children to use if their own does not provide enough protection

from inclement weather. Lots of spare mittens, socks and wellies are essential. There is no pain quite like the pain felt in tiny cold fingers! Opportunities for babies and young children to splash in puddles, dig in sand and earth pits, and even crawl in the outside environment can all be facilitated providing the environment is designed appropriately. Very young babies can be carried in slings or prams, wrapped up in warm blankets in winter and with sunshades in the summer, and allowed to roll and kick on a rug laid on the grass to ensure they are included, under the watchful eye of their close adult.

Questions for reflection

1. Standing back and reflecting, consider how many times and for how long, you expect very young children in your care to sit for 'group' sessions or 'activities'.
2. As in the case study, how could you offer these sessions in an alternative way?

Mills's (2007) study compared two- and three-year-old children's outdoor activity in a raised sand tray with their activity in a muddy area. He observed the children, using a fixed camcorder, digital camera, field notes and a reflective journal. In his interpretation of the data he drew on the work of Laevers (2005a) on children's involvement, Carr's study of learning dispositions (Carr and Lee, 2012), and schematic theory and practice (Atherton and Nutbrown, 2013; Athey, 2006; Nutbrown, 2011a). In the following observation sequences, which he refers to as 'fragments', it is possible to see how, by watching the children carefully, closely and in detail, sometimes with the aid of the camera, it is possible to 'tell their story'.

Fragment I

Annabella has chosen to join the digging area for the first time. She appears tense as she slowly and carefully scans the muddy area. Her knees are slightly bent and her hands dangle loosely from her arms that are held tight against the side of her body. She is standing in a mud pit and watches children take containers and tools from the storage baskets as they hunt for invertebrates, dig in the mud, and fill and empty buckets with an assortment of things (mud, water, stones, cones and sticks).

Annabella's facial expression and physical posture indicate that she is uncomfortable and unsure about how to react and respond to the environment. Annabella appears to be experiencing a low level of well-being. She is literally rooted and motionless as she observes other children and shows very little signs of activity or involvement (Laevers, 1998). Annabella is expressing her uncertainty in a quiet, powerful and understated way.

Interpretation

This behaviour was not representative of Annabella's overall experience in the muddy area but it did reflect a degree of uncertainty and cautiousness that most of the children expressed as they first explored this unfamiliar context. Secure attachments and relationships with educarers are paramount to very young children's well-being and ability to explore their environment (Goldschmied and Jackson, 1994; Trevarthen, 2002). It is likely that all the children felt inhibited in exploring this unfamiliar space with an adult that they had not seen for several months. This may also explain Annabella's initial hesitant response to the muddy area.

Fragment 2

Annabella is splashed as Darryl throws a clump of earth into the mud pit. Annabella stands up and wipes a little bit of mud on her face. Duncan brings a sieve filled with cones and empties it into the mud pit. Duncan squeals excitedly and looks towards me in the distance talking to Alice. Darryl picks up another clump of earth and throws it into the muddy water at the bottom of the mud pit. He looks at Annabella who seems to be okay. Alice stands near the edge of the mud pit and throws a cone into the mud pit. Darryl stands up and releases another clump of mud. From a height, Megan also drops a clump of soil into the mud pit. It creates a satisfying splat sound as it displaces muddy water around the sides of the mud pit.

Continues

Continued

Interpretation

In fragment 1, I notice that Annabella was feeling apprehensive and decided to help her find tools for digging. I stayed close to her as a way of reassuring her. Annabella slowly became curious and decided to explore. She squatted near a large bucket of water and used a small trowel to mix soil with water in a small bucket. She was quietly involved in a moment of experimentation until a clump of soil hit the bottom of the mud pit and splashed her.

To my surprise, Annabella did not recoil or protest. Annabella became interested in what other children were doing around her. Throughout fragment 2 she smiles, giggles and watches with curiosity and interest. She appears intrigued as children actively explore the mud pit by throwing and dropping objects. I wonder if my presence and non-verbal gesture (moving alongside Annabella) contributed to her apparent change in mood and expressions: 'The use of body language in adults and children contributes a significant role in effective practice' (Adams et al., 2002: 108).

Annabella is now enjoying the active form of exploration that other children are engaged in.

The understanding of gravity, of circulation of air, of movement of objects, of radiation of heat and light, and the myriad phenomena in the world of living things requires the capacity to cognitively reproduce experiences and their properties (Laevers, 1998: 77).

The group of children appear to be exploring the idea of 'height'. They could be exploring ideas relating to dynamic vertical trajectory continued over schema (Nutbrown, 2006). In fragment 2 they drop and throw objects as a vehicle for exploration. In the following fragment (fragment 3), three children explore a similar idea but their exploration appears to be a more collaborative notion that is both sophisticated and problematic. Annabella, Darryl and Megan explore the space by jumping. The mud pit is not big enough to accommodate all three children so they have to co-operate and negotiate as a means of facilitating their exploration.

Fragment 3

Darryl climbs out of the mud pit and I remove all the objects and debris that children have put into the pit. Annabella (middle), Darryl (right) and Megan (left) stand around the edge of the pit. Annabella spots her chance and does a two-footed jump into the pit. She lands the jump perfectly and shifts from foot to foot looking intently at her submerged feet.

Picture 5.1 *Annabella spots her chance and does a two-footed jump into the pit*

Megan jumps in and they stand side-by-side. Darryl circles but is reluctant to go in. Annabella reaches a hand towards him but Darryl looks away.

Interpretation

Annabella's confidence and self-esteem are beginning to grow. Her jump into the mud pit is literally a leap of faith. She has faith in her ability to perform a very expressive form of movement and she has faith in those around her. Without this sense of trust she would still feel inhibited and be unable to pursue her intrinsic motivation to explore this space (Greenhalgh, 1994). This is an important moment because Annabella has moved from observer to protagonist. In this context, movement is a vehicle for expression and an indicator that Annabella is feeling confident and secure. Gross motor exploration is an important aspect of young children's development: 'By nature children are closely linked with their motor system, they discover their environment through movement and action' (Laevers, 1998: 78).

After Annabella has landed her jump, she reaches out to Darryl with the offer of a hand to help him. Annabella may feel a sense of achievement and pride in her ability to take a risk and jump from a height. In this respect, the action of jumping not only relates to a physical realm but also contributes to emotional and social development: 'Although movement contributes in numerous ways to the physical domain, it is also critical to social/emotional (affective) and cognitive development' (Wang, 2004: 34).

Fragment 4

Annabella (right) loses her balance in the mud pit and gently puts her hand on Megan's back to steady herself. They smile warmly at each other. Darryl enters carefully into the mud pit. He marches in the mud briefly before clambering out sideways. Megan splashes enthusiastically: 'Wow, wibbly wobbly!' (Megan). Megan and Annabella laugh with each other. Annabella rests against the walls of the mud pit and watches Megan. Darryl sits on the edge of the mud pit. He gazes down and dangles his feet into the mud pit before climbing in. 'Get out now, get out now, get out now, get out now' (Megan in a sing-song voice). Megan and Annabella climb out leaving Darryl behind.

Picture 5.2 *Annabella (right) loses her balance in the mud pit and gently puts her hand on Megan's back to steady herself*

Carr and Claxton (2004) argue that the most urgent and fundamental purpose of education, particularly in early childhood, is to develop positive habits of mind or learning dispositions. The exchanges between Megan and Annabella could be evidence of one of these habits of mind; a learning disposition that Carr and Claxton (2004) refer to as 'reciprocity'.

Reciprocity (Carr, 2004) can be seen in fragment 4 through the exchange of smiles, laughter, tone of voice and the acceptance of each other's physical presence and physical contact. The tones of Megan's words are humorous, light and musical. I find it striking how gentle and thoughtful the exchanges between these children are. The close physical proximity between Annabella and Megan is a potential source of conflict. However, Annabella's hand on Megan's back is symbolic of their openness and reciprocity towards each other.

Fragment 5

Darryl looks as though he wants to get out. Annabella moves round to face Darryl and holds her hands out towards him. Darryl ignores her invitation by rubbing his hands together and glancing from side to side. Annabella retreats a little but decides to move forwards and again she offers her hands towards him. This time Darryl accepts and she pulls him out. They stand next to each other, pausing briefly as they gaze down into the mud pit. Darryl looks over to me and then looks at Annabella with a beaming smile. Annabella smiles at Darryl.

Interpretation

Annabella really persists with her offer of support and friendship. She shows a degree of resilience in accepting Darryl's initial rejection and persistence in deciding to reach out again to him. Annabella does not give up on Darryl and recovers fairly quickly from his 'rejection'. Carr and Claxton (2002) argue that 'resilience' is a key learning disposition.

There is a growing sense of 'linkedness' (Laevers, 2005b) in fragment 5. Darryl and Annabella have experienced diverse emotions. Initially, Darryl and Annabella felt unsure about how to relate to each other. Both Darryl and Annabella took a risk and reached out to each other. Their interactions and actions after this moment are in tune and suggest a sense of connection with each other and their environment.

Fragment 6

Megan has been sizing up the mud pit for a while. She studies the mud and the shimmering water below. In a seat drop position, she leaps into the air with outstretched arms and legs. The outline of her jump is momentarily embodied by her shadow and her weightless flowing hair captures the thrill and joy of flight. Darryl and Annabella are a receptive audience and show their appreciation with chuckles of delight.

Interpretation

Parrott (1997) has shown how physical play activities, such as swinging,

Continues

Continued

jumping, rolling and play involving others, have improved social and affective development for babies and pre-school children. The performance aspect of children's play and the sheer joy of being able to use their whole bodies to capacity certainly seems to have affected all three children. Movement is a source of delight and joy for many young children and a fundamental aspect of young children's development (Davies, 1995). The very physical nature of these fragments has not merely hinged upon physical mastery. These fragments illustrate how empowering the freedom of movement can be in spaces where children have the opportunity actively to explore natural elements.

(Mills, 2007)

There has been more emphasis recently on the benefit of outside learning opportunities for young children (Canning, 2010), particularly since the focus on the Danish Forest School approach has gained momentum (Joyce, 2012; Knight, 2011). In spite of this recent interest, for children aged three years and over there have been fewer examples of research with infants' and toddlers' exploration of the outside environment. However, in Scandinavian countries children of all ages spend much of the time playing outdoors, and the age of the child is not a barrier to outdoor learning (Moser and Martinsen, 2010). Nevertheless, with the advent of social media there has been an internet explosion calling for children to play, explore and expand their creative skills in the outside environment (Explorations Early Learning; Let the Children Play), alongside special features appearing in professional journals, for example, celebrating 'International Mud Day' (Mountain, 2012). For some further insight and challenge concerning the ways in which outside learning experiences for babies and toddlers are offered see Siren Films (2010). Settings with access to a covered outdoor space have the opportunity to offer experiences to the youngest children all year round regardless of weather conditions. This involves careful observation and planning to ensure that what is available meets the individual needs of the children.

As well as providing babies with experiences in the outdoor environment there is an argument that babies might sometimes be put outside to sleep. As Clare (2012) discusses, this practice is often questioned by parents because of safety issues, and while there is no suggestion that babies are left alone outside when sleeping, all nurseries have to be safe and secure. Ultimately, the advantages of fresh air uncontaminated by the germs that children pass on to one another, alongside the benefits of the noises of nature and everyday life outdoors, should outweigh these concerns, and practitioners should support parents to see the value of babies sleeping in outdoor environments.

In the 'fragments' above, Mills (2007) has captured the minute detail of the children's activities. In his careful and sensitive plan of the outside area he gave the children much needed time and space to carry out their explorations. In his analysis and interpretations, which he links to previous research, he was able to draw on the children's need for close attachments and the significance of the role and close proximity of the key person. Mills notes the impact of the relationships children form with each other and how they can shape the ways in which children may approach aspects of the curriculum, and their environment. In this example it was the outside muddy area, but it could also be applied to the indoor environment. Mills's work reminds us once again of the need for the familiar, as suggested by Thomas (2002), balanced with gradual introduction to the unfamiliar. The striking theme throughout the 'fragments' is the sense in which the children led the learning as he followed their interests and did not seek a predetermined outcome or rush the children on. The role of the practitioner in this example is to practise what is often referred to as 'sustained shared thinking' (Siraj-Blatchford et al., 2002). In other words, because he supported the children by gently promoting and encouraging their interests, he was gradually helping them to develop their creativity and critical thinking. The 'fragments' are quite short but it is the analysis and interpretation that aids Mills's ability to assess the learning. When practitioners are able to capture detailed observations of children in this way it is possible to map the information against any given framework to illustrate the children's progression across all the areas of learning. The fact that the children could return to the muddy area over a number of days is in line with the thinking of the nurseries in Reggio Emilia (Abbot and Nutbrown, 2001).

Picture 5.3 *Digging and gouging mud with tools and sticks*

Picture 5.4 *Hammering sticks and planks of wood into the ground*

Picture 5.5 *Exploring the properties of soil and water*

The most important point here is the skill of a highly competent practitioner who is attuned to the sensitive needs of very young children. Such a practitioner is able to carefully prepare and plan an appropriate enabling environment to facilitate deep-level learning, well-being, excitement, interest and involvement (Laevers, 1998). Through careful recording and analysis of the observations of children, the practitioner can make meaningful, individualized and informed judgements about children's progression which far outweigh the need for, indeed dispense with, checklists that would serve only to trivialize and undermine the depth and value of the children's explorations.

Pictures 5.3, 5.4 and 5.5 capture some of the ways in which the children approached and persevered in their own learning. Their involvement and competences are evident, as is the awe and wonder on their faces. Although not seen in the photographs, the children were always within the close proximity of their close, significant adult – the key person.

Questions for reflection

1. Thinking about your own practice, how do you currently provide meaningful outside exploration for the youngest children in your setting?
2. Do you take advantage of spontaneous opportunities to take children outside? For example to show your key children a hot air balloon that is flying overhead or to feel a snowflake for the first time?
3. How much freedom do the children in your setting have to explore a muddy area?
4. How do you work with parents who are reluctant to: (a) let their children go outside in the winter months? (b) get their children's clothes dirty?

In this chapter we have discussed the importance of the learning environments provided for young children. There are many combinations of early years and childcare settings, such as children's centres, that do not fit neatly into one category or another as we have described them in this chapter. By their very design, children's centres are intended to be a 'one-stop shop' offering a range of integrated services to parents and children at the hub of the community (DfE, 2010). More than one form of early education and care may be available running side-by-side in a children's centre. Practitioners will be able to draw on the examples which resonate most with their own working environments in developing their provision of enabling environments for babies and young children for whom they have responsibility.

Further reading

Dyregrov, A. (2008) *Grief in Young Children: A Handbook for Adults*. London: Jessica Kingsley.

Green, S. (2012) (series ed.) *Supporting Children from Birth to Three*. London: Routledge.

Rosen, M. (2008) *Sad Book*. London: Walker Books Ltd.

Sharp, A. (2011) *Enhance Learning when Working with Under Threes*. Special edition DVD boxset. London: Nursery World.

Useful websites

Winston's Wish: http://www.winstonswish.org.uk/

Explorations Early Learning: http://explorationsearlylearning.com/

Let the Children Play: http://progressiveearlychildhoodeducation. blogspot.co.uk/

Chapter 6

Understanding Every Child

This chapter will discuss:
- The subtleties of the key person approach
- Observation for planning
- Recording and assessing for planning and progressing
- What is meant by planning for learning?
- How to plan effectively

This chapter examines the importance of understanding every child so that the particular and distinct needs of each unique child can be understood and met. In particular, the chapter focuses on the role of the adult and how the key person approach can best be used to support young children and their families when gathering and sharing information and planning next experiences for the children.

In this chapter we consider the place of observation, record-keeping and assessment in the planning process and how highly skilled managers can support the positive development of potentially complex triangular relationships between the children, their parents and practitioners.

Subtleties of the key person approach

The role of the adult in young children's early education and care cannot be overemphasized (Page, 2005). The adult's role in relation to 'Tuning in to children' (NCB, 1994) and interpreting their needs is crucial (DfE, 2012a; Elfer et al., 2012). Moreover, in recent years studies have shown that it is the role of the key person (Elfer et al., 2012) which can make the greatest difference to young children's positive social and emotional development, to their health, well-being and ability to learn (Gopnik et al., 1999a). However, we suggest that the role of the key person is taken for granted in some circumstances and in aspects of policy. For example, the Early Years Foundation Stage (DfE, 2012a) makes numerous references to the importance of the key person role, and the examples given in the accompanying guidance (Early Education, 2012) seek to embed this into everyday work with children. However, we are left with the question as to whether all practitioners and managers have yet been able to understand and interpret the subtleties of the role of the key person and to put this complex role into practice. In policy and in practice there has been a change in terminology, and the 'key worker' (DfEE, 1990: 11) has been replaced by the 'key person'. This marks a change in emphasis from record-keeping and liaison with parents and services, to the responsibility to develop close relationships with each individual child and their family. Or as Elfer et al. (2012: 24) put it, the role of the key person 'refers to a professional relationship that has direct emotional significance from the point of view of the child and his or her family'.

What we are discussing is much more than a change in terminology and the responsibility for keeping records (although this is a fundamental). Elfer et al. (2012: 24) are quite specific in their definition of the key person and describe what they refer to as the *Key Person Approach* rather than a *Key Worker System* (Goldschmied and Jackson, 1994). They describe in some detail the vital importance of the role of the head of centre, manager, head teacher or other responsible person to offer support and supervision to the key person(s) to discuss the challenges and dilemmas of their role. The support they argue for does not replace traditional annual appraisals or monthly target reviews of the organization. It offers instead an opportunity for the key person(s) in the organization to address the professional boundaries of the role within the close and complex triangular relationship between the child, the parent(s) and themselves as the practitioner/carer/educator. Supervision was one of the recommendations in the Tickell (2011) review of early years policy in England and is now a mandatory requirement in the revised EYFS (DfE, 2012a). The EYFS is explicit, stating: 'Supervision should foster a culture of mutual support, teamwork and continuous improvement which encourages the confidential discussion of sensitive issues' (DfE, 2012a: 17). The Penn Green Research Centre has begun to offer a three-day supervision training programme with input from a trained psychotherapist and psychologist (John, 2008). It remains to be seen how a model of supervision such as that advocated by Elfer and Dearnley (2007) will be interpreted by providers; one that is intended to offer an appropriate space for early years professionals to talk about and reflect upon the emotional complexity of their unique care-giving role with infants and families.

The Early Years Foundation Stage documentation (DfE, 2012a) describes childminders, perhaps not surprisingly, as automatically considered to be the key person because they are usually the only adult working with the children in their care. But the role of the practitioner in a home setting will bring different challenges and dilemmas to those of the adult in a group setting, and the need to discuss professional boundaries alongside the complexity of the triangular child–parent–practitioner relationship is surely somewhat similar. Professional support for the childminder, then, should be of equal importance to that of those practitioners working in group settings if there is to be a shared understanding of the meaning of the terminology and subtle reality of the key person approach.

The EYFS guidance (Early Education, 2012) makes clear the expectation that the key person will provide warmth, affection and sensitive touch. However, Piper and Smith (2003) discuss the 'moral panic' experienced by some professionals who are concerned about physical holding and intimacy with young children. Some practitioners worry that if they cuddle and kiss the babies in their care, they will be accused of child abuse (Powell, 2010). As we discussed in Chapter 3, the protection of young children is the top priority, and all professionals, whatever their role, have a statutory duty as well as a moral obligation to act with the utmost integrity and respect whatever the age of the child. However, we suggest that it is far better to address concerns of a sensitive nature than to shy away from them – though we know it is not easy. A supervision time and space is likely to provide individual opportunities for practitioners to discuss their anxieties. However, it is important that a whole setting ethos is adopted to ensure the rights of children and of staff are protected. The challenge for providers is to have in place thoughtful policies and procedures that take full account of safeguarding and child protection (Elfer et al., 2012; Powell and Uppal, 2012) but afford infants and young children appropriate levels of intimacy, affection, and, some argue, love, from their key person.

Despite the evidence from research regarding the importance of close attachments in the form of a key person (Ebbeck and Yim, 2009; Elfer et al., 2012; Lee, 2006), many practitioners, it seems, can be caught up in the worry and fear engendered by previous research studies such as those by Bowlby (1953, 1969), whereby it was thought that if babies formed relationships with anyone other than the mother, their relationships with their mothers would be irretrievably damaged. And then there is the idea some hold that 'getting attached' is in some way 'unprofessional'. As we saw in Chapter 2, interpretation and reporting of this controversial theory has been a hot topic for debate and a cause of great distress to practitioners and parents. In a single intensive case study, Page and Elfer (2013) identified the importance of young children having close attachments with their familiar adults when cared for away from their parent(s). In the following practice example we can see how challenging it can sometimes be for practitioners to get it 'right' for children and their families.

> Lilia had been thinking about one of her key children — something seemed 'wrong'. Melissa had been attending the nursery for about two weeks and at eight months of age had been used to being at home with her mother with whom she shared a very close and loving relationship. Lilia thought about what she knew generally about child development and knew that from about six months of age it is quite usual for babies to show signs of concern when they lose sight of their significant adult and become 'more wary of strangers' (Lindon, 2012: 74). Lilia had tried gently to discuss this with Melissa's mother and to suggest why it might be a good idea for Lilia to gradually form a bond with Melissa. Melissa's mother, Florence, became quite alarmed and said somewhat accusingly to Lilia, 'under no circumstances are you to become close to Melissa, she is my baby do you understand?' Lilia felt nervous and shy and found it difficult to strike a balance between supporting Melissa's need for a close relationship while at nursery and her

mother's concern about her getting 'too close'. Lilia knew it was vital to be respectful of Florence and her views but she also recognized that not to meet Melissa's needs, if she failed to respond lovingly, could be potentially more concerning in the long term.

This came to a head one evening when Florence arrived early to collect her baby. Melissa was busily engrossed in her play at the treasure basket and Lilia was sitting next to her. Seeing Florence arrive, Lilia got up quickly from the floor to prepare Melissa's bottles and other items which she needed to take home. Melissa protested and started to cry, her mother sat down beside her and lifted Melissa on to her knee but Melissa protested even more, holding her arms out to Lilia who was desperately trying, with some embarrassment, to busy herself preparing the bag. With Melissa still crying in her arms Florence grabbed the bag from Lilia, rushed out of the baby room and bumped straight into Jane, the nursery manager. Noticing her distress, Jane said to Melissa, 'Oh dear what's all this then?' Florence looked up and said angrily 'I told her this would happen'. Jane invited Melissa and her mother to her office and listened to Florence's concerns about Melissa forming what she described as 'too close' a bond with Lilia. Jane explained why it was important for Melissa to feel secure and gave Florence some leaflets about the role of the key person. The literature explained how Lilia's role is important and how a key person can complement and build upon the relationship Melissa has with her mother, other significant adults and members of her family, without ever seeking to undermine or replace it.

With Florence's permission Jane asked Lilia to join the discussion. Lilia suggested to Florence that the reason Melissa might have been upset was the sudden change; she explained that usually if she was going to move away from Melissa she would indicate this with some sort of warning, while ensuring that Melissa could still see her, like 'I'm just going to get your things ready in your bag now Melissa, mummy will soon be here'. 'Knowing that you usually come to collect her at about 4.30 p.m. I usually make sure all her things are ready and then we look at the photographs of you and your husband and Dudley the dog in readiness for your arrival.' 'But where do you find the time? Do you only do this with my baby?' asked Florence. Lilia explained the careful thought and preparation that the baby room team put into ensuring that all the babies were given equal amounts of time and attention by their

Continues

Continued

key person, following their individual routines and patterns that were spe-cial to them and their families.

'I miss her dreadfully when I am away from her but I do want her to have a lovely time you know. My friend has not gone back to work since having her baby, she told me that Melissa will forget all about me and that she will pre-fer being with you. I just couldn't bear that to happen'. Lilia reassured Florence that she was in no way attempting to replace Florence but instead wanted to work with her to ensure she could best meet Melissa's needs while she was in the nursery. She confirmed her fondness for Melissa and went on to share an observation of Melissa that she had recorded earlier in the day.

Over the next few weeks Lilia and Florence built a trusting relationship. Jane met with Lilia for a one-to-one supervision session on a weekly basis to offer her support as she did with the other practitioners in the setting. This took the form of an informal discussion when Lilia could raise anything that had been either successful or challenging in her relationships with the babies and their families. Lilia overheard Florence proudly explaining to another parent how lucky she was that Melissa had formed such a good relationship with Lilia. 'It was really hard for me at first; I felt jealous and left out. It took me a while to realize that Lilia wasn't trying to take Melissa away from me. I still find it hard sometimes when I think about Lilia and Melissa together and I wish it could be me at home with Melissa all the time. I gave Lilia a really hard time at first but it's not her fault that I have to work. It's not Melissa's fault either and at the end of the day I want Melissa to feel loved and cared for. I think talking to Lilia about how I feel on a regular basis helps us both to understand one another. And, Lilia is so good – and thoughtful, and we talk everything through ... don't we?' she said, smiling and touching Lilia gently on the arm as she walked past.

In this example the practitioner used her solid understanding of child development theory as a basis for deciding how to approach her work with Melissa. Initially she was unsure how to strike the balance between the complexity of her relationship with Melissa and her mother, and could, perhaps, have used her manager's support at an earlier point. Her knowledge, instinct and observations of Melissa told her that her professional judgement was appropriate and sustaining as she gradually became familiar with her routine and her preferences. She had plenty of opportunity to observe Melissa and to build a relationship with her. However, Lilia had to some extent shied away from broaching the subject further with Florence, fearing she may upset her. She knew it was important to be respectful of Florence's wishes, but she was torn. The complexity of the situation is immense, and Lilia quite naturally was upset and perplexed. In this example, Jane, the manager, intervened and facilitated an opportunity to discuss the situation with Florence and listen to her concerns about the growing attachment that Melissa was forming with Lilia, and her fear that for Melissa, Lilia would somehow replace Florence.

In retrospect, such a discussion taking place before the 'tipping point' would have been preferable – Jane could have helped Lilia to explore her feelings further and suggested ways to discuss the situation with Florence. Had Jane encouraged Lilia to speak to Florence prior to the incident things may not have come to a head, but it can be difficult to gauge when the 'right time' might be, especially if a parent has expressed very strong views, as in this case.

Only through experience and support from the manager can practitioners seek to understand and balance the needs of the children they care for with the wishes and needs of their parents. Experience and sound knowledge of child development and relationships theory can help practitioners to work in ways which meet the needs of young children and their families. It is not impossible, but it is without doubt complex, emotionally demanding and challenging, which is perhaps why Elfer et al. (2012: 9), when referring to this case study of Melissa, say:

> We think Lilia is absolutely right that not to allow Melissa to make a bond with her could be very harmful. How important though that Jane had the time and skill to realize Florence's distress needed to be taken seriously, and responded to with time and careful attention. We think this is an example of highly sophisticated and sensitive practice but also an inevitable part of the key person approach.

Questions for reflection

Thinking about the example above and in relation to your own experience:

1. Can you imagine how it might have felt for: (a) Melissa? (b) Florence? (c) Lilia? (d) Jane?
2. Whose 'voice'(s) was/were heard?
3. How do you think you might handle a similar situation if you were the key person?

Observation for planning

> To assess attainment it must be observed in the round. Such observation is not easy. The observer has not only to use keenly his eyes and ears, but to know where to direct them: he has not only to see and hear the shape of an event but to perceive its quality. (Schiller, 1979: 3)

Many researchers and practitioners have followed observational practices in their studies of young children's learning and development because it is *actually* the only way of finding out what young children do. For example, the pioneering practice of Reggio Emilia in northern Italy has been developed largely through careful documentation which includes observations, notes, photographs and reflections upon the children's work as it unfolds in their learning communities (Abbott and Nutbrown, 2001; Clyde et al., 2006). To be meaningful and useful, observations need to be made with care and attentiveness. Insight into children's thinking requires practitioners to watch carefully and to attend to the fine detail of what they see children doing. The following versions of the same event illustrate this point.

Observation version I

Thirteen-month-old Samuel's father was talking to one of the other parents while holding Samuel in his arms so that he also could see the woman during the conversation. Samuel pointed to the woman's jewellery while his father continued the conversation.

Observation version 2

Thirteen-month-old Samuel's father was talking to one of the other parents while holding Samuel in his arms so that he also could see the woman during the conversation. Samuel first pointed to the woman's necklace which was made up of coloured squares of glass. He then looked at her wrist and fingered the glass beads on her matching bracelet. Finally, he pointed to her earrings which were made of similar matching glass beads. Samuel moved his gaze (and sometimes his fingers) between the necklace, the bracelet and the earrings for the five minutes while his father was in conversation. When the conversation was over, Samuel's father turned him to face him and carried him to the car, as he did so Samuel stared intently at his father's ear lobes.

The detail in version 2 gives more information about the connections which Samuel may have been making in his observations of the jewellery. And was he looking for earrings in his father's ears too? Version 1 simply notes that Samuel was interested in the woman's jewellery. Version 2 provides more insights into the nature of Samuel's interest, showing that he seemed to be exploring the beads quite intently.

Observation can also involve parents, as the following example illustrates:

Three-year-old Lulu was absorbed by and interested in circular shapes and motion. She toured the nursery looking for circular shapes, identifying circular objects – bowls, wheels, knobs, turning tap handles. The teacher told Lulu's mother about Lulu's interest, how staff were encouraging her to identify circular shapes and how this would support aspects of her mathematical development. The next morning Lulu and her mother arrived with a carrier bag filled with Lulu's 'circles'. Lulu had collected them together at her house on the previous evening – enlisting the help of her mother and baby brother! (Nutbrown, 2011a: 27)

This sharing of observations was later used to create further links between home and the setting. Ideas about children's learning can be reinforced as parents and practitioners draw on each other's observations of children playing in the home and in their settings. Together they can find ways of extending children's ideas. Lulu and her mother went with a small group of children and a nursery nurse to visit a working waterwheel which further extended their concept of 'going round' and roundness, and introduced the dynamics of movement. In the case of Lulu, the observations pointed to her intent interest in roundness and round objects, and were then used to plan an outing which further extended her learning opportunities.

Regular and frequent observation is necessary if practitioners are to build up a clear picture of individual children, the value of activities and group dynamics. Educators, who observe children, try to understand what they see children do. Watching children at their work of interacting with their environment will tell educators some of what they need to know about children's needs and development. Observation such as this needs to be planned and can be carried out more successfully when the adults who work with young children are prepared to watch with open eyes and keep open minds about the meaning and importance of what they see. Educators must think about what they see and hear children doing and saying. They must create meaning from their observations and be prepared to use what they learn from these processes in their interactions with children. They must trust children to show them what they are learning and they must trust themselves that time spent in observing children, though not an easy option, is an essential ingredient of effective teaching and learning partnerships.

In many cases practitioners are expert observers of young children. The examples above distinguish between noting the bare facts and detailing the minutiae as an objective note taker. Yet, as we have already discussed, when we think of observing babies and toddlers we need to take account of their emotions as well as their cognition and learning. The Tavistock Method (Miller, 2002) offers a model of observation whereby observer subjectivity is accepted and feelings are taken into account, as Peter Elfer explains: 'At the heart of this method of observation lies the fact that we are able not only to **see and hear** the reactions and responses of another person but also to have the capacity to have feelings evoked in us by another person'

(Elfer, 2005: 120, emphasis in the original). Although the Tavistock Method was originally designed to be used as a psychoanalytical tool to observe new-born babies in their own homes over a long period of time, Elfer suggests that with adaptation this method can work well in nurseries. The key features are summarized in Box 6.1.

Box 6.1 *Infant observation in the nursery*

- An early years practitioner observes for between 10 and 20 minutes focusing on one child and her or his interactions with adults, other children and with toys and objects.
- The practitioner observes without notebook, concentrating as far as possible on the chosen child, and being as receptive as possible to the smallest of details as well as emotional atmosphere and responses.
- After the observation, the practitioner makes a written record of the observation, writing in as free-flowing a way as possible, following the main sequence of events and recording details as they come back to mind.
- The written observations are shared with the supervisor/colleagues and discussed, differing interpretations and connections being considered and examined.
- The practitioner continues to observe, bringing further write-ups to the group to be discussed and compared.
Source: Elfer, 2005: 121

Elfer (2011) discusses his own use of this psychoanalytical tool to explore the nursery experience of a small boy, 'Graham'. In his discussion, Elfer exposes not only the vulnerability of the toddler's emotions but also explains how he felt watching Graham as he observed him experience moments of pleasure and of distress during his day at nursery. The use of psychoanalytic concepts is extended further in research in Germany which documents the transition to day care of 21-month-old Valentine (Datler et al., 2010). The two examples we have cited here do make for uncomfortable reading – it is preferable to conjure up images of happy children rather than those who are sad. Nevertheless, when observing young children it is important to be realistic and to record not just the things that go well but also the difficulties too. If we are to be respectful of the needs of our youngest citizens and if we want our observations to be believable to parents then we have to provide an honest, holistic view of the young child. As Miller (2004: 15–16) writes:

> Nothing is as abject as a downcast desperate toddler, and nothing so full of pure delight as an elated one. ...
>
> Toddlers are physically very small. We only need to think that we, the grown-ups, can be around three times their height, to imagine what giants we must look ...
>
> Sarah, who was capable and lively, was also highly strung and prone to collapse. It was as though at day-nursery she had to will herself on to ever greater efforts, speeding around, on the run from feelings of being unsure or little. When she got home she was frequently in a bad mood ... finally having a full-blown tantrum. Her father came to see that she was completely exhausted by the effort she was making to keep herself together and pretend that she was big.

Questions for reflection

1. Have you ever stopped to consider Miller's point about the size of a grown up compared to the size of a toddler?
2. When you are with young children, what proportion of your day is spent at adult height and what proportion is spent at child height?
3. Does this case study have any implications for practice in your own setting?

Recording for planning and progression

Recording for planning and progression is important for many reasons. For example, to:

- record babies' and young children's progress in line with developmental milestones

- ensure the appropriateness of the curriculum
- ensure practitioners are able to support babies' and young children's individual interests
- assist practitioners to offer babies and young children the appropriate level of support and challenge
- share with parents in their role as partners in their children's learning.

Less experienced practitioners (or even experienced practitioners who have many demands upon their time) may sometimes turn to pre-formulated checklists to assist them in recording for planning and progression. Unfortunately checklists can really only provide limited information and not a full picture of the child. The risky potential also exists for practitioners to be seduced into planning inappropriate experiences for children to enable them to tick off a point on the checklist. Checklists can really only serve a useful purpose when used alongside detailed observations which include the context of the learning experience and help to 'tell the story' of the baby or young child. One such way of capturing information would be to keep profiles (Figure 6.1). The profile could be linked to frameworks such as the EYFS (DfE, 2012a) or used to record particular areas of child development such as aspects of speech and language or social and emotional development. The important point is to ensure that any instrument used to demonstrate and record information about the child is used after the information is captured, thereby ensuring the framework fits around the child and not the child around the framework.

Information can be presented in a variety of ways for parents, but it is the meaningfulness of the information that is important, with the key person who knows the child being responsible for recording important entries. Photographs, particularly if used in a sequence, can capture detail and demonstrate even the youngest child's ability to concentrate and become absorbed as they persist in their own learning. The example of the things that Lucy 'can do' (Figure 6.1) provides her practitioners and her parents with details of her individual and specific achievements in a way more meaningful than pre-formulated tick lists.

Lucy is showing a growing awareness of self. She is curious about the face in the mirror although not yet aware that it is hers. (1/5/12) ML

Lucy was looking at the photos on the wall of her friends and paired key person (Mary) this morning before she arrived on her shift. She was kissing the picture. When Mary arrived today she said hello over the gate by the door and Lucy crawled over as quick as she could and pulled herself up on the gate and held out her arms to Mary.
(Noticing that she is able to gain attention and make contact) (7/05/12) RS

Lucy took two steps by herself today she showed confidence when moving forward, when she wobbled and dropped to her knees. I [key person] clapped and praised her. (Recognising that her contribution was valued and that she is developing healthy independence) (15/05/12) ML

Lucy joined in today at singing time she only has a few words at present but was able to contribute to the group using her hands to the song 'babies in the cradle'. She pointed to the ceiling and to the floor. (29/05/12) ML

Figure 6.1 *Extract from Lucy's profile*
Source: adapted from Page, 2006: 19

Assessment for planning – planning for learning

Assessment is central to the process of understanding what babies and young children know, understand and can do, so that future work with them can be appropriately planned. Assessment of their progress and development is part of any educator's role and those who have worked with babies or young children have always assessed their learning and development in one way or another.

The extracts from Lucy's profile in Figure 6.1 demonstrate how through observation a practitioner can assess the progress of a child's learning and development.

There will always be some things which practitioners need to know about all children, but they will find out most about young children as individual and dynamic learners if they develop a way of looking at children with open eyes rather than eyes which are blinkered because only certain aspects of young children's abilities are deemed to be of interest or significance by virtue of their place on an assessment check-list.

'Assessment' is not an easy, or even comfortable, word to use in respect of babies and toddlers, partly because it is often used to imply deficits. Carrying out an assessment can sometimes mean that there is a suspicion that something is 'wrong' and an assessment is needed to define the problem. Nutbrown (2011a) has suggested three different purposes for assessment in the early years, arguing that different tools are needed for different purposes: assessment for teaching and learning, assessment for management and accountability and assessment for research. Assessment for teaching and learning is the most important for practitioners and is used here to refer to the process of identifying the details of children's knowledge, skills, attitudes and understanding in order to build a detailed picture of the child's development and subsequent learning needs. Table 6.1 adapts the characteristics of Nutbrown's (2011a) view of assessment for teaching and learning with respect to work with babies and toddlers.

Assessment of young children raises a number of concerns in relation to their well-being and self-esteem. Roberts writes: 'How can we ascertain whether children's well-being is developing? Which aspects are thriving? In what areas do they need more support, and why?

Table 6.1   *Assessment to foster the learning and development of children under three*

Focus on individual children

Concerned with the fine detail about each child

Is always respectful

The voice of the child is paramount regardless of age or ability

Is always ongoing and 'takes as long as it takes' – is not rushed

Needs no numerical outcome or ticks in boxes to be meaningful

Is open-ended and the focus derives from meaningful interactions with and observations of the child

Informs the future planning by the key person and other practitioners

Information relates primarily to individual children

Assessments are needed for each child and may differ from child to child

The main focus is to help practitioners to support learning and development

Assessment is only useful if the information is used to guide work with the child

Requires professional insight into children's learning

Depends on established relationship with individual children and their families to be effective

To be shared with, commented on and contributed to by parents

Requires ongoing professional development and experience to be carried out effectively

These are "million-dollar questions" of assessment and planning' (2010: 128).

Observation is a crucial part of understanding and assessing children's learning. The following examples demonstrate the importance of involving parents in assessing their children's learning.

Freddie is 16 months old; he has a strong fascination for the water – continually tipping and pouring it, exploring how the water moves and flows in different places and contexts. He regularly demonstrates a high level of fine motor skills as he carefully tips the cups, so the water forms a constant trickle onto the ground, or to fill another container.

Divya is nine months old; she displays an interest in containing. She uses all her physical skills to stretch, reach, twist and turn her body to enable her to explore and pursue her interest in containing. The observations taken over a four-week period show how she has explored the concept of size, shape and volume, whilst gaining mastery of both her gross and fine motor skills.

Questions for reflection

1. Thinking about the two examples above, how can you build your understanding of what it means when young children become fascinated with their environment and begin to repeat patterns of behaviour?
2. How can you support parents who seem concerned about their child's persistence in following a specific interest?
3. In your setting discuss how you could gather information from parents about their child's interests at home and how this information could form part of your assessment of a child's learning and development.

Partnership with parents

Working with parents is an important and essential aspect of being a practitioner, but working *in real partnership* with parents may look quite different for different families. Earlier chapters have drawn on research to inform practice with the youngest children, and research is equally important when working with the parents of the youngest children. We have considered the role of the adult as the 'key person' (Elfer et al., 2012) and the close and complex triangular relationship among the children, the parents and the key person(s). We have suggested the importance of working within the diverse contexts of family cultures: their ethnicity, their faith, their languages, their moral frameworks, their way of parenting. Policy – in recent times – has helped to inform practice with regard to parenting programmes; for example, The Parents as Partners in Early Learning (PPEL; DCSF, 2007) project conducted in October 2006 and first reported in January

2007 considered a snapshot of policies across the 150 local authorities in England. The main purpose was to investigate projects already in existence and to build upon ways to work in partnership with parents to bring about better outcomes for children. The emphasis was on personal, social and emotional development, and communication, language and literacy. The project team identified the many established projects and suggested that some focused more on communicating with parents as opposed to working *in partnership with parents*.

Practitioners must be able to show deep, sensitive understanding of the needs of babies, young children and of their families. This can be a challenge for some practitioners who do not necessarily see the whole picture. For example:

> Mary seems to be completely at ease as she drops off her six-month-old baby, Dylan, with Wendy, his childminder. She is often in a rush and sometimes seems a bit aloof as she plants a quick kiss on his forehead and leaves him in Wendy's arms. But do we know how Mary really feels? Does she have a choice about being a working parent? Is she nervous to let her feelings show in front of the childminder?
>
> Mary writes lots of information in his contact book so that Wendy knows what Dylan has been doing when he is at home, but what sort of information does the childminder offer in return? Mary is pleased to know what she sees as the 'routine' stuff: that Dylan ate his lunch of peas and potato, had two dirty nappies, and so on. But what she really wants to know is how Dylan is. How is he doing during the day? What does he do? Is he happy? Is the childminder 'bringing Dylan on'? There never seems to be time to discuss these things – partly because Mary is in a hurry to beat the traffic to work in the morning and Dylan is tired when she picks him up and they both want to get home. Mary does not want Wendy to think she is checking up on her and what she does with Dylan, so she comforts herself in the knowledge that Wendy does appear to like Dylan. Mary has noticed when she has smiled at him. But is that enough? What Mary would really like is better communication with Wendy about her little boy – she needs a 'feeling' of how it is all going during the day. But how does she raise this with Wendy without risking causing upset or suspicion? Wendy seems oblivious to Mary's needs and on the surface all seems to be well. Mary continues to chat lightly when she picks Dylan up.

This is just one of many examples where parents want more of a 'sense' of their child's day and relationships with their carers. Parents are children's first and most enduring educators (DfE, 2012a) but some parents can feel at times as if it is they who have to seek approval from practitioners. Parents will always be concerned that their child's needs are not overlooked or ignored, and some parents resist asking questions or seeking more detail about their child because they do not want to 'make a fuss'. This may be a point for reflection for all practitioners.

For some parents (perhaps those who have not had good experiences of parenting themselves or for whom life is especially difficult) parenting may be a great challenge. Some parents hold strong views, even if these are not always considered to be in the best interests of the child. Practitioners can find that trying to meet the needs of the child is in conflict with the wishes of the parent. For example, at home a mother might allow her child to go to sleep with a bottle and fear her child will cry if not allowed the bottle to soothe her when she is in the nursery. There is no blueprint for working through such complexities, except to say that the health and safety of the child is paramount at all times and the practitioner has to be clear that such practice is unacceptable in the setting. Such a situation would need to be dealt with clearly and carefully so that the mother and practitioner can agree on a solution for the setting. Clarity and honesty are essential in communication with parents and, as has already been suggested, the practitioner will need regular one-to-one support from the manager or head of centre to seek solutions to which everyone agrees.

Lily had moved from another part of the country, but at two and a half had been attending nursery for nearly six months and had formed well-established relationships with the practitioners and her peers. Lily's mother, Leticia, seemed unusually upset when the manager informed her that Lily's key person, Melanie, was ill and Lily would be cared for by Sasha, her paired key person. Leticia was late for work and left in a hurry, Sasha having offered to take some photos of Lily during the session to share with her mother. During the morning Sasha used the digital camera, to record Lily's time in the nursery; several images featured Lily with her favourite green comfort blanket trailing behind her.

Continues

Continued

When Leticia arrived to collect Lily she was delighted to receive the pictures of Lily's day. Leticia apologized for her earlier concern and explained to Sasha that since Lily had started at nursery she had always relied on her main key person. She said that in Lily's previous nursery a similar situation had occurred but the paired key person had not known Lily at all and had not allowed Lily to have her comfort blanket during the day. This had caused Lily great distress, such that she spent the next three weeks clinging to her mother and her blanket whenever she arrived at nursery.

The following week Leticia read in the nursery newsletter that there had been an amendment to the role of the paired key person and an explanation of how this approach worked in Lily's nursery.

In this example the details of the paired key person in this setting had not been given to the mother. Because of a previously bad experience Lily's mum was upset when faced with a change to her daughter's routine. Spending time getting to know the family well (and not making assumptions) is particularly important if children previously have been cared for by a childminder or in an out-of-home setting. Sasha was a skilful and insightful practitioner who recognized Leticia's concern and, although there was no time for discussion when Lily was dropped at nursery, she was able to observe Lily and support her playful experiences. By capturing some of this on camera her mother was later able to see for herself that Sasha did indeed know Lily very well and she was in fact another close person in Lily's nursery life. The mother was reassured and could see that Sasha (in Melanie's absence) provided the security her daughter needed in order to play happily.

Ideas for practice

- There is no substitute for speaking with parents face to face and getting to know them. Admission forms can capture only part of the picture when new families join the setting. It is worth considering different ways of gaining information. Talking with families who are already well established in the setting is one way of anticipating the needs of prospective families and how best to collect the information which may be needed in order to build a fuller picture of the child.

- Some basic information is required on admission but additional information (the fine detail) can add depth and context to a particular situation. Parents may not wish to share some information and will not always want practitioners to know things that they may feel will be used to make judgements about them. A feeling of mutual trust is crucial.
- Settings create a range of opportunities to spend time talking with parents: informal coffee mornings, drop-in sessions, committee membership, staying to eat breakfast or tea with their child, and so on. Not all parents want this, some prefer more formal arrangements such as parents' evenings and annual questionnaires.
- Home visits, too, can provide an insight into family life, but, because they take time, are often viewed as a rare luxury and saved until the child is making the transition to school, when the class teacher often makes the home visit. In developing a mosaic of approaches to enhance dialogue with parents it is important always to be mindful of the differing needs and wishes of families.
- With permission from parents, communication with other adults who share in the care and education of a baby or young child can help to provide meaning to the lives of young children. It may be that the care is shared on a more regular basis; for example, the child may attend nursery two days and the childminder three days each week. A communication book can help to develop a fuller record of the child's days and aid meaningful continuity. Photographs, too, can help to foster a sense of belonging for the child and make the link between home and the setting(s).

Questions for reflection

Thinking about the case study above and your own practice:

1. How do you ensure parents are fully informed about the differing roles of the adults who they come into contact with within your setting?

2. What systems are in place to keep parents up to date with information, including media reports?
3. How do you enter into and balance your relationships with parents and the variation in parenting styles?
4. How do you listen to parents?

Assessment is about identifying points of need and progression in learning. Vygotsky argued that every piece of learning has a history, a base on which it was built, beginning before formal education and based on real-life experiences. We can, for example, trace early beginnings of writing back to the first time a pencil was held and the first time a mark is made on paper – often accidental and usually well before organized learning (for example, Goodman, 1980). Early and informal learning occurs when young children spend time with adults, in real situations and real explorations from which their learning can progress.

One of the clearest ways to understand progression in children's learning (and therefore to be able meaningfully to assess that learning), and how to plan for the next stages, is to look at individual children over a period of time, observe their interests, their learning patterns and preferences, and see how these relate to the development of their behaviour, their speech and their thinking. Assessment is not an end point, it is part of the cycle of planning holistically for the youngest children and is essential, and this was never better expressed than by Rouse and Griffin:

> We need the vision to plan for whole human beings who have a clear and realistic personal identity whatever combination of cultural or religious background, racial origins, gender, ability or disability that may be. Children who know who they are will have the confidence to love and learn and communicate in a world of mathematical, scientific, aesthetic and technological experiences. Children who can collaborate and learn together in harmony with other people are likely to respect and value differences. Children who are able to have intimate responsive relationships with their significant adult will have better access to relevant early learning experiences. Children who play in inspirational, safe and challenging environments will take these values into adulthood and pass them on to future generations.

An ethos of respect for and dignity in childhood may be set from the cradle. (Rouse and Griffin, 1992: 155–6)

Part of the practitioner's role is to assess children's learning, their developmental needs, their need for support, their achievements and their understanding. Through their work with children, adults make judgements about children's ideas, what children know, their motivation, their abilities and their thinking, and how their interests and ideas might be developed further. Such judgements are based more upon what adults see children do and hear children say than on formal assessments. Ongoing assessment begins with careful observation. Observation can help practitioners to identify children's achievements and their learning needs and strategies. Worthwhile curriculum content can be matched to children's learning needs, however young they are, once those needs have been identified.

Close observation 'little and often' is quite different in its form and its yield from observation 'more and seldom'. Assessment which makes use of detailed and focused observations of children should be an ongoing and dynamic process which illuminates children's thinking and their capabilities. To make effective and reliable assessments, practitioners need to be open to what babies and young children are doing, receptive to their needs and interests, and respectful of their learning agendas.

What is planning for learning?

Babies and toddlers love to explore with their whole bodies, and it is important to provide opportunities for their creativity. Through exploration babies and toddlers will discover the properties of sand, water, paint and glue, getting their hands and bodies messy and sticky, enjoying (or not!) the sensation of the textures against their skin. (Page, 2006: 14)

Early childhood practitioners need always to be aware that even very young children are capable of being patient observers, especially when given space and time to do so. Young children will, for example, explore scientific ideas, learn about mathematical concepts and develop their language while engaged in many different experiences in home and community situations, as well as through experiences specifically planned for such learning in early education settings. They need the constancy of provision which enables them to repeat the exploration of objects, sounds, spaces and so on in secure and familiar environments. Careful planning for meaningful learning involves making long-term decisions about what is always there, and more spontaneous and short-term decisions, based on observations of children, about what is provided for a single session or a short period of time.

We suggest that planning is much more than completing written documents about the choice of equipment, its location and the details of working with individual children on aspects of their learning. For us, planning is as much about knowing and understanding children and making events meaningful for them, as it is about further achievement in development and learning. And this kind of planning requires a deep knowledge not only of child development in general, but of individual children in particular.

In the following example, a child's key person has thought carefully about how to accommodate family wishes to celebrate his first birthday. This example, which at first sight might seem quite simple and uneventful, portrays several elements of detailed planning to make the birthday celebration special for the child concerned and acceptable for all the children.

'Wow don't you look lovely', Craig said as he scooped up Ashaq, one of his key children, responding to the little boy's outstretched arms. As Ashaq snuggled into Craig's shoulder, Craig read Ashaq's contact book. Craig had already made a point of learning about the family's customs and knew that Ashaq would not only have been celebrating his first birthday the previous week-end but would have had his very first haircut as is traditional for male children in his culture. The family also wanted Ashaq to celebrate his first birthday with his nursery friends and had previously discussed with Craig their desire to bring a birthday cake to nursery for Ashaq to share. Later that day Craig lit the candles on the cake and as agreed with all the baby room parents, the practitioners sang 'Happy birthday' to Ashaq while the babies clapped and waved their arms to the music. After helping Ashaq to blow out the candles, Craig cut up the cake, wrapping a piece for each child. He carefully peeled off the pre-prepared labels that Ashaq's mother had written out listing the cake ingredients and stuck them onto each piece. He then left a note in each child's bag informing the parents that a piece of Ashaq's birthday cake was ready to collect from the sealed container in the milk kitchen.

The role of the key person in this example is pivotal in working with not just the child but the whole family. Craig showed his sensitivity towards Ashaq, his family and the other babies and children in the group. He also holds a set of working principles in the way he plans the event for all children. He thoughtfully consults with all the families about preferences regarding the celebration of Ashaq's first birthday; in addition he warmly acknowledges the significance of Ashaq's first haircut, fostering his sense of self. By providing all parents with information about the ingredients in the cake, Craig ensures that choice about whether to give it to their child is left firmly with each family, ensuring they continue to be involved in decision-making when their child is being cared for out of their home. Craig's decision to offer the cake to parents to take home also overcame issues which may have arisen around dietary needs and preferences. Craig is a practitioner who has worked hard to foster a trusting relationship between himself and the families whose children spend their days with him.

This example of highly attentive thinking and planning from a thoughtful and attuned key person, we suggest, is an illustration of what planning actually is, involving a high degree of detailed knowledge of children, their lives, their cultures, their preferences and how best to make events meaningful for them.

Questions for reflection

1. What are the particular cultural perspectives that need to be borne in mind in your day-to-day practice with families in your setting?

2. How do you work professionally and inclusively with families whose cultural and religious beliefs are vastly different to your own experience and values?

How to plan effectively

Effective planning for babies, toddlers and young children begins with decisions involving what is *always* available and what always happens. An important 'constant' in early childhood settings is the provision made for children on a day-to-day basis. There need to be elements of consistency in those things which children see when they enter the nursery at the start of each session. They are better able to make use of and get involved in experiences that unfold when they are also surrounded by lots of familiar things. Young children can get on with the business of living and learning when they are not encumbered with such worries as where to find things or people, where to go, who will help, and so on. Babies and young children need to know that some things will remain the same each day, for example, that there will always be some paint, that those favourite books, or a story read today, will be available tomorrow. They need to be able to find familiar objects in predictable places and need to know that if they have enjoyed something today they will be able to find it again tomorrow if they need it, thus developing their own continuity of thought and action. This sort of continuity in materials is exemplified in the approach to curriculum and pedagogy developed in Reggio Emilia, where certain things are constant and predictable while new interest is brought in from time to time to add different tangents to explorations and learning (Abbott and Nutbrown, 2001).

Making learning meaningful has been a central focus of the work of those many educators who laid the foundations of early childhood education as it is known today. Knowledge of child development and learning theories can help practitioners to create environments for learning, and to work in ways such that quite little children are more likely to sustain their effort, and will struggle and persevere when they inevitably encounter learning which they find difficult.

India, 16 months, had been attending her day nursery regularly since the age of eight months. Her weekly attendance pattern on Tuesday and Thursday meant that her mother (a lone parent) could continue her part-time job at the newsagents. India was quite a shy, reserved child and her key person, Andrea, knew that India preferred to take her time to settle back into the nursery on a Tuesday after her four-day break. Andrea noted India's increased confidence in her surroundings and her approach to the offered environment on a Thursday.

On Monday, after a particularly challenging morning in the toddler room, one of the practitioners decided to change the layout of the room and removed the painting easel, swapping it instead for the water tray. The children, many of whom attended full-time, spent the afternoon exploring the properties of the water and one or two of them immersed themselves in it almost completely! But on Tuesday when India arrived she was very unsettled and clingy towards Andrea. She refused to eat her breakfast and kept staring at the water tray. Millie, one of the practitioners in the room, asked India if she wanted to play with the water but India shook her head furiously. Andrea was puzzled by India's behaviour and comforted her as they sat together in the book corner looking at the toddler room montage of photographs that had recently been assembled. India's face suddenly lit up as they turned to the page with the photographs of the children at the painting easel. 'I think India is upset because the easel is not out', said Andrea to Millie. 'But she never goes near the easel, she only ever watches the other children', replied Millie. 'Yes, but that's the whole point isn't it', said Andrea, taking out India's observation file. 'We have taken away her choice. Last week I recorded how much India had enjoyed watching Bobby as he explored the red paint, and just before she went home how she had traced her finger over the marks he had made on the paper. The painting wasn't quite dry and left a trace of red paint on her finger. She likes Bobby and maybe India would have tried out some painting this week.' Millie did not really seem to grasp the subtlety of Andrea's comments.

On Thursday the painting easel was back in the original space and the water tray had been moved to another equally appropriate and appealing part of the room. India was crying when she arrived. She stopped crying when she saw Andrea and smiled at Bobby who was at the painting easel up to his arms in red paint.

Continues

Continued

   Several weeks later Andrea took photographs of India to put in her profile. India had started to make marks on the paper with red paint. Only India herself would know when she, somewhat tentatively, would be ready to explore other colours. But in the meantime Andrea knew that ensuring the availability and consistency of the environment was her role and was essential for India who needed time to decide when she was ready to explore. Andrea worked with her colleagues to ensure support for the children who attended the setting full-time and planned a variety of opportunities to challenge and sustain their interests in line with their ongoing development and progression.

In this example the practitioners are using their experiences with the children to respond to their needs. Clearly children who attend the setting every day will be more familiar with their surroundings, and are more likely to require practitioners to offer more regular variations to support their continued and meaningful engagement with their environment and aid their learning. It can be a particular challenge for practitioners to strike an appropriate balance in offering appropriate yet differentiated learning opportunities to meet the individual needs of all the children. In this example it is not that Millie deliberately ignored or overlooked India's needs, but that she did not understand them. It is another example of the way in which the key person is able to facilitate the most appropriate experiences for the children in his or her care. Millie did not think India choosing to *watch* the children painting on several occasions was important; she thought India did not like painting and was surprised by her reaction to its unavailability. Andrea, India's key person, knew India, her preferences and her personality. She drew upon all these facets to come to the suggestion that by removing the painting easel, they were inadvertently removing something India liked. Andrea had a pivotal role in helping her colleagues to understand the situation. Her knowledge and observations of India (as we saw in Mills's work), and her relationship with her peers, made it possible for Andrea to make sense of the little girl's reaction. It would have been easy to have ignored India's upset and attribute it, for example, to her less frequent attendance pattern. Although this was a contributing factor, on its own, it was not enough. It is only when all the information is gathered and fitted together that the jigsaw is complete. Respecting children and their 'voice' is an essential part of working with all children, but listening to and *really hearing* the voice of all children requires the highest level of skill from the most sensitive and attuned significant adult (Page, 2006).

Questions for reflection

1. Have you ever noticed a young child that spends long periods of time watching the other children in the group?
2. Do you think Andrea should have encouraged India to join in with the room activities sooner?
3. Do you have a choice in the way the environment is set up for the children in your key group? Does this environment meet the individual needs of all your key children?
4. Do you have enough opportunities to discuss environment planning with your team colleagues?
5. Do you ever worry about your key children when you can't be with them, for example if you are on holiday?

Johnston (2005) in her study 'Who benefits from baby signing?' reports a case study of two eight-month-old babies in a full-day care setting in the UK. She shows how sign language with young children as a method of communication supports opportunities for babies to have a 'voice' and to choose aspects of how they spend their time in the setting. They can ask for food and drink and even when they want to have their nappies changed. This can only really happen when babies and young children are respected in their own right and encouraged by respectful, sensitive, knowledgeable and appropriately qualified practitioners. Ethics was an important consideration in Johnston's study, and, like Wailling, her attention to detail and ensuring respectful practices was a fundamental part of the research.

When teaching baby sign language to a child it is important that the word that you are teaching them has meaning. For example, if you are going to teach the child the sign for milk, it is imperative that you also offer them some milk, otherwise they will become confused and not know the meaning of the sign. 'Once a child has learned the sign they can tell you that they want some milk ... Some babies make clear statements that they do not like a certain person; this could be a visitor, a parent or even a member of staff from another room' (Johnston, 2005: 30–4).

In the following two vignettes we can see how Johnston recorded the progress of the babies. In her analysis and interpretations she is able to demonstrate how they are able to communicate with their key person and build upon their learning and enjoyment. Unsurprisingly the examples describe the babies' eating and drinking patterns, but this is exactly why it is so fascinating. The babies in this setting clearly set the agenda, and not the adults, making this research so powerful.

Mark's story

Mark's first sign was 'milk'. I had taken his milk out of the fridge and I asked him 'do you want some milk Mark?' and I showed him the sign for 'milk', as I always do. On this occasion Mark started to imitate the sign, we praised Mark, he was very excited and he laughed.

Although we are doing lots of signs with Mark, he watches and concentrates so intently but he is not yet picking up any of the signs. However Mark is playing with sounds and can copy many words such as 'hiya', 'tiger' and 'spider'. We do the signs for these words too.

Mark had finished his dinner and I asked 'have you finished Mark?' I showed him the sign for 'finished'. Mark laughed and waved his hands in the air, Mark's attempt was great and we gave him lots of praise even though he did not complete the correct sign.

Mark did the sign for 'milk' this morning as soon as he arrived at nursery; I asked Mark's mother if he had drunk any milk yet this morning. Mark's mother explained that he had not yet had any milk and she had brought an extra bottle. I warmed some milk for Mark and we sat down together, Mark drank the whole bottle of milk and we had a big cuddle. Mark was able to communicate his need this morning.

Mark has been attempting to smack his friends and some of the practitioners; we tell Mark 'no thank you' and show him the sign for 'no'. Mark stops immediately; he understands the word for 'no' and the sign, although he cannot copy it.

Mark is able to copy the sign for 'drink'; he usually does this sign when he is eating his dinner, and he sometimes does it while he is playing. Drinks are available throughout the day and not just when they ask for them.

While the practitioner Pam was helping Mark to eat his dinner, Pam asked him 'do you want some more Mark?' Pam showed him the sign for 'more'. Mark put his hands together and successfully completed the sign, he then started clapping he was so proud of himself. Mark can now do this sign competently, one of the other children was sharing some of their raisins with Mark, as soon as Mark ate one he carried on doing the sign for 'more'.

I was showing Mark the sign for 'Daddy', because his daddy was picking him up. Mark was able to do the sign and say the word. Mark completed this sign lots of times and was able to do the sign when his Daddy arrived. After mastering the sign for 'Daddy' we have been showing Mark the sign for 'Mummy'. Mark is able to do a very similar sign to the correct one.

I asked Mark 'where's the birdies?' I showed him the sign for 'bird'. I took Mark to the gate and opened the door so we could see the garden. There was a bird on the grass so I said 'birdie'. Mark was really excited by this, on another occasion I could see him sitting on the floor by the gate doing the sign for 'bird', he had spotted a bird outside, I went over and said 'bird'. Mark was so thrilled he stood up at the gate; he was laughing and still doing the sign for 'bird'.

Mark walked into the bathroom and did the sign for 'change'. I was interested to know if Mark associated the sign with the bathroom or if he needed changing. I checked his nappy and his nappy was soiled. I asked Mark 'shall we change your nappy?' Mark lifted his arms up so I could lift him onto the changing mat and I changed his nappy for him.

Sarah's story

Sarah is a very happy girl; she attends the setting full-time and she started her visits when she was five months old. Sarah has very strong relationships with all the key people in her room. Sarah loves messy play such as sand, gloop, jelly, water and paint. Sarah can get frustrated when she does not get her own way and throws herself back in temper. Generally, Sarah enjoys most

Continues

Continued

activities we offer her; she likes to interact with adults in the room but also spends lots of time with the other babies too. Sarah laughs at the other babies and likes very much to meet new people, her sense of belonging in the setting and trust of the practitioners is such that she is even prepared to go over to strangers and give them a cuddle, Sarah is very welcoming.

Sarah was sitting playing on the carpet area when she made her first sign; Sarah looked up at me and showed me the sign for 'milk'. I was really surprised as she had not made any signs yet and she did not normally have milk at this time. However in order for the sign language to be successful it is important that we can offer the things which the babies want at that particular time and respond positively, giving Sarah a sense of empowerment and choice. I went to warm up some milk for Sarah and we sat down together. Sarah likes to hold the bottle herself, Sarah drank the whole bottle of milk and sat with me as we had a big cuddle. Sarah then began to push me away clearly showing that she wanted to get down now. I took Sarah and placed her back on the carpet with her friends and some toys to play with.

Sarah is now getting used to using the sign for 'milk'. On another occasion Sarah was playing when she was doing the sign for 'milk' to herself while engaging with a toy. The practitioner, Erica, asked Sarah 'Do you want some milk Sarah?' while showing Sarah the sign for 'milk'. Sarah sat and did the sign for 'milk' continually, Erica picked Sarah up and she continued to do the sign until her milk was warm and ready for her to drink. Erica and Sarah sat down on the large comfy chair and snuggled in together as Sarah gave herself her milk.

While eating lunch today, I offered Sarah some food from the spoon, she took it and seemed really excited about her dinner. Maybe she really liked it or perhaps she was just really hungry. I asked 'do you want some more Sarah?' before her next spoonful, I also showed her the sign for 'more'.

Sarah was concentrating on my hands so much she put her hands together and tried to copy. Sarah was unable to copy this sign and she put her hands together and clapped instead. I continued to show Sarah the sign for 'more' throughout the rest of her lunch, I congratulated and praised her efforts for trying.

We were giving Sarah her breakfast today, when she refused it; Sarah made the sign for 'milk', so we sat down together for some milk instead, which she drank. Sarah is clearly communicating using this sign now, she knows when she wants milk and if we offer it before she is ready she refuses it.

I lifted Sarah onto the changing mat to change her nappy which was soiled. Sarah decided to throw herself back as she became frustrated. I said 'no thank you Sarah' and showed her the sign for 'no'. Sarah stopped her tantrum immediately, I offered her a toy to play with, as she lifted her hand up to take the toy, Sarah copied the sign for 'no'. Sarah was now clean and ready to get down, I said well done and gave her a cuddle before putting her on to the floor. On a few occasions a similar thing has happened and each time Sarah has stopped and repeated the sign for 'no'. Sarah will also copy this sign if she smacks or grabs one of her friends, again she stops and does the sign back to us.

Sarah concentrates so much on us doing the sign for 'more', she was able to close her fist and study it before she showed me the sign for 'more'. Sarah was so proud she had a big smile and she received lots of praise too. Sarah now does this sign very often while eating.

On one occasion we were doing a big group painting, all the babies were in their nappies, they were enjoying themselves so much. However, the paper had become ripped so I lifted it up and my team member Erica was putting a new piece down; as I walked out of the room with the picture Sarah shouted and showed the sign for 'more'. We put some more paper down and continued with the activity.

I asked Sarah 'do you want some milk Sarah?' Sarah did not repeat the sign, however, she crawled over to the comfy chair and waited for me to join her with her bottle.

Sarah has not yet mastered the sign for 'change', however, when I asked her 'shall we change your nappy Sarah?', I show her the sign for change, she crawls into the bathroom and puts her arms up to me for me to lift her on to the mat.

I asked Sarah did she want a drink and showed the sign for 'drink', she pointed to her cup, I passed it to her and she took a big drink. Sarah has picked up this sign and will ask for a 'drink' when she wants one.

When the lunch arrives I always ask the babies 'do you want something to eat babies?' and show them the sign for 'eat'. Sarah is now doing this sign and she associates it with the dinner trolley, as soon as she sees the trolley she does the sign.

We do the sign for 'finished' when the babies start to refuse their lunch or look away. Sarah is now able to tell us that she has 'finished' her lunch by showing the sign and she is also able to give us her bottle when she has finished her milk and then she does the sign for 'finished'.

Given Johnston's sensitivity in her research and how she reported the stories of what naturally occurred in the setting, it is perhaps no wonder that the following statement under the heading 'Helping children achieve well and enjoy what they do' appeared in their Ofsted Inspection Report:

> There are lots of smiles, laughter and giggling as staff cuddle, play and talk with the children, who are always really pleased to see their key worker and fling open their arms for the member of staff to lift them up … Babies have excellent opportunities to investigate natural products when they explore the contents of the treasure baskets and the sensory play area. They look at themselves in the mirrors, relish the feel of the shiny mobiles, energetically ring the chimes and splash water on and then feel the smooth and the rough rocks … They use lots of paint as they enthusiastically cover all the paper … Staff use their training well to provide interesting and fun opportunities for children, such as helping babies who cannot talk to communicate through signing when they are hungry, their food is all gone, their nappy needs changing or they see a bird. (Ofsted, 2008: 7)

This chapter has considered young children's natural curiosity, and their need to explore and investigate. It has examined the importance of practitioners being well informed in order to offer opportunities to babies and young children that extend their learning in a meaningful way. Examples show the importance of working in partnership with parents and how this aspect of every practitioner's role can be demanding, difficult, complex and rewarding. Children's natural curiosity and wonder in exploration must be supported by a trusted adult in environments which are more than just a 'space to play' but which are prepared with learning and interaction in mind. Where practitioners collaborate and develop their practice through the use of close, detailed and systematic observations of the babies and young children, the learning encounters which ensue can be sustained and meaningful.

Further reading

Abbott, L. and Langston, A. (eds) (2006) *Parents Matter: Supporting the Birth to Three Matters Framework*. Maidenhead: Open University Press.

MacNaughton, G. and Hughes, P. (2011) *Parents and Professionals in Early Childhood Settings*. Berkshire: Open University Press.

Nutbrown, C., Hannon, P. and Morgan, A. (2005) *Early Literacy Work with Families: Research, Policy and Practice*. London: Sage.

Whalley, M. (2007) *Involving Parents in their Children's Learning* (2nd edn). London: Sage.

Chapter 7

Planning for Positive Transitions

> This chapter will discuss:
> - Why we need to give thought to transitions
> - Settling into an early years setting
> - The emotional complexity of everyday transitions
> - How 'islands of intimacy' can encourage children's sense of belonging

When thinking about transitions for children it is natural to instantly think about a big or dramatic event in a child's life. The first day at nursery, moving house or the birth of a new baby are often planned for months in advance to ease the young child's uncertainty. Some transitions are inevitable and signal the norms of progression – for instance, a child moving from the baby room to the toddler group space. For little children, transitions signify the end of something familiar, whereupon feelings of loss and bewilderment may be experienced as well as the excitement of looking forward to the beginning of something new.

Settling into an early years setting – easing transitions

Goldschmied and Jackson (1994) draw attention to the anxieties faced by both parents and children when initial separation takes place and settings can create opportunities for children gradually to settle in. Regular visits and opportunities to spend time getting to know the adults, other children and the new surroundings are all helpful strategies to overcome the period when the time to part finally arrives.

Parents seeking advice and information about suitable childcare arrangements prior to the birth of their baby and putting his or her name onto a waiting list may feel very different when the reality of 'leaving' a baby dawns.

Turning up on the doorstep of the large purpose-built day nursery with four-month-old baby Dora all snuggled up in her car seat with Buggley Wuggley Bunny (the birth toy with the name that seemed quite amusing when Grandma first gave it to Dora – but now seemed a bit silly!), Molly was wondering if she should call the rabbit by some other name. 'What would they think!' Molly had walked what seemed like miles with the car seat in the crook of one arm and the massive 'changing' bag slung over the other shoulder with everything in it but the kitchen sink – just in case! She had to park quite a long way from the nursery and could not understand why she had not noticed how far the car park was from the nursery when she had put Dora's name on the waiting list – but she was not carrying Dora in the awkward car seat carrier then. Molly remembered that day well – she had just had her scan and she was on a high. All was well, and the nursery seemed perfect, exactly what they were looking for. Molly had liked the bright cheerful young manager and had even commented on the red blouse she was wearing. She thought this was the best place for her baby and was confident that working three days per week would give her the balance she needed to continue working in the town hall and spend time with the baby. She had chatted to her friends and family about the best time to return to work and when the baby was six months old seemed to be the best time and they could just about manage financially.

Molly battled against the wind and rain, wishing that William was with her. Dora was not a difficult baby but she had cried more than Molly had expected. Colic, the health visitor said, was 'normal', but Molly could not bear to see her daughter in pain and when she drew her knees up to her chest and squealed, nothing would soothe her except when Molly paced up and down the room, rubbing her back and singing 'You are my sunshine' with Buggley Wuggley Bunny tucked underneath Dora's left cheek. Molly wished she could afford to have had nine months at home with her. She was too little, but that was how it was and Lucinda the manager at the nursery had

Continues

Continued

suggested Molly should bring Dora along to settle her into nursery and meet Rebecca, her key person, several weeks before Molly had to return to work.

Lucinda answered the door and looked as young and attractive as ever compared to Molly's dishevelled appearance. Dora kicked her legs vigorously and the toy rabbit fell onto the floor unnoticed. Molly bent down to unwrap Dora's blankets and as she did so was aware of a small child standing next to her. Two-year-old Elliot, on the way to the toilet, held out Dora's rabbit and said 'Wabbit, I like wabbit, I got Joey – ook' and he held out a rather tatty-looking kangaroo. 'He won't go anywhere without Joey – will you Elliot?' Elliot gently laid the rabbit on top of a now wide awake Dora and said 'Bye baby, bye wabbit' and ran off to the bathroom holding Joey by the ear and trailing him along the ground firmly behind him.

Molly was struck by the confidence and self-assurance of this small boy who seemed so content. She later discovered that Elliot had been attending the setting since he too was a baby. Molly went to meet Rebecca who was to be Dora's key person and they got on well. Molly explained all about Buggley Wuggley Bunny and Rebecca did not laugh or make her feel silly, and somehow meeting Elliot had given Molly the confidence to suggest that it did not really matter what the rabbit was called, it was just important for Dora to have him close to her. Molly explained in detail all about Dora's likes and dislikes and the way she liked to be held.

After about an hour of chatting and, in between playing and feeding Dora, Molly realized that she had stopped feeling so tense and was enjoying telling Rebecca about Dora. Rebecca seemed genuinely interested and explained all the practical things about the nursery. Molly could feel the tears begin to prick her eyes as Rebecca showed her Dora's coat peg and 'cubby' – both with the photograph of Dora which she had previously sent in with her admission forms. Sensing her mixed emotions Rebecca suggested perhaps Molly and Dora might have had enough for one day. Molly smiled gratefully at Rebecca who helped Molly to gather Dora's things together and walked with her to the entrance. Lucinda looked up and seeing them both, smiled warmly at Molly and said 'No one can really prepare you can they? ... for how you might feel'. Molly knew that Lucinda was right. She was exhausted from her two-hour visit to the nursery, and she did not know how long it would take her, let alone Dora, to settle in. And she couldn't begin to imagine how she could possibly concentrate on going back to work. But she knew that, despite its glossy exterior and Lucinda's elegant dress, in the nursery was a deep sense of caring and respect towards the adults and the children.

As she reflected on her afternoon, she thought deeply about how the practitioners in the baby room had spoken to the babies. It did not seem like it was just a performance for her ... but only time would tell. Later that evening when William arrived home from work and asked Molly how it went – Molly burst into tears with relief, exhaustion, guilt and delight ... a whole range of emotions. Lucinda, Molly thought, was an experienced manager with a deep understanding of children and adults, but no one could have prepared Molly for how she might feel.

It was some two months later that Molly finally left Dora and returned to work, she cried all the way to the car. She cried every day for the first week. A year later, when it was time to change rooms, Molly could feel the wave of emotions rise in her again as Rebecca suggested Dora could spend some time settling into the toddler room ... Dora's next transition.

In this example we have only really touched the surface of how it might be for babies, children, families and practitioners. Goldschmied and Jackson (1994) suggest that the initial period can be very demanding for practitioners. When building a relationship with the parents it is the (often small) detail which can play a big part. It is commonplace for settings as well as childminders to invite parents and children for an introductory visit to enable the parent to help settle their child. It is virtually impossible to know how long the settling-in process will take because each child and family is unique and has differing needs. Some settings suggest that children attend for two or three short visits with their parent until the parent feels confident to leave the child for a short period (anything from 10 minutes to an hour) depending on how the child and parent feel. Separation time is often increased over a series of visits until the parent leaves for the whole length of their session. The process can be painful for all concerned, including the practitioner, who must try to manage the situation as well as possible for everyone. In the example above, the manager knew that it is impossible to predict how the introductory visits will go. Some parents find the process too painful and decide not to take up the intended place at all. Such decisions are entirely personal. All human beings handle parting and separation differently, and this must be borne in mind in the context of the family, their culture and the place of the child in the family. A mother once wrote in a note about her daughter – the youngest in a family of four elder brothers:

> Please treat her gently, don't judge her too harshly and forgive her roughness or tantrums – she has to fight for her voice to be heard and sometimes this results in what others might think as 'naughtiness'. She is a lively high-spirited girl who challenges us all – but she is my daughter and I love her!

On meeting this mother it would have been easy to assume that after experiencing leaving four boys and knowing the setting well, she would have been used to transitions and partings. While she appeared to be a confident parent, she knew her daughter would display traits in her personality which would not always be the most endearing. Goldschmied and Jackson (1994) remind us that parents and practitioners will be watching and assessing each other. It is important for the practitioner not to be judgemental or critical of the parents' child-rearing practices, especially in this early phase when the parents may have a particularly strong desire for their child to be not only liked but indeed loved by the practitioner.

Transition, continuity and coherence are three words that appeared in the original EYFS (DCSF, 2008) and which seem at first glance to be at odds with one another. 'Transition' is about change, while 'continuity' is about keeping things the same. However, 'coherence' helps children to make sense of transition. The supporting guidance (Early Education, 2012) to the newly revised EYFS (DfE, 2012a) points out the importance of saying goodbye to their key children when practitioners change shift. It might seem remarkable that adults who work with young children might need to be reminded to say 'goodbye' or 'hello' to the children in the setting. Most practitioners are very generous with their time, ensuring the children are settled with their paired key person before departing. Nevertheless, leaving a baby with a practitioner for the first time will not necessarily make much sense to the child as he or she feels lost and bewildered, crying bitterly for the loss of their most special person and not knowing if they will ever return. How the practitioner reacts to the child's distress is of the utmost importance:

> Unless there is a substitute for the parent with whom they can make a relationship, they may sink into depression, not wanting to play or eat … Once our eyes have been opened, we can understand that for the child too young to have a concept of time, a separation short in adult terms may feel the same as losing a loved person for ever. (Goldschmied and Jackson, 1994: 46)

Separation anxiety will undoubtedly be more problematic for the child who has experienced insecure attachments in the past or many separations. This may manifest itself in various ways and expert help may need to be sought from other professionals.

Ideas for practice

- Develop ways of communicating with parents that really help them to feel that they have a voice.
- Draw on experiences of established parents to help make times and periods of transition more manageable for all concerned.
- Consider whether a transitions policy has a place in the setting:
  - o What would be its purpose?
  - o How would it help to inform new parents?
  - o How would it be kept up to date?
  - o How would it help practitioners to work with families and to plan for periods of transition?
  - o How can setting managers help and support practitioners through the phases and transitions of their key children?
- How can parents support each other? Consider developing a 'buddy' system among parents who can discuss their experiences at first hand and help to ease the burden, or a more experienced parent can befriend a new parent or one who is experiencing the trauma of settling in/transition.

Questions for reflection

1. How do you ensure that parents' feelings are taken into account when they come to drop their children off for the first time?
2. Reflect on how welcoming your setting is to all people, respecting their individual family lives.
3. How do you accommodate the personal belongings of babies and children so that they have their 'own space'?

The emotional complexity of everyday transitions

We must consider not just how many physical transitions there are from the home to nursery, but also how many emotional transitions a young child will experience in the course of their day. How many people will a child come into contact with and how many partings will a child experience throughout a 'normal' day or week? Once again this suggests to us the need for close attachments and respectful sharing of information as an essential ingredient in the nurturing of a young child to ensure both consistency and constancy.

Let us imagine for a moment a toddler called Simon. His mother wakes him up at 7 a.m. to say 'goodbye' as she rushes off to catch the train to work. Simon's dad dresses him and drops him off at nursery at 7.30 a.m. Simon has been attending nursery for six months. As he is one of the 'early' children his dad hands him over to the nursery manager. She is in the large group room with three other children (whose ages range from two to four years) and another practitioner who works with the pre-schoolers. They wait together until the toddler room leader comes on duty at 8 a.m. She greets Simon and takes him with her to the toddler room to prepare his breakfast. Over the course of the next two hours, 11 other toddlers arrive with their parents, and three other staff come on duty into the toddler room, including Jude, Simon's key person. Jude is on a late shift and is the last one to arrive at 10 a.m. Throughout the day there are more arrivals and departures of children and adults. After lunch, four of the 'morning' children go home and two more 'afternoon' children arrive. The 'full-timers' like Simon start to be collected around 4.30 p.m. and the toddler room leader leaves at 5 p.m. At 5.30 p.m. Simon is re-united with his mother who arrives to collect him. By this time Simon is grumpy and tearful. Jude, who is still on duty, reassures Simon's mum that he has been 'fine' all day, and for the most part he has managed to 'hold himself together'. However, if we pause to reflect on the number of transitions Simon has had to cope with since he got out of bed, it is quite staggering. For the majority of the nursery day, Simon was able to rely on the close presence of Jude. However, for at least two hours in the morning, although he was being cared for by other caring practitioners, they were frequently involved in other organizational tasks and therefore unable to attend in any meaningful way to Simon's specific emotional needs. Furthermore, Simon witnessed the arrival and departure of many other people big and small throughout his 'normal' nursery day.

Questions for reflection

1. How can the adults involved in a scenario such as this build a picture or profile of the child?
2. Have you ever paused to think about the emotional as well as the physical transitions that take place for some children in your setting?
3. How can adults help children to feel a sense of belonging throughout their day?

David et al. (2003) suggest the following list as an example of the depth of knowledge and understanding required by those who work with our youngest children.

Practitioners need to be able to:

• understand attachment and the importance of a child being special to at least one significant person in order to promote resilience
• be informed about young children's development
• provide opportunities to explore and play in a safe and secure environment – children's mobility and movement are important for their development

- know about brain development and the importance of 'nourishment' (a good diet – in both the form of food and of physical and psychological stimulation)
- help parents see that intimate behaviours such as bugging and nudging, pet names and idiosyncratic behaviour are important and that children's development sometimes seems difficult because they are trying to become independent people with a sense of self
- have reasonable rules which fit with children's rhythms and give a pattern to life
- know that parents, as well as children, need support
- know about child abuse and neglect and have other colleagues to consult
- recognise the additional requirements of babies and young children with special needs, and plan how to ensure these children have access, in a philosophical, as well as practical, sense, to similar experiences and opportunities to their peers
- help communities and the public understand the importance of positive interactions and experiences in the first three years for all areas of development, including brain development, and for enjoyment in the here and now
- access the education and training necessary in order to fulfil their important role.
(David, et al., 2003: 9–10)

We have already discussed the importance of children being 'held in mind' (Barlow and Svanberg, 2009), and the rationale for close attachment relationships. Robyn Dolby, a leading psychologist in the field of infant mental health, has been conducting research with a group of early years practitioners in Australia, to develop an intervention programme intended to support children during times of transition. 'The Circle of Security'[1] map helps parents and carers to follow children's relationship needs and so know how to become more emotionally available to them. 'The map draws a very clear link between attachment and learning' (Dolby, 2007: 1). Dolby uses the 'two row boats

[1] The Circle of Security©® International Early Intervention Program for Parents and Children, devised by Glen Cooper, Bert Powell and Kent Hoffman, http//circleofsecurity.net

metaphor' (Cooper, 2011) to highlight the critical importance of providing children with enough emotional support at the moment of transition. The metaphor is used to stress the point that in order for the young child to step safely and securely from one metaphorical boat (the parent) into another (a nursery practitioner) the two boats need to be perfectly aligned. If the two 'boats' are too far apart, the child effectively 'falls' through the gap. As Dolby points out, when little children are moving from being with one adult to being with another there is a moment, when they are unsure about who is 'holding' them. Thus, in effect they have 'one foot in each boat'.

When children are being prepared for a more formal transition, it is likely that a sensitive approach will be taken to the event. However, it is often the everyday transitions which are overlooked, largely because after the initial planning they can seem mundane and unnecessary. However, practitioners must consider how to ensure smooth transitions, be they daily, weekly, monthly or at a particular formal phase or stage.

For example:

- How can Jenny's new key person really ensure she understands Jenny's idiosyncratic behaviour at sleep time?
- Will William be able to take turns with the tractor and will his new key person understand his interest in trajectory schema?
- Will Michael's new key person understand that he is not being 'naughty' when he gets upset at lunchtime if the gravy is put on his lunch, covering his potato? Will his new key person in the tweenies room sensitively support his preference to pour the gravy himself just the way he likes it, next to the vegetables?

This is not about children being 'fussy' or 'difficult', or even 'spoiled'. The adults in any organization need to plan for these periods of transition with the utmost integrity and sensitivity to ensure that little children's individuality is understood. Every child's entitlement to be treated with respect and dignity regardless of their age, stage or point of transition can be realized through sensitive understanding, commitment and patience. Practitioners will need to draw on their detailed record-keeping and documentation of children (including their discussions with parents, their observations, profiles/learning stories and photographs) to help them to make informed judgements and to ensure children's well-being and emotional support is catered for during these times of change. Routine and normality alongside rhythms and routines to suit the child (rather than the practitioner or the organization) are important. This is not easy, in fact it requires careful thought, planning and flexibility – always in discussion with parents and on many occasions with the child as well.

Johnston (2005) was able to ensure the voices of the babies in her setting were heard and understood by responding to a request from one mother to teach her baby baby-signing. Johnston and the other practitioners learned signing and taught some signs to the baby. This truly meant that the voices of babies were heard and that they were included. It was so successful that she negotiated with other parents and used signing with their babies also. It was found to be the most powerful form of communication for the babies who used it to convey their needs and wants to the practitioners and with each other. Johnston writes:

> After a discussion with the other members of our team and the next room (one- to two-year olds), we decided that this was something that we would continue to offer to all the babies and toddlers in our care on a regular basis. Within a short space of time many of our babies were picking up the signs and using them at the relevant times. For example asking for more whilst eating lunch, or asking for milk after they wake up, if this is part of their routine.
>
> When I went into the next room I could see that these children were using sign language really well and also using oral language for the words too. They were using the sign language in a really positive way, I could see them telling their friends 'no' if they were pushing them or trying to take a toy from them. I realised for the first time that this must really reduce frustration for these toddlers all of whom are learning to talk. (Johnston, 2005: 4)

In this example Johnston could clearly see how the babies and toddlers could be active partners in their own learning. This is important at any time, but perhaps more so during periods of transition. Many experienced and skilled practitioners will support children by carefully planning 'visits' to the next room for a baby who may be ready to move to the toddler room. Recognizing when the child has had enough and is ready to return to their familiar person or space is an important consideration. Indeed, it is sometimes the parents who, having formed close sustaining bonds with their child's key person, find the change difficult and may resent and even resist the change. This can be equally difficult for the key person too. After months of nurturing a young child s/he has to prepare for the moment when a child moves on. Some settings work in such a way as to ensure that children retain the same key person who moves through the setting with them, although this remains unusual. However, even in the settings where the key person approach is respected and a shared understanding has been reached, it is still possible to identify the practitioner who was a child's first key person.

Diane knew Alice well. She had, after all, cared for her every day in the nursery since she was six weeks old. She had a very good relationship with her parents and was well respected among the baby room team – 'a good role model' the manager had written on Diane's annual appraisal. Diane was aware how difficult she found it when 'her' babies moved from the baby room to the toddlers' but she also knew that it was essential to work with the baby's new key person to ease the transition for the baby and his or her family. Diane had been working closely with Alice's new key person – June. Alice was very content in the baby room and Diane waited until she *really* was sure that Alice was emotionally ready to detach from Diane as well as being able to reach all the other developmental milestones. Diane often took Alice to visit the toddler section, at first she stayed with her and then she gradually started to leave Alice with June. She was careful to ensure Alice gave her 'permission' to leave (usually in the form of a wave or a spontaneous kiss). This gradual introduction worked well and coincided with the transition of another baby, Felix, who Alice liked and who had a similar pattern of attendance. Once settled into the toddlers' room with (what seemed to Alice's parents) apparent ease, they continued their regular dialogue with Diane

Continues

Continued

whenever they saw her, generally chatting about how Alice was progressing.

About 14 months later when Diane arrived at the nursery one morning, Alice ran up to Diane and hugged her. Diane bent down, stroked Alice's hair and smiled at her, affirming and acknowledging her every breath as she excitedly told Diane all about her new shoes. To the attentive observer it was clear that Diane had sustained her relationship with Alice from her first days in the baby room and throughout her time at nursery. She responded naturally to Alice and the little girl was secure in her trust and expectation of Diane's reaction to her in the way that she smiled and smoothed her hair as she had done when she was a baby. Diane had been able to continue her relationship because she had understood and prepared Alice in her earliest transition, and was able to respond to Alice's need to continue her relationship with her even though Diane was no longer her key person. It was an important point for discussion at team meetings and it had been agreed for some time that the children should be allowed to return to the company and comfort of a previous key person at times of the child's choosing. This was facilitated by the manager to ensure the adults in the setting were secure and not made to feel awkward or uncomfortable if a child needed a more familiar significant adult to share their excitement and/or distress.

A recent parent questionnaire indicated this as one of the strengths of the setting and said it helped to foster a 'family type of atmosphere'.

In the case study example we can see how Diane had been secure from the start about her relationship with Alice. She had always taken her cues from the child and her parents, and had an open and honest relationship with them. This was partly due to Diane's knowledge and understanding of the holistic needs of young children, and the importance of ensuring children's readiness for transition is indicated in relation to their emotional well-being, not just their intellectual and physical capabilities. The manager engaged the whole team in regular dialogue about the importance of close attachment and openly discussed the advantages and disadvantages of the children and the adults being comfortable about their relationships. New or less well established relationships were also fostered by the adults, who, inevitably in the context of the transition, were less familiar to the children. Because the children knew they could return to their significant adult, they were secure and comfortable in their explorations (Cassidy, 2008; Elfer et al., 2012). David et al. (2003) highlight the point that when children have strong, secure attachments they are more likely to be curious, self-assured, resilient and emotionally strong:

> During the very early years, support for babies and young children is extremely important, as they begin on a journey of self-discovery from a base of secure relationships with parents and a key person. The beginnings of autonomy can be seen in the relationships which exist as babies and young children play and explore in the context of a close, attentive and emotionally present adult. In order to become strong, the baby needs a nurturing environment in which their key person plays an essential role. By encouraging and supporting decision making, empathising and providing opportunities for children, the key person helps them grow emotionally and respond to successes and challenges. (David et al., 2003: 34–5)

Questions for reflection

1. How will the points we have raised here about transitions impact on your practice?
2. Thinking about the children in your setting, how do you think they cope with their daily/weekly transitions?
3. Is there anything you could do differently to provide a greater level of emotional support during times of transition?
4. Who could you talk to at your setting if you are concerned about how a young child is coping?

When little children spend much of their time away from their homes and families it can be a challenge for practitioners to give them a sense of belonging. Toys and equipment in the setting become jointly owned and have to be shared with lots of other children. Therefore, it is important to incorporate opportunities for children to feel 'special', 'cherished' and 'individual' whenever possible. Infants and toddlers are frequently expected to 'share' group belongings long before they have reached the appropriate developmental milestone to understand what it is to 'share'. Thus it is crucially important that sensitive and attuned practitioners who have a good understanding of child development provide special times with their key children. 'Islands of intimacy' provide one such example.

'Islands of intimacy'

Much of the time babies and young children spend out of their own homes in day care settings can be taken up with the routines and organization of the setting (Goldschmied and Jackson, 2004). As practitioners become more aware of the need to ensure babies and young children are offered opportunities that flow with their rhythms and patterns, individualizing as opposed to institutionalizing children, then the quality of their experiences is likely to improve. The *Birth to Three Matters Framework* (DfES, 2002a) helped practitioners to think more deeply about the principles that underpin quality learning experiences for very young children. These principles, with some adaptation, are now firmly embedded within the EYFS (DfE, 2012a).

The day can be very long for children and adults in settings; 8 a.m. to 6 p.m. is a usual length of day for many settings, and for some 7 a.m. to 7 p.m. is the norm. Practitioners need to be alert, motivated and insightful but they also need to be able to sit and relax with the children and change the 'mood' and 'pace' of the day, perhaps also to share something of their own interests. Goldschmied and Jackson (1994, 2004) suggest 'islands of intimacy' as an alternative to children spending time waiting for things to happen. For example, at lunchtime a key person can give her group of key children her undivided attention. Also, they suggest, 'Children require time and space and an available adult to enable them to develop their power of speech' (Goldschmied and Jackson, 2004: 46). In the following example the practitioner offers her children an opportunity to share her own collection of shells, using the time for talking and extending their interest and their language.

Carmel took her special collection of shells from the top shelf of the cupboard. She had previously set up an area with comfy cushions and her three excited 18-month-old key children sat down. Carmel put the basket on the floor and the children proceeded to help themselves to some of the shells, touching, smelling and handling them with impressive care. They were so absorbed in their experience that they were oblivious to the clatter of the lunch trolley arriving. Carmel sat close to the children acknowledging and affirming their intimate discoveries. The shells held the children's interest while another practitioner made final preparations for lunch. After about 10 minutes Carmel suggested that the children take it in turns to wash their hands in readiness for their meal. The children seemed disappointed to leave their 'island of intimacy' but were beckoned by the welcoming smell of food! As the children put the shells back in their basket, Carmel thought about how much more meaningful this period of the day had become since she had introduced 'islands of intimacy'.

Children in nurseries often spend considerable amounts of time waiting for things to happen. Lunchtime in particular can be a challenge when quite a lot of organization is needed before the meal can begin. However, as this example demonstrates, practitioners can work together to plan special times of the day to capture and engage even the youngest child's interest. This reduces the waiting in highchairs and at tables for food to arrive, and reduces the noise of impatient and hungry children. Goldschmied (2004) suggests that each practitioner should have his or her own collection of items which are unique to that person and never borrowed by other adults in the setting. The emphasis is on the sharing of some special items that are personal to the practitioner – a box of buttons, shells, coins, turned wood carvings, lace bobbins, and so on. The practitioner can convey his or her own pleasure in handling the collection – telling little stories about how they were obtained and thus engaging the children with the personal intimacy that this time offers. Children in group settings spend much of their day sharing toys and activities. 'Island time' provides a unique time for children with their key person and his or her distinctive collection.

Ideas for practice

■ Consider the differing interests of the practitioners in the setting and the items of interest she or he could bring to the setting. Think carefully about the times of the day where children would gain most benefit from 'island time'.

■ As with aspects of the treasure basket and heuristic play, the ethos and philosophy of the *islands of intimacy* are fundamental to its successful implementation. It may be tempting to borrow Maggie's box of buttons, Mandy's selection of pebbles or Isaac's marbles, but to do this would be to miss the point of a personal sharing of something special.

Infants and young children need time: to watch, to explore, to create, to rest, to giggle, to cry, to relax and to learn, and practitioners' attachments with them are essential in offering opportunities to do all these things. Page (2006) suggests we can only really claim to value and wonder at a small child's competence, concentration and involvement, when we give them the time to explore, and we can only respect and understand the individuality of their creative minds when we allow them time to construct their own knowledge alongside their close adult.

Transitions can be challenging, difficult and even painful – but they can also be exciting and positive, opening up new possibilities. The examples in this chapter have shown how practitioners can support children, their families and each other. Where practitioners are offered support and supervision from managers or heads of centres to manage their own emotions (DfE, 2012a; Elfer and Dearnley, 2007) they are better able to support each other. When babies and young children are separated from their parents, their attachments to one or two people in the nursery will help them to become resilient and more fully equipped to cope with transition (Goldschmied and Jackson, 2004). Sometimes in large settings, where there is a need constantly to consider the capacity and occupancy levels of children, managers can be seduced into offering vacancies to new families by rushing babies and children on to the next room or space before they are really ready. But such transitions need to be managed, and hurried transitions can add to the anxiety and stress of transition because the constancy and consistency are missing. Transitions have to happen in life, they are often much anticipated and exciting 'rites of passage', and young children experience many transitions in their first few years. But it is the practitioner's responsibility to really tune in to the needs of the children and to take their cues from them. This is not always easy, but as Johnston's study illustrates, letting children set the agenda can reap the rewards for children, practitioners and their families.

Further reading

Gonzalez-Mena, J. and Widmeyer Eyer, D. (2011) *Infants, Toddlers and Caregivers*. Buckinghamshire: Open University Press.

Kernan, M. and Singer, E. (eds) (2010) *Peer Relationships in Early Childhood Education and Care*. London: Routledge.

Rich, D. (2004) *Listening to Babies*. Listening as a Way of Life Series. London: National Children's Bureau.

Siren Films (2010) *All About Attachment* (Series of 5 DVDs on Attachment). Newcastle Upon Tyne: Siren Films Ltd.

Chapter 8

Permission to Love Them

Throughout this book we have discussed some key values and key issues of practice in working with babies, toddlers and young children. In this final section, Jools Page returns to her recent research which sets out what she sees as the essential ingredient in caring for and educating young children, and why practitioners need permission to love the children they work with.

For some time now I have been arguing for a place and space to talk about what it is to love babies and young children in professional roles. As we discussed in the Introduction on p. 8, for professionals, the idea of loving children who are unrelated, if it is discussed at all, is discussed with caution. However, babies and children **do need love**, and in the context of paid child care, I have begun to think about this as *'professional love'* or even *'pedagogy of love'* (Page, 2011a). However, although I believe love exists in early years settings, my view of love goes far beyond what Stonehouse (1989) once called 'nice ladies who love children'. I agree with Goldstein (1998) when she suggests that to talk about caring, and love, in this way oversimplifies caring and undermines the complex work of professionals into a somewhat trivialized view of the caring professions. Nevertheless, love is not easy to talk about in professional roles with children; especially given the sensitivity surrounding safeguarding and child protection, as we discussed in Chapter 3. This is for me precisely why I think there is a need to discuss what love means to practitioners, and parents and children too. For me, not talking about love is a refusal to acknowledge it exists — which in my view in western society is just not true. Of course there can be no requirement to love

children in practice or policy terms, but I believe that infants and toddlers deserve the opportunity to be loved by those practitioners with whom they spend so much of their time in a way that is accepted and acknowledged, always with the rights of the child at the centre of the practice.

In a recent radio interview (BBC, *Woman's Hour*, 2012) a retired Norland Nanny recounted her experience of caring for countless babies and young children during the Second World War. When asked to sum up the one thing that she thought was the essential ingredient for young children, 80-year-old Brenda Ashford responded without hesitation 'Love, love and more love'. And in the opening chapter of her autobiography, Ashford says:

> Children are born uniquely vulnerable with a love they never outgrow. A baby has a special way of adding joy every single day and can flood your heart with love like nothing else. They say that you can never truly love a child that is not your own, but that goes against every instinct that runs though me. For I have loved children born to other women all my life, and every child that I have cared for, I have adored with all my heart. Many I would have laid down my life for, in fact on some memorable occasions when I fled to air raid shelters clutching my charges to my chest, I very nearly did. (Ashford, 2012: 1)

This heart-warming story of one woman's love for her 'charges' conjures up a somewhat romanticized image of a homely individual who to all intents and purposes gave up her own life and dedicated it to others. In this regard I both applaud but also challenge this view of love in early childhood. Nanny Ashford both worked and lived in the family homes of the children for whom she was responsible. The role of nanny is one that still continues, and yet there are many professional roles that exist in childminder homes and group settings beyond that of caring for a child in their own family environment. It is in these complex roles that we might wonder how today's practitioners, and parents for that matter, view love and relationships between young children and the practitioner – the key person.

In the professional roles I have held in the early years' sector – practitioner, policy-maker, academic – I have witnessed parents, essentially mothers, faced with decision-making regarding childcare solutions when deciding whether to return to work following the birth of a baby. The younger the child the more

Continues

Continued

challenging the dilemma seems to be. Of the many conversations I have had with mothers, the importance of close reciprocal relationships between the adult carer and the child has played a key factor in their decision-making. However, how the mothers reached their decisions were in my experience complicated and unique to their individual circumstances. These are questions I have been attempting to explore in my own research.

I recently conducted a life historical study (Page, 2010) which investigated the deeply held views, values and beliefs of six participant mothers which informed their decision-making about returning to work when their babies were under a year old, and what importance, if any, the mothers placed on having carers in day care settings who 'love' their children. I have drawn on Noddings's (1984/2003, 1992) work on the intellectual aspect of caring in relation to ethics of care and education, specifically in relation to babies and children under three. I have suggested that the work of early childhood professionals involves not only 'care' and 'education' but '*love*', care and education. I argue that when a mother is able to recognize Noddings's notion of a 'reciprocal intellectual encounter' at first hand, this is the point at which she may be more readily able to identify with the intellectual experience of love as an attachment that is deeply in tune with her own wishes for her child, rather than a feeling that it is threatening to her mother-child relationship.

Very young babies, because of their age and stage of development, frequently need a great deal of care and attention to their personal needs: nappy changing, feeding and settling to sleep. Sometimes this reliance shrouds the developmental progress which is naturally happening in parallel. Robinson (2003) suggests this may be one reason for what she describes as the 'perpetuation of the sad myth that anyone (especially anyone female) can look after babies' (2003: 10). The role of the key person as defined by Elfer et al. (2003) became a mandatory requirement of the Early Years Foundation Stage (EYFS) (DfE, 2012a): '... how one or two adults in the nursery, while never taking over from the parents, connect with what parents would ordinarily do: being special for the children, helping them manage throughout the day, thinking about them, getting to know them too ...' (Elfer et al., 2003: vi).

Although research by Elfer (2007; Elfer and Dearnley, 2007) confirms the complexity and challenge which practitioners in day care have faced in the implementation of the key person approach (KPA), in a recent study (Page and Elfer, 2013), practitioners upheld the importance of close relationships, even when the Key Person Approach is difficult to implement within particular organizational structures in some early years settings. As we have discussed throughout this book it takes an enormous amount of determination and integrity on the part of the practitioner to work sensitively with infants, toddlers, young children and their families in a respectful, equitable and professionally appropriate manner. Yet, it seems to me that a critical dialogue that examines terms such as love can only help to better equip those who work in professional roles that include all children. I hope that the notion of supervision as advocated in the revised EYFS (DfE, 2012a) will provide a suitable space to talk about the complexity of personal and professional anxieties involved in working with babies and young children.

In addition to this individual space I believe that what is needed is an open and transparent debate whereby the complex notions of caring for and loving young children are discussed at *all* levels; with parents, managers, politicians, with each other, not just in training but as an ongoing debate wherever we want high quality education and care of very young children to exist. Gerhardt (2004) is clear about the dangers of not providing children with loving relationships in relation to 'how affection shapes a baby's brain'. However, love is rarely explicitly spoken about, especially within the context of policy. In fact in a round table discussion on Sure Start the former shadow minister said: 'You don't talk about love in government, or in public policy. This has got to change, because so many of the mothers who use Sure Start and most other public services are looking for just that. Love, validation, nurture and support' (Gerhardt et al., 2011: 154). Whilst Adamson (2008) contends:

> ... neuroscience is beginning to confirm and explain the inner workings of what social science and common experience have long maintained – *that loving, stable, secure, stimulating and rewarding relationships with family and caregivers in the earliest months and years of life are critical for almost all aspects of a child's development.* (Adamson, 2008: 6, emphasis in the original)

The findings of my research into mothers' views of love in childcare confirmed to me that although the mothers did not always use the term love, their ways of expressing the type of relationship they craved for their child

Continues

Continued

was in fact in line with my notion of 'professional love' (Page, 2010, 2011a). There is without doubt a need for more research which examines not only the terminology of love, but perhaps more importantly the meaning of the use of the term love in professional care and education roles with infants and young children. As Noddings (2003: 184) points out, 'it is absurd to suppose that we are educating when we ignore those matters that lie at the very heart of human existence'. And for me, to deny the place of love is to deny what lies at the heart of human existence; further justification perhaps of why I firmly believe that love *really does* matter; never more so than to our youngest children who need love and affection to help their minds, bodies and souls grow strong, to be equipped to learn and to be emotionally resilient throughout their whole lives.

Jools Page
December 2012

References

Abbott, L. and Langston, A. (eds) (2006) *Parents Matter: Supporting the Birth to Three Matters Framework*. Maidenhead: Open University Press.

Abbott, L. and Nutbrown, C. (eds) (2001) *Experiencing Reggio Emilia: Implications for Pre-school Provision*. Buckingham: Open University Press.

Abbott, L., Ackers, J., Gillen, J. and Moylett, H. (2000) *Shaping the Future: Working with the Under-Threes*. Video. Manchester: Manchester Metropolitan University.

Acredolo, L. and Goodwyn, S. (1996) *Baby Signs: How To Talk with Your Baby before Your Baby Can Talk*. Vacaville, CA: Babysigns.

Adams, S., Moyles, J. and Musgrove, A. (2002) *SPEEL Study of Pedagogical Effectiveness in Early Learning*. Norwich: Department for Education and Skills.

Adamson, P. (2008) *The Child Care Transition: A League Table of Early Education and Care in Economically Advanced Countries*. Florence: The United Nations Children's Fund.

Alanen, L. (2001) 'Explorations in generational analysis', in L. Alanen and B. Mayall (eds), *Conceptualizing Child–Adult Relations*. London: Routledge Falmer.

Alderson, P. (2008) *Young Children's Rights* (2nd edn). London: Jessica Kingsley.

Alderson, P., Hawthorne, J. and Killen, M. (2005) 'The participation rights of premature babies', *The International Journal of Children's Rights*, 13: 31–50.

Allen, G. (2011). *Early Intervention: The Next Steps*. London: Cabinet Office.

Appell, G. and David, M. (1973) *Lóczy: An Unusual Approach to Mothering*. New York: Bruner-Mazel.

Ashford, B. (2012) *A Spoonful of Sugar: A True Story of a Norland Nanny in Wartime England*. London: Hodder and Stoughton.

Atherton, F. and Nutbrown, C. (2013) *Understanding Schemas and Young Children: From Birth to Three*. London: Sage.

Athey, C. (1990) *Extending Thought in Young Children: A Parent–Teacher Partnership*. London: Paul Chapman Publishing.

Athey, C. (2006) *Extending Thought in Young Children – A Parent–Teacher Partnership* (2nd edn). London: Paul Chapman Publishing.

Australian Association for Research in Education (1998) 'Code of ethics for research in education', in M. Bibby (ed.), *Ethics and Education Research*. Melbourne: Blackwell.

Australian Association for Research in Education (1999) *Code of Ethics*. New South Wales: University of New South Wales. Available at: http://www.swin.edu.au.aarc.ethcfull.html (updated 26 July 2000) (accessed 3 January 2005).

Bain, A. and Barnett, L. (1986) *The Design of a Day Care System in a Nursery Setting for Children Under Five*. London: Tavistock Institute of Human Relations Document number 2T347.

Barlow, C. (1997) 'Ooooh baby, what a brain! The early impact of books and libraries', *School Library Journal*, 43(7): 20–2.

Barlow, J. and Svanberg, P.O. (2009) *Keeping the Baby in Mind: Infant Mental Health in Practice*. Hove: Routledge.

Bartlett, F.C. (1932) *Remembering: A Study of Experimental and Social Psychology*. Cambridge: Cambridge University Press.

BBC *Woman's Hour* (2012) Brenda Ashford – Norland Nanny. Presented by Jane Garvey, 18 June.

Berthelson, D., Brownlee, J. and Johansson, E. (2009) (eds) *Participatory Learning in the Early Years: Research and Pedagogy*. London: Routledge.

Bibby, M. (ed.) (1998) *Ethics and Education Research*. Victoria: Australian Association for Research in Education.

Bookstart (2011) 'A research update from Louise Chadwick, Head of Public Policy and Research, Booktrust'. Retrieved 17 July 2012 from http://www.bookstart.org.uk/professionals/news-and-blog/professionals-blog/84

Bowlby, J. (1953) *Child Care and the Growth of Love*. Baltimore, MD and London: Pelican/Penguin.

Bowlby, J. (1969) *Attachment and Loss: Vol. 1.* Attachment. New York: Basic Books.

Brierley, J. (1994) *Give Me a Child Until He is Seven: Brain Studies and Early Childhood Education* (2nd edn). London: Falmer Press.

British Educational Research Association (BERA) (1992) *Ethical Guidelines for Educational Research.* Nottinghamshire: BERA.

British Educational Research Association (BERA) (2011) *Ethical Guidelines for Educational Research.* Nottinghamshire: BERA.

Broadhead, P., Howard, J. and Wood, E. (2010) *Play and Learning in the Early Years: From Research to Practice.* London: Sage.

Brooker, E. and Woodhead, M. (eds) (2010) *Culture and Learning.* Early Childhood in Focus, 6. Milton Keynes: The Open University.

Bruner, J. (1983) *Child's Talk.* New York: Norton Press.

Calder, P. (1999) 'The development of early childhood studies degrees in Britain: future prospects', *European Childhood Education Research Journal*, 7: 45–67.

Canning, N. (2010) 'The influence of the outdoor environment: den-making in three different contexts', *European Early Childhood Education Research Journal*, 18(4): 555–66.

Carr, M. (2004) *Assessment in Early Childhood Settings: Learning Stories.* London: Sage.

Carr, M. and Claxton, G. (2002) 'Tracking the development of learning dispositions', *Assessment in Education*, 9(1): 9–25.

Carr, M. and Claxton, G. (2004) 'A framework for teaching learning: the dynamics of dispositions', *Early Years*, 24(1): 87–97.

Carr, M. and Lee, W. (2012) *Learning Stories: Constructing Learner Identities in Early Education.* London: Sage.

Carroll, R. (2001) 'An interview with Allan Schore – the American Bowlby'. Available at: http://www.thinkbody.co.uk/papers/interview-with-allan-s.htm

Cassidy, J. (2008) 'The nature of the child's ties', in J. Cassidy and P. Shaver (eds) *Handbook of Attachment: Theory, Research and Clinical Applications* (2nd edn). New York: Guilford Press, pp. 3–22

Caulfield, R. (2002) 'Babytalk: developmental precursors to speech', *Early Childhood Education Journal*, 30(1): 59–62.

Children's Workforce Development Council (CWDC) (2006a) FAQs. http://webarchive.nationalarchives.gov.uk/20120119192332/http:/cwd.council.org.uk/ (accessed 3 December 2006).

Children's Workforce Development Council (CWDC) (2006b) http://webarchive.nationalarchives.gov.uk/20120119192332/http:/cwd.council.org.uk/ (accessed 3 December 2006).

Chilvers, D. (2002) 'Thinking in reflective practice in early years', unpublished Diploma/MEd dissertation, University of Sheffield.

Christensen, P. and James, A. (eds) (2000) *Research with Children: Perspectives and Practices*. London: Routledge.

Christensen, P. and James, A. (2008) *Research with Children: Perspectives and Practices* (2nd edn). London: Routledge.

Clare, A. (2012) *Creating a Learning Environment for Babies and Toddlers*. London: Sage.

Clark, A. (2005) 'Listening to and involving young children: a review of research and practice', *Early Child Development and Care*, 175(6): 489–505.

Clark, A. and Moss, P. (2005) *Spaces to Play: More Listening to Young Children Using the Mosaic Approach*. London: NCB.

Clark, A. and Moss, P. (2011) *Listening to Young Children Using the Mosaic Approach* (2nd edn). London: NCB.

Clough, P. and Nutbrown, C. (2002) *A Student's Guide to Methodology: Justifying Enquiry*. London: Sage.

Clyde, J.A., Miller, C., Sauer, S., Liebert, K., Parker, S. and Runyan, S. (2006) 'Teachers and children inquire into Reggio Emilia', *Language Arts*, 83(3): 215–26.

COAG (2009) *Investing in the Early Years – A National Early Childhood Development Strategy. An initiative of the Council of Australian Governments*. Available at: http://www.acecqa.gov.au/storage/national_ECD_strategy.PDF (accessed 13 July 2012).

Cohen, L., Manion, L. and Morrison, K. (2003) *Research Methods in Education* (5th edn). London: Routledge.

Coles, R. (1997) *The Moral Intelligence of Children*. London: Bloomsbury.

Community Playthings: Lindon, J. and Langston, A. (2003) *Creating Places for Birth to Threes: Room Layout and Equipment*. Robertsbridge, E. Sussex: Community Playthings.

Cooper, G. (2011) The Two Row-Boats Metaphor, Personal communication with Dolby, R., Hughes, E. and Friezer, B. as part of working association on the Attachment Matters Project in Dolby, R., Hughes, E. and Friezer, B. (2011) 'Playspaces Educators, Parents and Toddlers', paper presented at a Symposium on Infant–Toddler

Education and Care: Exploring Diverse Perspectives on Theory, Research, Practice and Policy. Infant, Toddler Symposium, Charles Sturt University, Bathurst, Australia, 21–25 November.

Cooper, G., Hoffman, K. and Powell, B. (2009) Circle of Security Parenting. ©® A relationship based parenting program. http://circleofsecurity.net

Cortazar, A. and Herreros, F. (2010) 'Early attachment relationships and the early childhood curriculum', *Contemporary Issues in Early Childhood*, 11(2): 192–202.

CPS (2009) *Safeguarding CPS*. Available at: www.cps.gov.uk/news/press_releases/161_09/

Crain, W. (2003) *Reclaiming Childhood: Letting Children Be Children in Our Achievement-Oriented Society*. New York: Henry Holt.

Cremin, H. and Slatter, B. (2004) 'Is it possible to access the "voice" of pre-school children? Results of a research project in a pre-school setting', *Educational Studies*, 30(4): 457–71.

Cunningham, H. (2006) *The Invention of Childhood*. London: BBC Books.

Dahlberg, G., Moss, P. and Pence, A. (2007) *Beyond Quality in Early Childhood Education and Care: Languages of Evaluation* (2nd edn). Abingdon: Routledge.

Dalli, C., White, E.J., Rockel, J., Duhn, I., with Buchanan, E., Davidson, S., Ganly, S., Kus, L. and Wang, B. (2011) *Quality Early Childhood Education for Under-Two-Year-Olds: What Should It Look Like? A Literature Review*. Wellington: Ministry of Education, New Zealand.

Datler, W., Datler, M. and Funder, A. (2010) 'Struggling against a feeling of becoming lost: a young boy's painful transition to day care', *Infant Observation*, 13(1): 65–87.

David, T. (1999) 'Valuing young children', in L. Abbott and H. Moylett (eds), *Early Education Transformed*. London: Falmer Press.

David, T. (2006) 'Grandparents matter', in L. Abbott and A. Langston (eds), *Parents Matter: Supporting the Birth to Three Matters Framework*. Maidenhead: Open University Press.

David, T., Goouch, K., Powell, S. and Abbott, L. (2003) *Birth to Three Matters: A Review of the Literature*. London: DfES.

Davies, M. (1995) *Helping Children to Learn Through a Movement Perspective*. London: Hodder and Stoughton.

Dearing, E., McCartney, K. and Taylor, B. (2009) 'Does higher quality early child care promote low-income children's math and reading achievement in middle childhood?', *Child Development*, 80(5): 1529–349.

Degotardi, S. and Pearson, E. (2009) 'Relationship theory in the nursery: attachment and beyond', *Contemporary Issues in Early Childhood*, 10(2): 144–5.

Department for Children, Schools and Families (DCSF) (2007) *Parents as Partners in Early Learning (PPEL) Project – Parental Involvement – a Snapshot of Policy and Practice PPEL Project Phase 1 Report*. London: DCSF/HMSO.

Department for Children, Schools and Families (DCSF) (2008) *The Early Years Foundation Stage: Setting the Standards for Learning, Development and Care for Children from Birth to Five*. London: DCSF.

Department for Education (DfE) (2010) *Sure Start Children's Centres Statutory Guidance*. London: DfE.

Department for Education (DfE) (2011) *Families in the Foundation Years: Evidence Pack*. London: DfE and DoH.

Department for Education (DfE) (2012a) *Statutory Framework for the Early Years Foundation Stage: Setting the Standards for Learning, Development and Care for Children from Birth to Five*. London: DfE.

Department for Education (DfE) (2012b) *Early Education for Two-Year-Olds*. Available at: http://www.education.gov.uk/childrenandyoungpeople/earlylearningandchildcare/delivery/free%20entitlement%20to%20early%20education/b0070114/eefortwoyearolds (accessed 7 July 2012).

Department for Education (DfE) (2012c) *Provision for Children Under Five Years of Age in England – January 2012*. Available at: http://www.education.gov.uk/rsgateway/DB/SFR/ (accessed 28 June 2012).

Department for Education and Employment (DfEE) (1990) *Starting with Quality: Report of the Committee of Inquiry into the Educational Experiences Offered to 3 and 4 Year Olds*. London: HMSO.

Department for Education and Employment (DfEE) (1996) *Nursery and Grant Maintained Schools Act*. London: HMSO.

Department for Education and Employment (DfEE) (1997) *Excellence in Schools*. White Paper. London: DfEE.

Department for Education and Employment (DfEE) (1998) *Meeting the Childcare Challenge: A Framework and Consultation Document*. London: DfEE.

Department for Education and Employment (DfEE) (1999a) *New*

Qualifications Framework: A Newsletter for the Early Years Development and Childcare Partnerships, Partners 5, September. London: DfEE.

Department for Education and Employment (DfEE) (1999b) *Tomorrow's Children – Review of Pre-schools and Playgroups*. London: DfEE.

Department for Education and Employment (DfEE) (2000a) *Curriculum Guidance for the Foundation Stage*. London: DfEE/ Qualifications and Curriculum Authority.

Department for Education and Employment (2000b) *Select Committee on Education and Employment*. London: DfEE.

Department for Education and Science (DES) (1990) *Starting with Quality: Report of the Committee of Inquiry into the Educational Experiences Offered to 3- and 4-Year-Olds*. London: HMSO.

Department for Education and Skills (DfES) (2001) *National Standards for Under Eights Day Care and Childminding: Full Day Care*. Nottingham: HMSO.

Department for Education and Skills (DfES) (2002a) *Birth to Three Matters: A Framework to Support Children in their Earliest Years*. London: DfES/Sure Start.

Department for Education and Skills (DfES) (2002b) *Together from the Start – Practical Guidance for Professionals Working with Disabled Children (Birth to 2) and Their Families. Consultation Document*. London: DfES/ Department for Health.

Department for Education and Skills (DfES) (2002c) *Spending Review 2005/06*. London: DfES.

Department for Education and Skills (DfES) (2003) *Every Child Matters*. Green Paper. London: HMSO.

Department for Education and Skills (DfES) (2004a) *A Choice for Parents, the Best Start for Children: A Ten Year Strategy for Childcare*. London: HMSO.

Department for Education and Skills (DfES) (2004b) *Every Child Matters: Change for Children*. Nottingham: DfES Publications.

Department for Education and Skills (DfES) (2005) *Common Core of Skills and Knowledge for the Children's Workforce*. London: HMSO.

Department for Education and Skills (DfES) (2006a) *The Early Years Foundation Stage: Consultation on a Single Quality Framework for Services to Children from Birth to Five*. London: DfES/DWP.

Department for Education and Skills (DfES) (2006b) *Seamless Transition: Supporting Continuity in Young People's Learning*. London: DfES.

Department for Education and Skills (DfES) (2007) *Early Years Foundation Stage: Setting the Standards for Learning, Development and Care for Children from Birth to Five*. London: DfES/Sure Start.

Department of Health (DoH) (1991) *The Children Act 1989, Guidance and Regulations, Volume 2, Family Support, Day Care and Educational Provision for Young Children*. London: HMSO.

Dolby, R. (2007) *The Circle of Security: Roadmap to Building Supportive Relationships*. Canberra: Early Childhood Australia.

Donaldson, M. (1978) *Children's Minds*. London: Hodder and Stoughton.

Drummond, M.J., Rouse, D. and Pugh, G. (1992) *Making Assessment Work: Values and Principles in Assessing Young Children's Learning*. Nottingham: NES Arnold/National Children's Bureau.

Dunn, J. (1987) 'The beginnings of moral understanding', in J. Kagan and S. Lamb (eds), *The Emergence of Morality in Young Children*. Chicago, IL: University of Chicago Press.

Dyer, P. (2002) 'A box full of feelings: emotional literacy in a nursery class', in C. Nutbrown (ed.), *Research Studies in Early Childhood Education*. Stoke-on-Trent: Trentham.

Dyregrov, A. (2008) *Grief in Young Children: A Handbook for Adults*. London: Jessica Kingsley.

Early Education (2012) *Development Matters in the Early Years Foundation Stage*. London: Early Education.

Ebbeck, M. and Yim, H. (2009) 'Rethinking attachment: fostering positive relationships between infants, toddlers and their primary caregivers', *Early Child Development and Care*, 179(7): 899–909.

Edwards, C., Gandini, L. and Forman, G. (eds) (1993) *The Hundred Languages of Children: The Reggio Emilia Approach to Early Childhood Education*. Norwood, NJ: Ablex.

Elfer, P. (2002) 'Babies as scientists, artists, and communicators', *Montessori International*, January–March: 32–5.

Elfer, P. (2005) 'Observation matters', in L. Abbott and A. Langston (eds), *Birth to Three Matters: Supporting the Framework of Effective Practice*. Maidenhead: Open University Press.

Elfer, P. (2007) 'Babies and young children in nurseries: using psycho-analytic ideas to explore tasks and interactions', *Children and Society*, 21: 111–22.

Elfer, P. (2011) 'Psychoanalytic methods of observation as a research tool for exploring young children's nursery experience', *International Journal of Social Research Methodology*, 15(3): 225–38.

Elfer, P. and Dearnley, K. (2007) 'Nurseries and emotional well-being: evaluating an emotionally containing model of continuing professional development', *Early Years: Journal of International Research and Development*, 27(3): 267–79.

Elfer, P., Goldschmied, E. and Selleck, D. (2003) *Key Persons in the Nursery: Building Relationships for Quality Provision*. London: David Fulton.

Elfer, P., Goldschmied, E. and Selleck, D. (2012) *Key persons in the Early Years: Building Relationships for Quality Provision in Early Years Settings and Schools* (2nd edn). London: David Fulton.

Every Child Matters (2005a) Aims and outcomes. Archived information available at: www.education.gov.uk/publications/standard/publicationDetail/Page1/DfES/1081/2004 (accessed 25 April 2005).

Every Child Matters (2005b) Every Child Matters: Change for Children. The vision. PowerPoint slide 2. www.everychildmatters.gov.uk/content/documents/ECMCFC%20presentation%20A%20v0.1.ppt#270,2 (accessed 25 April 2005).

Field, F. (2010) *Foundation Years: Preventing Poor Children Becoming Poor Adults*. London: Cabinet Office.

Filippini, T. and Vecchi, V. (eds) (2000) *The Hundred Languages of Children: The Exhibit* (2nd edn). Reggio Emilia: Reggio Children.

Fonagy, P., Gergely, G. and Target, M. (2008) 'Psychoanalytical constructs and attachment theory and research', in J. Cassidy and P. Shaver (eds) *Handbook of Attachment: Theory, Research and Clinical Applications* (2nd edn). New York: Guilford Press, pp. 783–810.

Fraser, S., Lewis, V., Ding, S., Kellett, M. and Robinson, C. (eds) (2004) *Doing Research with Children and Young People*. London: Sage.

French, G. (2007) *Aistear: the Early Childhood Curriculum Framework: Children's Early Learning and Development*. Dublin: National Council for Curriculum and Assessment (NCCA).

Froebel, F. (1912) *Froebel's Chief Writings on Education Rendered into English by S.S.F. Fletcher and J. Welton*. London: Arnold.

Gammage, P. (2006) 'Early childhood education and care: politics, policies and possibilities', *Early Years*, 26(3): 235–48.

Gardner, H. (1993) *The Unschooled Mind: How Children Think and How Schools Should Teach*. London: Fontana.

Gerhardt, S. (2004) *Why Love Matters: How Affection Shapes a Baby's Brain*. London: Routledge.

Gerhardt, S., Jowell, T. and Stewart-Brown, S. (2011) '"You don't talk about love in government" – a roundtable discussion on Sure Start and the first three years of life', *Soundings: A Journal of Politics and Culture*, 48 (Summer).

Goldschmied, E. (1987) *Infants at Work*. Video. London: National Children's Bureau.

Goldschmied, E. and Hughes, A. (1992) *Heuristic Play with Objects: Children of 12–20 Months Exploring Everyday Objects*. Video. London: National Children's Bureau.

Goldschmied, E. and Jackson, S. (1994) *People Under Three: Young Children in Day Care*. London: Routledge.

Goldschmied, E. and Jackson, S. (2004) *People Under Three: Young Children in Day Care* (2nd edn). London: Routledge.

Goldschmied, E. and Selleck, D. (1996) *Communication Between Babies in their First Year*. London: National Children's Bureau.

Goldstein, L.S. (1998) 'More than gentle smiles and warm hugs: applying the ethic of care to early childhood education', *Journal of Research in Childhood Education*, 12(2): 244–61.

Golinkoff, R.M. and Hirsh-Pasek, K. (2004) *Einstein Never Used Flashcards: How Our Children Really Learn – and Why They Need to Play More and Memorize Less*. Emmaus, PA: Rodale.

Göncü, A. (2010) 'Cultures of caregiving – mothers and others', in L. Brooker and M. Woodhead (eds) *Culture and Learning*. Early Childhood in Focus 6. Milton Keynes: Open University. pp. 12–13.

Gonzalez-Mena, J. (2007) 'What to do for a fussy baby: a problem solving approach', *Young Children*, 62(5): 20–1.

Goodley, D. (2007) 'Becoming rhizomatic parents: Deleuze, Guattari and disabled babies', *Disability & Society*, 22(2): 145–60.

Goodman, Y. (1980) *The Roots of Literacy*. Claremont, NJ: Claremont Reading Conference Year Book.

Goodwyn, S., Acredolo, L. and Brown, C. (2000) 'Impact of symbolic gesturing on early language development', *Journal of Nonverbal Behavior*, 24(2): 81–103.

Goouch, K. and Powell, S. (2010) *The Baby Room Project*. Report on Phase 1 to the Esmé Fairbairn Foundation.

Goouch, K. and Powell, S. (2012) 'Orchestrating professional development for baby room practitioners: raising the stakes in new dialogic encounters', *Journal of Early Childhood Research*, 1–15, DOI: 10.1177/1476718X12448374.

Gopnik, A. (2009) *The Philosophical Baby: What Children's Minds Tell Us About Truth, Love, and the Meaning of Life*. New York: Farrar, Straus and Giroux.

Gopnik, A. and Schulz, L. (2004) 'Mechanisms of theory-formation in young children', *Trends in Cognitive Science*, 8(8): 27–39.

Gopnik, A., Meltzoff, A. and Kuhl, P. (1999a) *How Babies Think*. London: Weidenfeld and Nicolson.

Gopnik, A.N., Meltzoff, A. and Kuhl, P. (1999b) *The Scientist in the Crib: Minds, Brains and How Children Learn*. New York: William Morrow.

Goswami, U. (1998) *Cognition in Children*. Hove: Psychology Press.

Graham, A.-M. (1997) '"Have experience; want to learn" – creating a new pathway to professionalism with a little European money and a lot of hard work from our friends', in L. Abbott and H. Moylett (eds), *Working with Under-3s: Training and Professional Development*. Buckingham: Open University Press.

Graue, M.E. and Walsh, D.J. (1998) *Doing Research with Children*. London: Sage.

Greenfield, S. (1997) *The Human Brain*. London: Weidenfeld and Nicolson.

Greenhalgh, P. (1994) *Educational Growth and Learning*. London: Routledge.

Greenough, W.T., Black, J.E. and Wallace, C.S. (1987) 'Experience and brain development', *Child Development*, 58: 569–82.

Grieg, A. and Taylor, J. (1999) *Doing Research with Children*. London: Sage.

Grieg, A., Taylor, J. and Mackay, T. (2007) *Doing Research with Children* (2nd edn). London: Sage.

Hamer, C. (2012) 'NCT Research overview: parent–child communication is important from birth', *Perspective* (March): 15–20. Available at: http://www.literacytrust.org.uk/assets/0001/3375/Hamer_NCT_rese arch_overview_Parent_child_communication_p15-20_Mar12.pdf (accessed 13 July 2012).

Hannon, P. (2003) 'Developmental neuroscience: implications for early childhood intervention and education', *Current Paediatrics*, 13(2): 17–23.

Hennessy, E., Martin, S., Moss, P. and Melhuish, E. (1992) *Children and Day Care: Lessons from Research*. London: Paul Chapman Publishing.

Henry, L., Michael, B., Crowther, C., Evans, J., Mortimer, H. and Phillips-Green, J. (2007) *Senses – Play Foundations*. Dublin: Folens Publishers.

Her Majesty's Stationery Office (HMSO) (1998) *School Standards and Framework Act, 1998. Ch. 31*. London: HMSO.

Her Majesty's Stationery Office (HMSO) (2000) *Care Standards Act 2000*. London: HMSO.

Her Majesty's Stationery Office (HMSO) (2004) *Children Act 2004*. London: HMSO.

Her Majesty's Stationery Office (HMSO) (2006) *Childcare Act 2006*. London: HMSO.

Holland, R. (1997) 'What's it all about? How introducing heuristic play has affected provision for the under-threes in one day nursery', in L. Abbott and H. Moylett (eds), *Working with Under 3s: Responding to Children's Needs*. Maidenhead: Open University Press.

Holmes, R. (1998) *Fieldwork with Children*. London: Sage.

Hutchby, I. and Moran Ellis, J. (eds) (1998) *Children and Social Competence*. London: Falmer.

Hutt, J., Tyler, S., Hutt, C. and Cristophersen, H. (1989) *Play, Exploration and Learning*. London: Routledge.

International Federation of Library Associations and Institutions (2007) *Guidelines for Library Services to Babies and Toddlers*. IFLA Professional Reports, No. 100. International Federation of Library Associations and Institutions NJ1.

Isaacs, S.S. (1933) *Social Development of Young Children*. London: Routledge and Kegan Paul.

Jackson, S. (1992) 'Benign or sinister? Parental responsibility in Great Britain', in P. Close (ed.), *The State and Caring*. Basingstoke: Macmillan.

James, A. and Prout, A. (1997) *Constructing and Reconstructing Childhood* (2nd edn). London: Routledge.

Jenkinson, S. (2001) *The Genius of Play: Celebrating the Spirit of Childhood*. Stroud: Hawthorne Press.

John, K. (2008) 'Sustaining the leaders of Children's Centres: the role of leadership mentoring', *European Early Childhood Education Research Journal*, 6(1): 53–66.

Johnston, A. (2005) 'Who benefits from baby signing?', unpublished

MA dissertation, University of Sheffield.

Joyce, R. (2012) *Outdoor Learning: Past and Present*. Berkshire: Open University Press.

Kandel, E.R., Schwartz, J.H. and Jessell, T.M. (2000) *Principles of Neural Science* (4th edn). New York: McGraw-Hill.

Kapoor, S. (2006) 'Early childhood care and education: an Indian perspective', in E. Melhuish and E. Petrogiannis (eds), *Early Childhood Care and Education*. London: Routledge.

Katz, L. (1995) *Talks with Teachers of Young Children: A Collection*. Norwood, NJ: Ablex.

Knight, S. (2011) *Forest School for All*. London: Sage.

Kowalski, H.S., Wyver, S.R., Masselos, G. and de Lacey, P. (2005) 'The long-day childcare context: implications for toddlers' pretend play', *Early Years: An International Journal of Research and Development*, 25(1): 55–65.

Laevers, F. (1997) *A Process-Orientated Child Follow-up System for Young Children*. Leuven: Centre for Experiential Education.

Laevers, F., Vandenbussche, E., Kog, M. and Depondt, L. (1997) *A Process-Oriented Child Monitoring System for Young Children*. Experiential Education Series No 2. Leuven: Centre for Experiential Education.

Laevers, F. (1998) 'Understanding the world of objects and people: intuition as the core element of deep level learning', *International Journal of Educational Research*, 29(1): 69–86.

Laevers, F. (2005a) *Deep-Level-Learning and the Experiential Approach in Early Childhood and Primary Education*. Leuven: Leuven University Department of Educational Sciences.

Laevers, F. (2005b) *Observation of Well-being and Involvement in Babies and Toddlers*. A video training pack. Belgium: CEGO.

Lally, J.R. and Mangione, P.L. (2006) *New Perspectives in Infant/Toddler Care* (DVD). Sacramento: California Department of Education Press.

Lancaster, Y.P. (2006) *RAMPS: A Framework for Listening to Children*. London: Daycare Trust.

Lancaster, Y.P. (2010) 'Listening to young children: enabling children to be seen and heard', in G. Pugh and B. Duffy (eds), *Contemporary Issues in the Early Years* (5th edn). London: Sage.

Lancaster, Y.P. and Broadbent, V. (2003) *Listening to Young Children*. Maidenhead: Open University Press.

Landry, S.H., Smith, K.E. and Swank, P.R. (2006) 'Responsive parent-ing: establishing early foundations for social, communication, and independent problem-solving skills', *Developmental Psychology*, 42(4): 627–41.

Learning and Teaching Scotland (2010) *Pre-Birth to Three: Positive Outcomes for Scotland's Children and Families*. Glasgow: LTL Scotland.

Lee, B.Y. (2010) 'Investigating toddlers' and parents' storybook read-ing during morning transition', *Early Childhood Education Journal*, 38(3): 213–21.

Lee, S.Y. (2006) 'A journey to a close, secure and synchronous relation-ship: infant–caregiver relationship development in a childcare con-text', *Journal of Early Childhood Research*, 4(2): 133–51.

Levy, R. (2008) '"Third spaces" are interesting places: applying "third space theory" to nursery-aged children's constructions of them-selves as readers', *Journal of Early Childhood Literacy*, 8(1): 43–66.

Levy, R. (2009a) '"You have to understand words … but not read them": young children becoming readers in a digital age', *Journal of Research in Reading*, 32(1): 75–91.

Levy, R. (2009b) 'Children's perceptions of reading and the use of read-ing scheme texts', *Cambridge Journal of Education*, 39(3): 361–77.

Lewis, A. and Lindsay, G. (eds) (2000) *Researching Children's Perspectives*. Buckingham: Open University Press.

Lindon, J. (2012) *Understanding Child Development: 0–8 Years*. Linking Theory and Practice (3rd edn). Abingdon: Hodder Education.

MacNaughton, G. and Hughes, P. (2011) *Parents and Professionals in Early Childhood Settings*. Berkshire: Open University Press.

McMullen, M. and Dixon, S. (2009) 'In support of a relationship-based approach to practice', in D. Berthelson, J. Brownlee and E. Johansson (eds), *Participatory Learning in the Early Years: Research and Pedagogy*. London: Routledge.

Macrory, G. (2001) 'Language development: what do early years prac-titioners need to know?', *Early Years*, 21(1): 33–40.

Mahadevan, J. (2012) 'Plans to raise professional standards at the heart of early years review', *Children and Young People Now*, 26 June 2012.

Makin, L. (2006) 'Literacy 8–12 months: what are babies learning?', *Early Years*, 26(3): 267–77.

Malaguzzi, L. (1993) 'History, ideas, and basic philosophy', in C. Edwards, L. Gandini and G. Forman (eds), *The Hundred Languages of*

Children: The Reggio Emilia Approach to Early Childhood Education. Norwood, NJ: Ablex.

Mandler, J. (1999) 'Preverbal representation and language', in P. Bloom, M. Peterson, L. Nadal and M. Garrett (eds), *Language and Space*. Cambridge, MA: A. Bradford Book/MIT Press.

Marsh, J. (2003) 'Ethical issues in early childhood research', Module 4, Unit 9, *Research Methods and Methodology: Early Childhood Education*. Sheffield: University of Sheffield, Department of Education Studies.

Mathers, S., Ranns, H., Karemaker, A., Moody, A., Sylva, K., Graham, J. and Siraj-Blatchford, I. (2011) *Evaluation of the Graduate Leader Fund*. London: DfE.

Mayall, B. (2002) *Towards a Sociology for Childhood*. London: Routledge Falmer.

Mead, M. (1962) 'A cultural anthropologist's approach to maternal deprivation', in M.D. Ainsworth (ed.), *Deprivation of Maternal Care: A Reassessment of its Effects*. No. 14. Geneva: World Health Organization.

Melhuish, E.C. and Moss, P. (eds) (1991) *Day Care for Young Children: International Perspectives*. London: Routledge.

Melhuish, E.C. and Petrogiannis, K. (2006) 'Introducing international perspectives on early childhood care and education', in E. Melhuish and K. Petrogiannis (eds), *Early Childhood Care and Education: International Perspectives*. London: Routledge.

Meltzoff, A.N. and Moore, M.K. (1999) 'A new foundation for cognitive development in infancy: the birth of the representational infant', in E.K. Scholnick, K. Nelson, S. Gelman and P.H. Miller (eds), *Conceptual Development: Piaget's Legacy*. Mahwah, NJ: Erlbaum Press.

Meltzoff, A.N. and Prinz, W. (2002) *The Imitative Mind: Development, Evolution, and Brain Bases*. Cambridge: Cambridge University Press.

Miller, L. (1992) *Understanding your Baby*. London: Rosendale Press.

Miller, L. (2002) *Observation Observed: An Outline of the Nature and Practice of Infant Observation* (videos and booklet). London: The Tavistock Clinic Foundation.

Miller, L. (2004) *Understanding your Two-Year-Old*. London: Jessica Kingsley.

Mills, C. and Mills, D. (1998) *Britain's Early Years*. London: Channel 4 Television.

Mills, J. (2007) 'What are the significant differences between children's play and exploration in an outdoor raised sand tray compared with children's play and exploration in a muddy area?', unpublished MA dissertation, University of Sheffield.

Ministry of Education, New Zealand (1995) *Te Whāriki*. Wellington: MoE.

Miyakawa, Y., Kamii, C. and Nagahiro, M. (2005) 'The development of logico-mathematical thinking at ages 1–3 in play with blocks and an incline', *Journal of Research in Childhood Education*, 19(4): 292–302.

Mooney, A. and Blackwell, T. (2003) *Children's Views on Childcare: Talking and Listening to Children: DfES Research Brief No. RB44482*. Nottingham: DfES Publications. www.education.gov.uk/publications/eOrderingDownload/RR482.pdf

Morrow, V. and Richards, M. (1996) 'The ethics of social research with children: an overview', *Children and Society*, 10: 90–105.

Morss, J. (2002) 'The several social constructions of James, Jenks, and Prout: a contribution to the sociological theorization of childhood', *The International Journal of Children's Rights*, 10: 39–54.

Moser, T. and Martinsen, M. (2010) 'The outdoor environment in Norwegian kindergartens as pedagogical space for toddlers' play, learning and development', *European Early Childhood Education Research Journal*, 18(4): 457–71.

Mountain, J. (2012) 'A right mess', *Nursery World*, 112(4295): 28–9.

Munro, E. (2008) *Effective Child Protection* (2nd edn). London: Sage.

Munro, E. (2011) *The Munro Review of Child Protection: Final Report. A Child-Centred System*. Available at: http://www.education.gov.uk/munroreview/downloads/8875_DfE_Munro_Report_TAGGED.pdf (accessed 13 July 2012).

Murray, L. and Andrews, E. (2000) *Social Baby*. London: Richmond Press.

National Association for the Education of the Young Child (NAEYC) (1996) *Developmentally Appropriate Practice Early Childhood Programs Serving Children from Birth through Age 8*. Washington, DC: NAEYC.

National Association for the Education of the Young Child (NAEYC) (2005) 'Developmentally Appropriate Practice with infants and toddlers'. Available at: www.naeyc.org/dap/infants-and-toddlers (accessed 7 July 2012).

National Children's Bureau (NCB) (1994) *Tuning in to Children*. London: National Children's Bureau.

National Literacy Trust http://www.literacytrust.org.uk/

Neisser, U. (1976) *Cognition and Reality*. San Francisco, CA: W.H. Freeman.

NICHD Early Child Care Research Network (2002). 'Child-care structure → process → outcome: direct and indirect effects of child-care quality on young children's development', *Psychological Science*, 13(3): 199–206.

Noddings, N. (1984) *Caring: A Feminine Approach to Ethics and Moral Education*. Berkeley, CA: University of California Press.

Noddings, N. (1992) *The Challenge to Care in Schools: An Alternative Approach to Education*. Advances in Contemporary Educational Thought Series, Vol. 8. New York: Teachers College Press.

Noddings, N. (2001) 'The care tradition: beyond "add women and stir"', *Theory into Practice*, 40(1): 29–34.

Noddings, N. (2003) *Caring: A Feminine Approach to Ethics and Moral Education* (2nd edn). Berkeley, CA: University of California Press.

Nutbrown, C. (1996) *Children's Rights in the Early Years. Respectful Educators – Capable Learners*. London: Paul Chapman Publishing.

Nutbrown, C. (1999) *Recognising Early Literacy Development: Assessing Children's Achievements*. London: Paul Chapman Publishing.

Nutbrown, C. (2006) *Threads of Thinking: Young Children Learning and the Role of Early Education* (3rd edn). London: Sage.

Nutbrown, C. (2010) *Children's Views of their Early Years Settings: Summary of Findings*. Sheffield: University of Sheffield.

Nutbrown, C. (2011a) *Threads of Thinking: Schemas and Young Children's Learning* (4th edn). London: Sage.

Nutbrown, C. (2011b) *Key Concepts in Early Childhood Education and Care* (2nd edn). London: Sage.

Nutbrown, C. (2012) *Foundations for Quality. The Independent Review of Early Education and Childcare Qualifications*. Final Report. Available at: http://media.education.gov.uk/MediaFiles/A/0/9/%7BA098ADE7-BA9A-4E18–8802-D8D4B060858D%7DNUTBROWN%20FINAL%20REPORT%20-%20final.pdf (accessed 13 July 2012).

Nutbrown, C. and Carter, C. (2010) 'The tools of assessment: watching and learning', in G. Pugh and B. Duffy (eds), *Contemporary Issues in the Early Years* (5th edn). London: Sage.

Nutbrown, C. and Clough, P. (2009) 'Citizenship and inclusion in the early years: understanding and responding to children's perspectives on "belonging"', *International Journal of Early Years Education*, 17(3): 191–206.

Nutbrown, C. and Clough, P. (2013) *Inclusion in the Early Years: Critical Analyses and Enabling Narratives* (2nd edn). London: Sage.

Nutbrown, C. and Hannon, P. (2003) 'Children's perspectives on family literacy: methodological issues, findings and implications for practice', *Journal of Early Childhood Literacy*, 3(2): 115–45.

Nutbrown, C. and Jones, H. (2006) *Daring Discoveries: Arts Based Learning in the Early Years*. Doncaster: DARTS/University of Sheffield.

Nutbrown, C. and Page, J. (2008) *Working with Babies and Children from Birth to Three*. London: Sage.

Nutbrown, C., Hannon, P. and Morgan, A. (2005) *Early Literacy Work with Families: Research, Policy and Practice*. London: Sage.

Nyland, B. (2009) 'The guiding principles of participation: infant, toddler groups and the United Convention of the Rights of the Child', in D. Berthelson, J. Brownlee and E. Johansson (eds), *Participatory Learning in the Early Years: Research and Pedagogy*, London: Routledge, pp. 26–43.

Oates, J., Karmiloff-Smith, A. and Johnson, M. (2012) *Developing Brains*. The Hague: Bernard van Leer Foundation. Available at: http://bernardvanleer.org/Developing-Brains (accessed 13 July 2012).

Office for Standards in Education (Ofsted) (2005) *Annual Report of Her Majesty's Chief Inspector of Schools 2004/2005*. London: Ofsted.

Office for Standards in Education (Ofsted) (2008) *Oaklands Day Nursery Report*. London: Ofsted.

Oxfordshire LEA (1991) *Curriculum Guidance for Oxfordshire*. Oxford: Oxfordshire LEA.

Page, J. (2005) 'Working with children under three: the perspectives of three UK academics', in K. Hirst and C. Nutbrown (eds), *Perspectives on Early Childhood Education: Contemporary Research*. Stoke-on-Trent: Trentham.

Page, J. (2006) 'Planning for under-threes', *Nursery World*, 106(4031): 13–20.

Page, J. (2007) 'Heuristic play', *Nursery World*, 107(4074): 15–18.

Page, J. (2010) 'Mothers, work and childcare: choices, beliefs and dilemmas'. Unpublished PhD Thesis Volumes 1 and 2, University of Sheffield, School of Education.

Page, J. (2011a) 'Do mothers want professional carers to love their babies?', *Journal of Early Childhood Research*, 9(3): 310–23.

Page, J. (2011b) 'Where is the "professional love?": investigating notions of love and loving relationships between practitioners and young children in early years and childcare settings', Symposium on Infant-Toddler Education and Care: Exploring Diverse Perspectives on Theory, Research, Practice and Policy, Charles Sturt University, Bathhurst, Australia, November.

Page, J. and Elfer, P. (2013) 'The emotional complexity of attachment interactions in nursery', *European Early Childhood Education Research Journal*.

Paley, V.G. (1981) *Wally's Stories: Conversations in the Kindergarten*. Cambridge, MA: Harvard University Press.

Parker, C. (2002) 'Working with families on curriculum: the development of shared understandings of children's mark making', in C. Nutbrown (ed.), *Research Studies in Early Childhood Education*. Stoke-on-Trent: Trentham.

Parker-Rees, R. (2007) 'Liking to be liked: imitation, familiarity and pedagogy in the first years of life', *Early Years*, 27(1): 3–17.

Parrott, K. (1997) *The Contribution of the Kiwi Baby Programme to Meaningful Health Gains*. Auckland: Waikato.

Pascal, C. and Bertram, T. (2009). 'Listening to young citizens: the struggle to make real a participatory paradigm in research with young children', *European Early Childhood Education Research Journal*, 17(2): 249–62.

Pearson, B. (1998) 'Assessing lexical development in bilingual babies and toddlers', *International Journal of Bilingualism*, 2(3): 347–72.

Pence, S. and McCallum, M. (1995) 'Developing cross-cultural partnerships: implications for child care quality research and practice', in P. Moss and A. Pence (eds), *Valuing Quality in Early Childhood Services*. London: Paul Chapman Publishing.

Penn, H. (ed.) (2000) *Early Childhood Services: Theory, Policy and Practice*. Buckingham: Open University Press.

Penn, H. (2011) *Quality in Early Education and Care: An International Perspective*. Maidenhead: Open University Press/McGraw Hill.

Physick, R. (2005) 'Changes and challenge: pre-school practitioners' responses to policy change and development', in K. Hirst and C. Nutbrown (eds), *Perspectives on Early Childhood Education Contemporary Research*. Stoke-on-Trent: Trentham.

Piaget, J. (1937/1954) *La construction du réel chez l'enfant/The Construction of Reality in the Child*. New York: Basic Books.

Piaget, J. (1955) *The Language and Thought of the Child*. London: Routledge and Kegan Paul.

Piaget, J. (1969) *The Mechanisms of Perception*. London: Routledge and Kegan Paul.

Piaget, J. (1977) *The Essential Piaget*. Eds H.E. Gruber and J. Jacques Vonèche. New York: Basic Books.

Pikler, E. (1940) 'What can your baby do already?', Hungary. English translation, Sensory Awareness Foundation's winter 1994 bulletin.

Pikler, E. (1971) 'Learning of motor skills on the basis of self-induced movements', in J. Hellmuth (ed.), *Exceptional Infant. Vol. 2*. New York: Bruner-Mazel.

Pikler, E. (1973) 'Some contributions to the study of gross motor development of children', in A. Sandovsky (ed.), *Child and Adolescent Development*, 52–64. New York: Free Press.

Piper, H. and Smith, H. (2003) 'Touch in educational and child care settings: dilemmas and responses', *British Educational Research Journal*, 29(6): 879–94.

Post, J. and Hohmann, M. (2000) *Tender Care and Early Learning: Supporting Infants and Toddlers in Child Care Settings*. Michigan: High Scope.

Powell, S. (2010) '"Not allowed to kiss the babies". Complexities and contradictions in "baby room" policies and practice', in European Conference of the World Organisation for Preschool Education (OMEP), April 2010, Chester, UK.

Powell, J. and Uppal, E. (2012) *Safeguarding Babies and Young Children: A Guide for Early Years Professionals*. Berkshire, England: Open University Press.

Pugh, G. (2001) 'A policy for early childhood services', in G. Pugh (ed.), *Contemporary Issues in the Early Years: Working Collaboratively for Children* (3rd edn). London: Paul Chapman Publishing.

Qualifications and Curriculum Authority (QCA) (1998) *Education for Citizenship and the Teaching of Democracy in Schools*, Crick Report. London: DfEE/QCA.

Qualifications and Curriculum Authority (QCA) (2000) *Curriculum Guidance for the Foundation Stage*. London: QCA.

Ravi, L. (2007) 'Evaluation of better beginnings: from birth to toddler', in A. Bundy (ed.), *Learning Futures: Public Libraries for the New Generations in Australia and New Zealand*. Conference proceedings, Adelaide, 9–10 March 2007. Blackwood: Auslib Press.

Rich, D. (2004) *Listening to Babies*. Listening as a Way of Life Series. London: National Children's Bureau.

Riedl Cross, J.R., Fletcher, K.L. and Speirs Neumeister, K.L. (2011) 'Social and emotional components of book reading between caregivers and their toddlers in a high-risk sample', *Journal of Early Childhood Literacy*, 11(1): 25–46.

Rinaldi, C. (1999) 'The pedagogy of listening', paper given in Reggio Emilia, 28 April.

Roberts, R. (2002) *Self-Esteem and Early Learning* (2nd edn). London: Paul Chapman Publishing.

Roberts, R. (2010). *Well-being from Birth*. London: Sage.

Robinson, M. (2003) *From Birth to One: The Year of Opportunity*. Buckingham: Open University Press.

Rogoff, B. (2003) *The Cultural Nature of Human Development*. Oxford: Oxford University Press.

Rosen, M. (2008) *Sad Book*. London: Walker Books Ltd.

Rouse, D. and Griffin, S. (1992) 'Quality for the under threes', in G. Pugh (ed.), *Contemporary Issues in the Early Years: Working Collaboratively for Children*. London: Paul Chapman Publishing.

Rutter, M. (1972) *Maternal Deprivation Reassessed*. Harmondsworth: Penguin.

Rutter, M. (2002) 'Nature, nurture and development: from evangelism, through science towards policy and practice', *Child Development*, 73(1): 1–21.

Salford EYDCP (2004) *Birth to Three in Salford*. Salford: Salford EYDCP.

Schiller, C. (1979) *Christian Schiller in his Own Words*. London: National Association for Primary Education/A&C Black.

Schools Curriculum and Assessment Authority (SCAA) (1996) *Nursery Education – Desirable Outcomes for Children's Learning on Entering Compulsory Education*. London: SCAA/DFEE.

Schore, A. (1997) 'Early organization of the non-linear right brain and development of a predisposition to psychiatric disorders',

Development and Psychopathology, 9(4): 595–631.

Scott, W. (1996) 'Choices in learning', in C. Nutbrown (ed.), *Children's Rights and Early Education*. Respectful Educators – Capable Learners. London: Paul Chapman Publishing.

Shenglan, L. (2006) 'Development of kindergarten care and education in the People's Republic of China since the 1990s', in E.C. Melhuish and K. Petrogiannis (eds), *Early Childhood Care and Education: International Perspectives*. London: Routledge.

Shin, M. (2010) 'Peeking at the relationship world of infant friends and caregivers', *Journal of Early Childhood Research*, 8(3): 294–302.

Shonkoff, J. and Phillips, D. (2000) *From Neurons to Neighbourhoods: The Science of Early Childhood Development*. Washington: National Academy Press.

Siraj-Blatchford, I., Sylva, K., Muttock, S., Gilden, R. and Bell, D. (2002) *Researching Effective Pedagogy in the Early Years*. London: DfES.

Siren Films (2010) *All About the Outdoors*. Newcastle Upon Tyne: Siren Films Ltd.

Smith, A.B. and May, H. (2006) 'Early childhood care and education in Aotearoa – New Zealand', in E.C. Melhuish and K. Petrogiannis (eds), *Early Childhood Care and Education: International Perspectives*. London: Routledge.

Society for Research in Child Development (1991) *Ethical Standards for Research with Children*. Michigan: University of Michigan: Department of Educational Studies. Available at: http://www.srcd.org/ethicalstandards.html (updated autumn 1991, accessed 25 February 2005).

Stevens, C. (2003) 'The value of Early Years Development Officers' support for voluntary pre-school playgroups', in K. Hirst and C. Nutbrown (eds), *Perspectives on Early Childhood Education Contemporary Research*. Stoke-on-Trent: Trentham.

Stephenson, A. (2009) 'Horses in the sandpit: photography, prolonged involvement and "stepping back" as strategies for listening to children's voices', *Early Child Development and Care*, 179(2): 131–41.

Stone, L.J., Smith, H.T. and Murphy, L.B. (eds) (1974) *The Competent Infant: Research and Commentary*. London: Tavistock Publications.

Stonehouse, A. (1989) 'Nice ladies who love children: the status of the early childhood professional in society', *Early Child Development and Care*, 52(1–4): 61–9.

Sumsion, J., Barnes, S., Cheeseman, S., Harrison, L., Kennedy, A. and Stonehouse, A. (2009) 'Insider perspectives on developing Belonging, Being and Becoming: The Early Years Learning Framework for Australia', *Australasian Journal of Early Childhood*, 34(4): 4–13.

Sumsion, J., Harrison, L., Press, F., McLeod, S., Goodfellow, J. and Bradley, B. (2011) 'Researching infants' experiences of early childhood education and care', in D. Harcourt, B. Perry and T. Waller (eds), *Researching Young Children's Perspectives*. London: Routledge, pp. 113–27.

Sure Start (2002) *Delivering for Children and Families – 2002. Interdepartmental Childcare Review*. London: Sure Start.

Sure Start (2003a) *Childminding: National Standards for Under Eights Day Care and Childminding*. Nottingham: DfES Publications Centre.

Sure Start (2003b) *Full Day Care: National Standards for Under Eights Day Care and Childminding*. Nottingham: DfES Publications Centre.

Sure Start (2003c) *An Introduction to the Birth to Three Matters*. London: Sure Start.

Sure Start (2006) *Personal, Social and Emotional Development Training Materials – Birth to Five*. London: DfES Sure Start Unit.

Sylva, K., Melhuish, E.C., Sammons, P., Siraj-Blatchford, I. and Taggart, B. (2004) *The Effective Provision of Pre-School Education (EPPE) Project: Technical Paper 12 – The Final Report: Effective Pre-School Education*. London: DfES/Institute of Education, University of London.

Sylva, K., Stein, A., Leach, P., Barnes, J., Malmberg, L.E. and the FCCC-team (2012) 'Effects of early child-care on cognition, language, and task-related behaviours at 18 months: An English study', *British Journal of Developmental Psychology*, 29: 18–45.

Thomas, S. (2002) *Familiar Things*. London: Thomson.

Thompson, R., Cotnoir-Bichelman, N., McKerchar, P., Tate, T. and Dancho, K. (2007) 'Enhancing early communication through infant sign training', *Journal of Applied Behavior Analysis*, 40(1): 15–23.

Thoreau, H. (1995) *Walden; or; Life in the Woods*. London: Dover Publications.

Tickell, C. (2011) *The Early Years: Foundations for Life, Health and Learning*. London: DfE.

Touraine, A. (2000) *Can We Live Together? Equality and Difference.*

Stanford, CA: Stanford University Press.

Trevarthen, C. (1977) 'Descriptive analyses of infant communication behaviour', in H.R. Schaffer (ed.), *Studies in Mother–Infant Interaction: The Loch Lomond Symposium*. London: Academic Press.

Trevarthen, C. (2002) 'Learning in companionship', *Education in the North: The Journal of Scottish Education*, new series (10): 16–25.

Trevarthen, C. (2004) 'Making friends with infants', paper presented at Penn Green Conference, 3 July.

Trevarthen, C. (2010) 'What Is It Like to Be a Person Who Knows Nothing? Defining the Active Intersubjective Mind of a Newborn Human Being', *Infant and Child Development*, 20(1): 119–35.

University of Sheffield (2004) *Master of Arts in Early Childhood Education: Dissertation Guidelines*. Sheffield: The University of Sheffield School of Education.

Vakil, S., Freeman, R. and Swim, T.J. (2003) 'The Reggio Emilian approach and inclusive early childhood programmes', *Early Childhood Education Journal*, 30(3): 187–92, 210.

Vallotton, C.D. (2009) 'Do infants influence their quality of care? Infants' communicative gestures predict caregivers' responsiveness', *Infant Behavior and Development*, 32: 351–65.

Vallotton, C.D. (2010) 'Support or competition? Dynamic development of the relationship between pointing and symbolic gestures from 6 to 18 months of age', *Gesture*, 10(2–3): 150–71.

Vallotton, C.D. (2011a) 'Babies open our minds to their minds: How "listening" to infant signs complements and extends our knowledge of infants and their development', *Infant Mental Health Journal*, 32(1): 115–33.

Vallotton, C.D. (2011b) 'Sentences and conversations before speech? Gestures of preverbal children reveal cognitive and social skills that do not wait for words', in G. Stam and M. Ishino (eds), *Integrating Gesture: The Interdisciplinary Nature of Gesture*. Amsterdam and Philadelphia: John Benjamins.

Vorria, P., Papaligoura, Z., Dunn, J., van IJzendoorn, M.H., Steele, H., Kontopoulou, A. and Sarafidou, Y. (2003) 'Early experiences and attachment relationships of Greek infants raised in residential group care', *Journal of Child Psychology and Psychiatry*, 44(8): 1208–20.

Vygotsky, L.S. (1978) *Mind in Society: The Development of Higher Psychological Processes*. Cambridge, MA: Harvard University Press.

Vygotsky, L.S. (1980) *Mind in Society: The Development of Higher Psychological Processes* (2nd edn). Cambridge, MA: Harvard University Press.

Vygotsky, L.S. (1986) *Thought and Language*. Boston, MA: MIT Press.

Wade, B. and Moore, M. (2000) 'A Sure Start with books', *Early Years*, 20(2): 39–46.

Wailling, K. (2005) 'What visually attracts two babies: the value of studying babies in their homes and child care settings', unpublished MA, University of Sheffield.

Wang, J. (2004) 'A study on gross motor skills of preschool children', *Journal of Research in Childhood Education*, 19(1): 32–43.

Ward, L. (2007) 'Is your baby playing with its toes yet? If not the government wants to know why', *Guardian*, 14 March.

Welsh Government (2011) Flying Start. http://wales.gov.uk/topics/childrenyoungpeople/parenting/help/flyingstart/?lang=en (accessed 12 June 2012).

Whalley, M. (2007) *Involving Parents in their Children's Learning* (2nd edn). London: Sage.

Whitburn, J. (2003) 'Learning to live together: the Japanese model of early years education', *International Journal of Early Years Education*, 11(2): 155–75.

Winnicott, D.W. (1953) 'Transitional objects and transitional phenomena', *International Journal of Psychoanalysis*, 34: 89–97.

Winnicott, D.W. (1957) *Mother and Child. A Primer of First Relationships*. New York: Basic Books, Inc.

Winnicott, D.W. (1964) *The Child, the Family and the Outside World*. Harmondsworth: Penguin.

Wood, E. and Attfield, J. (2005) *Play, Learning and the Early Childhood Curriculum*. London: Sage.

Woodhead, M. (1996) *In Search of the Rainbow: Pathways to Quality in Large Scale Programmes for Young Disadvantaged Children. A Report to the Bernard van Leer Foundation*. The Hague: Van Leer.

Yoshinaga, I.C. and Stredler-Brown, A. (1992) 'Learning to communicate: babies with hearing impairments make their needs known', *Volta Review*, 94(2): 107–29.

Web addresses

Koester, O. (2005) *Seeing Babies in a New Light: The Life of Hans Papousek*, London: Routledge. http://www.routledge.com/books/details/9780805842708/

Gonzalez-Mena, J. and Widmeyer Eyer, D. (2011) *Infants, Toddlers and Caregivers*, Mcgraw Hill: Berkshire. http://mcgraw-hill.co.uk/html/0078024358.html

http://us.macmillan.com/BookCustomPage_New.aspx?isbn=9780312429843

Johnson, J. (2009) *Babies in the Rain: Promoting Play, Exploration and Discovery with Infants and Toddlers*. Redleaf Press. http://www.amazon.co.uk/Babies-Rain-Promoting-Exploration-Discovery/dp/1933653841/ref=sr_1_1?ie=UTF8&qid=1341099570&sr=8–1

http://www.cps.gov.uk/news/press_releases/161_09/ (safeguarding CPS)

http://webarchive.nationalarchives.gov.uk/20120119192332/http://cwdcouncil.org.uk/

https://www.education.gov.uk/publications/standard/publicationDetail/Page1/DfES/1081/2004

https://www.education.gov.uk/publications/eOrderingDownload/RR482.pdf

Useful websites

Useful website to consult on early years peer to peer support:
http://ncb.org.uk/what-we-do/early-years/early-years-peer-to-peer-support

Useful website to consult on aspects of the Early Years Foundation Stage: http://www.foundationyears.org.uk/

Useful website to consult on aspects of the Early Years Foundation Stage guidance development matters: http://www.early-education.org.uk/

Useful website to consult on support for language and literacy support for babies and young children: http://www.literacytrust.org.uk/talk_to_your_baby

Useful website which is home to the National Children's Bureau, a charity organisation which reports on all aspects of early years and childcare: http://www.ncb.org.uk/

For policy documents and press releases for England consult the Department for Education website: http://www.education.gov.uk/

Useful website to consult for those who want to know more about supporting children across a range of services in early years and childcare: http://www.c4eo.org.uk/themes/earlyyears/default.aspx?themeid=1

Useful website for this national charity which is the government partner organisation aimed to help develop policy for children and families: http://www.4children.org.uk/

Reports on current policy and the state of Early Childhood Education in many countries are available via the OECD iLibrary which can be located on the OECD website at: http://www.oecd-ilibrary.org/

Index